# Up To
# Scratch

*Also by Diana Cooper*

ANIMAL HOTEL

# UP TO SCRATCH

# DIANA COOPER

St. Martin's Press   New York

Library of Congress Catalog Card Number  83-50946

ISBN: 0-312-83391-1

First published in Great Britain in 1981 by Michael Joseph Ltd.

First U.S. Edition

10 9 8 7 6 5 4 3 2 1

*To Genevieve and Jeremy*

# 1

'Maybe his legs are too short,' I suggested timidly. I doubt if the bridegroom was listening. He stood looking thoroughly disconsolate near the open drinks cabinet, as anyone might after failing at the very altar itself. I think we both felt it would have been all right on the night, though.

'You mean her's are too long,' snapped Mrs Mince. She spelt her name with a 'z' but she would always be Mince to me. Her face was the hue and consistency of a pound of the stuff, topped by hair like mashed potato. She may have been some Shepherd's Pie but she certainly wasn't mine. I bit back the urge to tell her that his coat looked lousy to me. He had funny ears, too, watery eyes and a drip on the end of his nose. I daresay his pedigree was crooked as well, if only I could have got a good look at it. All *my* sympathies were with little Tallulah, banished to the car: how she must have looked forward to this, Her Day, all for nothing.

'Anyway,' went on Mrs Mince triumphantly, 'there's something wrong about her rump.' I opened my mouth to protest, but she continued, 'It peaks.'

'Others have admired it,' I claimed boldly, 'often.'

One hears of arranged marriages, shotgun weddings, complex dowries. Of families falling out about the cost of the nuptials, the number of guests to be invited, even the quality of the champagne or choice of brewery, but never in my life had I heard the final flaw being the tilt of the bride's bottom. I wondered how Mrs Mince herself had managed to qualify.

'Won't you have a drink before you go?' she asked pleasantly, as if the insults counted for nothing and this had just been a routine social call. I shook my head with muttered thanks and added that it was getting late. The room smelled of boiled paunch and linament. It was small and fetid rather than cosy and warm. Rosettes of all colours, silver cups and smaller trophies shone bravely through murky light from a dusty lampshade. Somewhere I could hear a cacophony of whines and yelps and barks, and I longed to be home where the kitchen would smell only of Ben's baking, and where dogs used their voices for nothing but welcome or warning.

Mrs Mince lifted her own rump from the edge of the table where it had been threatening to act like a catapult and send a vase of six weeping chrysanthemums through the window. We walked to the front door together, sharing a mutual, but tacit, disappointment. I could also add outrage, but why apportion blame in a clear case of incompatibility?

We paused by a heavy chenille draught curtain and faced one another. I did hope she wouldn't try to shake hands. Hers were cushiony, like grasping a pound of sausages left in the sun.

'Maybe you got the day wrong,' she suggested, 'or maybe she would have appealed more to my Puddisey Pinto, or Puddisey Pussifoot Hambone. They are, I think, a little less discriminating.' She opened the front door a few inches. 'Still, we would hardly want to throw anything *bigger,* would we!'

It was just what we did feel like by then, but I said coldly No, of course we wouldn't, though I was shaking with resentment at the implications behind every word. The whole thing began to sound like a very amateur wellie-bunger contest rather than what should have been a joyous mating.

It was good to get outside where the air was sharp and cold and clean. Tallulah the Third, known at home as Lulu, stood seething with impatience and frustration, two fat and furry paws resting on the ledge of the car windscreen, gazing out to find me. The freshly laundered bridal white of her coat was ruffled. Her neat ears were alert. I think she was telling me she hoped never to set eyes on her intended again. I got in the car and kissed the top of her head. Her nose was cold and damp but without any bit of a drip. 'You were a good girl and you've got a gorgeous rump,' I said as I started the engine. 'You were just too good for him.' I tried hard to convey as much comfort as one can possibly muster when the wedding's been cancelled at the last minute. She climbed on my knee, whimpering a bit with relief at my return, and we drove away into the icy night over rapidly freezing roads. I said, 'We'll put the whole unsavoury affair behind us, darling,' and the bartered bride fell asleep with a sigh and snored a little.

Actually, I remembered, the groom had quite fancied her when they first met. He was very nice to her. It was hard to see what was going on in that murky parlour with Mrs Mince insisting that I admire her scrapbook of cuttings, blurred photographs and award cards. Perhaps if we had withdrawn altogether over the appalling sherry, all might have gone according to plan. One can manoeuvre a meeting, manipulate a marriage, but when it comes to consummation it would seem prudent to step out of the scene and leave the rest to the couple concerned. Perhaps if Mrs Mince hadn't waded in with a helping hand and shrieked after a well-deserved bite from the bride, all would have been well, and the groom might have stayed the course instead of sulking off to idle the time away with a rubber rabbit under the sideboard. That way we could have avoided the slanging match later. I had, of course, saved myself a stud fee, but only at the expense of a heartbroken bride, a shattered groom, a valuable litter of puppies and a wasted afternoon. It was no consolation at all.

I noticed the final demand from the Rates Office as I let myself in through my front door, and left it where it was while I parked Lulu in her basket, strategically placed in purdah behind the bureau in the office. There would be no shortage of willing suitors rushing to prove Mrs Mince wrong had I taken her through to the kitchen where Lulu's attractions had already been recognised.

Ben was busy at the table making a batch of pet snacks from his latest canine recipe – fancifully called 'In a Pig's Ear'. Two or three lay around on the floured board, each filled with brown breadcrumbs. I averted my gaze. Ben enjoyed cooking. He was into an idea for dominating the Pets' Package market when he left school. Meantime, he worked out various ways of using the weekly assortment of odds and ends rejected by our Friendly Butcher. It kept Ben and the dogs happy, even though I suffered a few uneasy moments when he served up our own speciality suppers.

I glanced across the table bravely. 'All up to scratch?' I asked, which was an in-joke we used when checking on the general welfare of our fluctuating dog population. Ben grinned. He was fifteen and suddenly quite attractive. 'Almost fanciable,' Hetty, my vet and close friend (about whose good looks there was no doubt at all) had muttered a few days previously, one hand lingering on her enviably groomed hair. When Ben had first arrived, spotty and gauche, to stay with us for a few weeks during a memorable summer, neither of us had remotely foreseen such satisfactory developments.

'Well,' I said wearily, sinking into the rocking-chair and accepting sundry forms of enthusiastic welcome from the dogs, 'Old Mother Mince Pie didn't seem to fancy Lulu at all. Didn't want her barking up their family tree. So it's now back to square one, I suppose.'

Frilly, the grown-up kitten, stalked the back of the rocker, while

Rosie tried to clamber on my knee, and Treacle, rolling on her back, eyes narrowed in ecstasy, small neat feet waving in the air, exploded in little cries of joy. Rosie and Treacle were mongrels, sisters, utterly different, entirely adorable. Mattie, the very old bobtail sheepdog, lumbered over and dropped her head on my arm. It felt like a Christmas pudding full of lead. Come to think of it, that's a pretty accurate description. She grumbled a bit at the other two and then appeared to fall into a doze. Every day she looked and acted more and more like Grandma from a Giles cartoon.

'I thought it wasn't up to her to do the fancying,' said Ben, adding more Marmite to what looked like a thick white sponge mixture.

'She's very fussy about what gets thrown into the Puddisey coat of arms,' I explained, 'and you're out on your elbow if you don't pass the rump test.'

Ben took the tray of ears and put them carefully in the oven. Then he closed the door with the air of genius proved again. 'So it was a waste of time?'

I nodded and kicked off my boots. The kitchen was hot and heavy with that indefinable atmosphere that was home. Comfort and familiar things and the clutter of convenience.

'Well, that's sex for you,' concluded Ben, with the worldly wisdom of six lessons a term. 'Your Body as a Precious Tool,' headed the leaflet shown to me with glee and issued with *The Mill on the Floss* for holiday reading (plus a complete playground survey of the softer porn glossies). Then he added, casually, 'By the way, you've a customer in the office.'

I shot out of my chair and scattered dogs in all directions. 'Why on earth didn't you say so?' I was shedding my coat, recovering my boots, pushing a hand through my hair. 'Who is it? How long have they been there? Did you put the fire on and hide the Accounts file?'

Ben nodded to the first two and muttered about the third. 'Who on earth would think of looking through the pages of an encyclopaedia? 'Some people enjoy encyclopaedias,' I said crossly, though I would have been pushed to name one. For me, encyclopaedias seem to be the ideal place to file things. You've got a selection of pages for each letter of the alphabet. Books that size can't be as easily mislaid as everything else I've used, and they look quite innocuous on a shelf. Finally, no Inland Revenue invader would ever suspect such a hiding-place. Not that I ever cheat the

10

Inland Revenue. I've never yet made enough money to raise a flicker of interest over their teapots, but I'm not a born optimist for nothing.

The woman waiting for me was still wearing her coat. One of those black, closely-curled furs for all the world like burnt tripe, and though I'm sure it quite suits lambs in Persia, it doesn't do a thing for elderly ladies who so often adopt it as winter uniform when they can afford it. I rushed in stumbling over my apologies. I switched on a third bar to the electric fire, I expressed remorse at keeping her waiting, despair at failure to be serving tea and abused myself because Charlie, all long legs and shaggy hair, appealing brown eyes and drool, was resting against her knee pleading for just a little kindness. Without moving his head he took in my arrival and flattened his ears back as if expecting me to run at him brandishing a whip. On our own, Charlie, left in my care by a friend called Jenny who was making hay with her lover in the Hindu Kush, spent all his time trying to convince me of his single-minded devotion. But immediately anyone else noticed him, he fell on them with silent pleas, all but verbally accusing me of neglect, ill-treatment and starvation. Boarding dogs brings you up against far more complex neuroses than any analyst's couch.

The woman reached out a hand to protect him and I could see her measuring me up for a report to the RSPCA as soon as she got back home. 'Poor thing,' she murmured, 'he seems very dejected. Quite scared.' It was an accusation. Then, 'Don't worry about keeping me waiting. I should have made an appointment only I happened to be passing this way and we do want to get things settled.' She exuded Devon Violets and utter authority.

Twelfth Night was past but I always leave just one piece of tinsel up somewhere to carry me through the year to come. You can't simply dismiss Christmas as if it never happened. I like a link to remind me there's another one ahead.

The woman's eyes took in everything – me, Charlie's nicked ear, encyclopaedias out of order – and finally the tinsel star where they settled as she went on, 'Anyway, I always think it best to have frank discussions face to face.'

Who on earth was she? An enraged wife whose husband took too long delivering a boarding Pom? Was I to be accused of his infidelity? I'd sooner have had the Pom than any husband of hers.

'Sattersthwaite-Pells,' she said suddenly, beaming at me at last. It sounded as if she were bestowing a blessing. 'Monica Sattersthwaite-Pells.' She gave a saucy giggle and said, 'At school they

11

called me Knickers, but I'm known in the trade as Monty.'

Trade? What trade? And she was the most unlikely contender for the name of Knickers. I smiled weakly. I noticed her elegant slender feet. Mine are broad and serviceable. The world's divided into race-horses and cart-horses and the cart-horses are the ones in slippers shuffling to the Co-op. The race-horses have delicately high arches and prepare the shopping lists. They also pay the bills, of course, but that's because they're born into 'A' type shoes. 'A' fittings, I've noticed, are ahead of me every time. After some months during the off-season trying out a sideline in clipping, stripping and grooming (dogs) and with most of the proceeds going back into Elastoplast (bites), I found an 'A' fitting foot was always prepared to pay a fair fee but expected a perfect result. The dog would be as tractable as a stuffed hedgehog – so long as the owner was there. I'm wary of 'A' fittings. They're smarter than I am, speaking generally.

We shook hands. I could see it was a preliminary to battle. The kick-off, the toss, the bugle call to arms. Charlie put his head on one side and warned me, with a long look, to watch it. I frowned at him for acting as double agent.

'I represent The Friends of Beowulf,' Monty Sattersthwaite-Pells said proudly, as I made myself moderately comfortable and as close to the fire as politeness allowed without blotting it from sight. 'I thought first of writing to you. Then, being in the vicinity as it were, decided on this confrontation instead.'

'Good,' I said, not meaning a bit of it. Friends of Beowulf were going to be no friends of mine, I could see that. The end of her nose had a small blemish which leapt about as she spoke, like a squirrel on a griddle. I don't like the word 'confrontation'. It indicates something I'm going to be asked to defend, deny, explain or accept.

'I'll come straight to the point then,' she said. 'We want this house.' I stared at her. The squirrel settled warily for a moment, but remained alert. Pa and I had lived in the house for about two years and before that *nobody* wanted it. I didn't want it much myself at first but it was the only one we saw among dozens of others that we could afford and that also offered some scope for contributing towards the dreaded Rates. I like to know that any house I occupy is going to help support itself, so it has to offer something more than adequate shelter. Something such as an orchard, greenhouses, a machine in the cellar for counterfeiting banknotes or, as in this case, kennels outside which I had seen at

12

once would contribute to a splendid dog-boarding business. Beautiful kennels, almost new, immaculately kept, timbered and wired with ample runs, an exercise yard and a sick-bay. Trees beyond gave shadow and any dog lucky enough to take up residence on a temporary basis would probably have second thoughts about going home again.

The boarding had been pretty successful, even though the kennels remained unoccupied. It was just that every arrival had very good reasons for preferring to be inside the house with me. As I'm not one of those ruthless tycoons who make fortunes at the cost of their clients, and as I was alone that first summer anyway (my husband being in hospital), I put up less than a token resistance. I was, to be honest, jolly glad of the company. In the meantime, the kennels looked impressive and efficient to customers, and acted as a constant reminder that I was running a business and not just entertaining a few friends.

The house, an old rectory, though shabby and dim, was big enough to sleep a pack of hounds if necessary and by the end of that summer I was taking any pet at all, provided it paid its way. Snakes, tortoises, canaries, rabbits, hamsters, kinkajous and frogs. We adopted a pig, goats and a donkey, not to mention the welcome I gave to the three children – not mine, of course. Ben, then thirteen, had parents who were occupied elsewhere and he now came back to us for every school holiday. Emily, then nine, arrived with her dog Rajah, and eventually elected to live with us in term time so she could go to our friendly village school instead of her huge local one. Then there was Adam who had brought me his dog, Lady, to board because she was unpopular at home. Lady and Rajah boarded full time, and the rest of the permanent intake had settled down in their respective quarters and gave us little or no trouble at all. We were all very happy in a very ordered existence, routine but rarely dull. Adam, now thirteen, came to us as often as his divorced parents would surrender him.

The house had become home to us all and here was someone eager to snatch it away. What, I cried to myself, what had I done to make the place so attractive to Squirrel-nose and her Friends? Did they know something about it that I didn't? Gold bullion deep 'neath the daisies somewhere, anybody's for the want of a metal-detector? Oil slurping under the hen-run perhaps? 'Well,' I said modestly, 'it's nice of you to want it, but it's not for sale, I'm afraid.'

'We are aware of that, of course. Even so, I'm sure you'll

reconsider when I explain. You're a reasonable woman.'

Did she mean I was a woman of sweet reason? or that I was cheap at the price? The sweet reason bit I am, of course, and it's funny but when people tell you you're something you know you're not, you're more inclined to believe them than your own inside information. I immediately found myself being tolerant and benign. I adopted an air of understanding and eager accord. If she had then said she could see I was a woman of filthy temper amounting to murderous instincts, I would have had her begging for mercy as I thumped her head on the floor. I told you those 'A' fittings made her a lot smarter than I was.

'What we are prepared to do,' she went on, 'is offer you a Figure You Can't Refuse.' I bridled. How had she found out there was hardly any price at that moment that my bank manager would have refused on my behalf? What with the boarding season months ahead, the number of local dogs begging to be stripped, clipped or even groomed in January negligible, and the new breeding venture seemingly governed by unsuitable leg length on the part of my only suitable applicant, times were bleak indeed.

'We are, of course, a Registered Charity.' She handed me a card.

I waited, holding it in my hand, the dead white card like a flag of surrender supplied by the enemy. 'An Animal Welfare Trust,' she explained. 'We rescue pets smuggled into this country and appre- hended by authorities at Customs level. Where no one can be found to foot the six months' quarantine, these poor creatures are often destroyed. We have set ourselves up to save them. We either assist with kennel fees where owners can afford to contribute or we pay the entire cost and, provided owners keep in touch, visit and help where possible, hand back the pet if wanted or find good homes when the time comes. We raise funds from appeals both here and overseas and this house, with its ideal range of kennels, is in an excellent position between London and the Channel ports.' She beamed, the matter settled as far as she was concerned. I could see Knickers was used to getting her own way and keeping her elastic straight.

Charlie stiffened. He sensed undercurrents, but to me it was all plain sailing.

'I'm very sorry,' I said firmly, 'but it's out of the question. We've been here less than two years. The kennels form part of *my* business, too.'

'You don't use them,' she accused me. We stared at one another. It was undeniable, of course, and indefensible. Yet, for all she

14

knew, I might be keeping midgets there, or growing mushrooms; running a murderer's mortuary on the rent-a-plot basis or preparing to throw the place open to the public on summer Sundays. Things like that can be big business nowadays. They flock to nose round anything from a parsonage to a palace, provided they can go back home knee-deep in sour grapes and convincing themselves with constant repetition that they much prefer their own bijou bungalow and quite exquisite taste. I think I'd rather have the mortuary.

I stood up. 'I'm so sorry I can't help you,' I said icily.

'Do you really think,' she tried persuasively, 'it is fair to leave that range of lovely kennels unused, when poor, sad creatures, such as this one' – Charlie gave an instant imitation of a poor, sad creature – 'unwanted, neglected, starved even,' – Charlie ran through a repertoire of anguish and then fell over as Mrs Sattersthwaite-Pells stood up – 'are so desperate?' It was a very emotive moment. We stared at one another, then she rested a hand clothed in dead goat on my arm for a moment.

Her car was purring down towards the motorway when I went back to the kitchen and stuck the card behind a pile of bills on the dresser. 'She only wanted to take away my home,' I told Ben bitterly. He was washing-up at the sink. I put on the kettle and collected the teapot. Ben had stopped and turned towards me and I felt myself close to tears. I was glad I could be ready with the right sort of emotion though I had a sneaking fear it was motivated by anger more than anything.

Ben and I sat down and shared what his aunts – the Misses Priddle, late owners of our village shop but now running a home for the aged called 'Rainbow's End' at Newhaven – used to refer to as 'one of our strong Indians'. 'My dear,' the elder Miss Priddle had said to me once, recommending their Special Blend, 'a good, strong Indian can do more for you than a weak Chinese any day.' I didn't doubt it for a moment, but even a strong Indian couldn't have lifted my present flagging spirits. Once Pa heard about The Offer We Couldn't Refuse, he wouldn't refuse it.

After retiring early, he had decided to start making the fortune he always knew could be his once he got work out of the way. He chose Speculation or Property Development, although up till now he had done most of it lying back in a chair with his eyes closed. Small differences of opinion started erupting when he finally set off to view possible starting-points and I had to make it quite clear that I had no idea of moving into riverside warehouses in the

Liverpool Dock area, or Highland byres with a view of Aurora Borealis, even if they did have Vast Potential. Selling our old wrecktory (more apt spelling than the original) was his plan to raise capital. At all costs, he would have to be kept from Beowulf's Friend. I get very wary of people in skinned goat. And she was lean, too. Lean people – not thin, or skinny, or slender, but lean – are symbolic of all the word implies, or rhymes with, like mean, preen and much too keen. Lean people are like the thin end of a wedge. We tubbier types can't even squeeze in, let alone pass them. (Kindly hand me another sour grape.)

Ben said uneasily, closing the cupboard door on the final clean dish, 'she won't get it, will she? The lady with the electric nose?' He regarded it as home as much as I did. Ben, indeed, had helped me create what it had become, and London, where his mother lived, was somewhere to be in term time, like local boarding. I often wondered if it might have been better had we been less available, and then I reasoned it was the sort of thing people *say* simply because it's so often been said – the way they repeat it's good news to have family rows. 'Clears the air,' they say smugly, surveying the broken crockery. No row, argument or heated discussion ever cleared so much as it clouded, if you ask me. They simply plant seeds for further recrimination in the future.

So I could be happy with Ben coming to stay every holidays, and keep a clear conscience. And so could his mother, who then indulged her nervous breakdowns without feeling guilty and could recuperate in Spain without dragging along a reluctant son together with two Janet Reger nighties, a bottle of valium and the very latest in lovers.

The strong Indian was certainly doing its best. Ben had drawn the curtains and the old 'dog-walker' – a moth-eaten fur coat of vast proportions kept hanging behind the back door for general use when exercising residents and boarders three times a day – was over the back of a chair. Ben saw me look at it and nodded. 'They've been out,' he said. 'By the way, Pa rang, and said he'd ring again later. He's viewing some negotiable real estate, he says.'

We grinned. Pa always had the right professional terms even if he didn't seem too sure about the rest of it. One of his spies, another retired opportunist, had highly recommended something for immediate inspection and he'd gone haring off earlier that morning. They would doubtless discuss it over a few pints before and after, by which time both would have made a theorectical fortune.

Ben said, 'Why tell him about the wart-nosed woman? Keep her

16

a secret. Send her away if she comes again. Ignore her, forget her. Burn all correspondence.' No Mole could have been more ruthless. But I rather hoped we could discuss things rationally, like they advise in magazines manned by a staff of divorced neurotics usually showing hysterical tendencies.

'I'd never surrender this admirable little empire, this incredible gold-mine, this unique establishment, Ben, not even for a Figure he couldn't Refuse. Not a hog's hoof in hell of a chance . . .'

He relaxed and grinned. Then he said, 'Did you know it took a Norwegian fifteen years to train a trout to leap into a beer mug?'

'Go on!' I invited, impressed. 'Well, jug, actually, it says here,' he admitted, 'but that was in Norway, of course. I thought mug would sound more authentic, perhaps.' I could only think it had to be a mug who spent a quarter of his life wasting good beer. The things I liked best about Ben were his wide range of interests, his ability to dismiss gloom and despondency, and his strong Indians – all of which he could put together with a timing which was nothing short of miraculous.

Outside, the day was finishing with a rising gale and a falling temperature. It was wonderful to sink into a soporific stupor urged by the heat from our old Aga, the wafted aroma of Ben's baking and the steady, or unsteady, beat of Radio 1.

'They've got a Scottish DJ,' said Ben. 'He's just said he'll be away until next weekend because he's got a wee cough.'

'OK,' I said, 'I'm not falling for that one. A week off . . .'

Ben grinned. 'And they're still sending pea stalks to Bulgaria.'

I blushed, but I really had thought it was one of our biggest export earners: though what they did with the pea stalks when they got there really baffled me. Were they popular, like bamboo shoots for pandas? It was Ben who finally sorted me out and explained it was 'peace talks'. Ben was growing smarter than me, in spite of feet like flounders.

He passed me a slice of Bananabake, an original recipe tried out, unfortunately, at the same time as his Catfish Crumble. The Bananabake had a distinctly fishy taste and I slipped it quickly to Charlie who was prepared to eat anything from a bootlace to a set of false teeth if offered. The Catfish Crumble had been quite a successful experiment with a glut of cods' heads from the fishmonger plus stale bread donated by the baker following an undersubscribed Christmas. The dogs found it a change from the butcher's off-cuts or cast-offs or whatever it was he sent in sinister bulk and Oxo cartons every week. Ben spread his own Bananabake liberally with butter from the farm up the lane where, with free-range eggs, we paid a bit more than the usual price for what I often suspected they themselves bought from the same supermarket I scorned.

'Do you still want to go back and live in town?' asked Ben. He was over the stage of speaking through a barrage of crumbs, and I no longer ducked as he opened his mouth. Just as it was his ambition to get away from the big city so, for a long time, it had been mine to get back in there among remembered lights and delights.

'No,' I said, surprised yet again that it was true. 'Odd, isn't it? Came here against my will and now I'm fighting to stay. What on earth would I do now, in a city?'

'What did you do when you lived there before?'

It was a good question. What didn't I do? I did a lot of things, and loved every minute. Now I did a lot of other things and loved every minute twice as much. Maybe it makes very little difference where you are. Being happy hasn't much to do with the accessibility of buses and beer mats on the one hand, nor with farms and fieldmice on the other.

'I did a lot of things,' I said defensively. Ben knew about my various horticultural and agricultural experiences with apples, tomatoes, herbs, lilies and canine exploitation, which was about to be joined by breeding, but nothing about my sundry civic and cultural efforts. 'I was a PRO once,' I claimed.

'What's a PRO?'

'Funny you should ask that,' I began, agreeably recalling more lofty occupations than feeding the motley lot now living and boarding under my present roof. Charlie wriggled over, trying his eye-appeal act, so successfully paraded for the attentions of Beowulf's Friend. I ignored it. Then I couldn't ignore it any longer. I began the long, slow stroke that sends him into ecstatic bliss. Rosie rested her chin on my left foot so I could wiggle my toes under her chin. Treacle drew up close the other side, claiming my spare hand. I felt like a one-man band. The rest were snoozing, but Mattie kept up a low rumble of complaint as she dozed. Outside, snow drifted, hesitated, settled, vanished. Advance armies reconnoitring for troops obviously massing in the night sky. 'I didn't know what it was myself, actually. I still wonder if I got it wrong. It was just that I wanted a different job from the one I was in and it represented A Challenge.' The clock ticked, the anthracite crackled, the cuckoo put his nose out of the clock and yawned.

'What sort of job were you in?'

'Organising exhibitions for an art gallery. A small private one. But of some distinction, I do assure you. The first invitations I sent out were fine. Gilt lettering, deckle edges, Gothic print, dark blue card. The lot. Except I forgot to put the address. The Private View was very private indeed. Wine ran like the rivers of Babylon with just four of us to get through fifty filled glasses.'

'Did you get the elbow?'

'No, just sloshed. They were quite keen for me to stay by the time the evening was over. But I was a bit worried about the next morning.'

'Go on.'

'So I resigned. And then I rejected Harold Pinter.'

'You did *what?*'

'Rejected Harold Pinter. I didn't know who he was, then. It was some years ago, of course. They told me at the agency he wanted a secretary but I was worried I might miss The Baker's Oven breadshop if I waited to ask questions and make an appointment, so I rejected him. I often wished afterwards that I'd got a Mother's Pride at Sainsbury's instead. Still, that's prudence for you. Better safe with the sliced and wrapped than rushing to grasp at the fresh and tempting.'

We both pondered the wisdom of it. Then Ben said shortly, 'I prefer sliced and wrapped.' He sounded puzzled. I didn't admit I prefer it too. But then I like ice cream better than Beaujolais and 'Coronation Street' better than 'Panorama' and it's only in admitting it that I'm at all unusual. There are things to be scorned, like convenience foods, and things to be admired, like wholefood diets, or you might just as well emigrate.

'Then you were this PRO thing?'

'That's it. They said the job was going in a new outfit up near Berkeley Square. The girl in the agency, who wanted to get her commission, I expect, said I'd be simply sensational, and you know what a sucker I am for flattery. I told a few people about the job and they all said I'd be terrific at it. Such scope, too. So exciting. Things like that.'

'And was it?'

'I'm not sure. It began to dawn on me the initials might be an abbreviation for something rather unsavoury. Then I had the interview with a Mr de'Ath. I didn't like to admit I hadn't a clue what it was, so I decided to wait and find out as I went along.'

'And did you?' Ben finished the Bananabake, the butter and the boiled beetroot I'd bottled in the summer. I was sick of reminiscing. With my future career in the breeding business off to a non-start, my home almost under the hammer and a pile of ironing to do, I decided to finish the story quickly.

'Sort of. Mr de'Ath congratulated me on his choice. He asked if I would like to become a partner in the business and invest a lump sum. I didn't have a lump sum but I agreed enthusiastically just the same. Agreeing enthusiastically is a very easy way of extending one's horizons, I've found, so long as you don't sign anything.'

I never give advice, only what's good for *me*. There's a lot of difference. I was thinking, 'Suppose Knickers meets Pa on his way back from the station – she determined to get her friends in and he determined to get his family out? What then?' There weren't many offers he couldn't refuse if he had to get his hands on a lump sum for a deposit elsewhere. I lost the thread of what I was saying, my mind being as dissolute as a Tudor monastery.

'Go *on*,' urged Ben crossly.

'Oh, yes, well, I had a telegram which said, 'Monday Welcome Death' and it put me off a bit. After that it sort of fell apart. . . . ' I shrugged. 'I'd agreed to do a promotion job on a hairdresser so I went round, had my hair done, noted the floral nylon overalls and dirty floors and began my Frank and Fearless Report. My hair looked awful too.' It was no good: my mind was on Monty Sattersthwaite-Pells and my husband planning a takeover. I went to the back door and looked out down the drive towards the motorway. Small strong lights hastened towards unknown destinations, no longer calling me to follow as they once had, but leaving me glad and grateful to be here in a place I'd grown to love like a second skin, where I'd made friends and established myself as an identity to be recognised. The shabby old house had become very precious to me. Ben waited impatiently. It was much more amusing than Careers Class.

Then the phone began to ring. Phones always do when you're unprepared, the way places on maps lurk in the fold or totter off the edge of a page out of sight. Points I want to make get drowned by thunder or a sneeze. We all stagger through life under mighty blows or teeny nips, and if I didn't get so many nips, the mighty blows would have left me with one leg and bifocals by now. So who's complaining?

I finished quickly. 'I went off home at teatime and wrote up my notes, with observations, ideas and suggestions including a colour scheme of grey and ginger, and took them back to Berkeley Square next morning, but there was nobody there. De'Ath and my dream of a directorship had vanished.' I picked up the phone and said crisply, 'One moment, please,' put my hand over the mouthpiece and finished, 'The party was over. I never got any wages and I never found out what PRO really stood for and I never went back to the hairdressers.' I took my hand away and trilled apologetically, 'So sorry to keep you waiting. Now, can I help you?'

'Yes!' shouted my husband angrily, just as the pips interrupted, ending any chance of letting me know how. The dialling tone began and I put down the phone and felt guilty. How was I to have known who it was – and from a call box too?

Charlie had taken over the rocking-chair. Charlie's mania for movement stretched to anything at all. Any wheels led to heaven for Charlie. More than once he'd been fetched or brought back from outlying villages where he'd managed to arrive via the post van, baker's van or visitor's car. He was the only dog I knew who could successfully hitch a lift. Lorry drivers, businessmen in Rovers, sympathetic old ladies in velvet hats or punks in a hurry, they all stopped for Charlie. He did it by limping and panting and hanging about on the edge of the road as if he'd been hit by traffic. He enjoyed being handed over to the police who usually gave him a biscuit, a saucer of tea and a lot of attention.

'I had an afghan once who was always running away,' I remembered, trying to dismiss a picture in my mind of Pa vandalising the phone box in rage. 'He was a bit like Charlie.' I leant against the Aga and waited for the phone to ring again. I was determined to see my story got there first. 'He always legged it to the Battersea Dogs' Home the minute he was loose. We lived a couple of miles away but Cawston-Grieves (that was his name when we had him) ignored traffic, pedestrians, one-way streets and all other dogs, he was so eager to get there. They kept a special place for him in the end. I believe it's still known as "The Cawston-Grieves" Corner.' I hesitated, listening for the phone but nothing happened. Had Pa given up and gone away, bought some abandoned supermarket or crumbling tower block going at A Price He Couldn't Refuse? Or was he just asking strangers in the street for change?

Ben was still eating crumbs from the Bananabake. With some asperity he asked, 'But *why*?'

'Why what?'

'Why did he go to the Dogs' Home?'

'Why do people book in at Butlins? He liked the company there and the activity and possibly the food. He was saved all that bother

21

of wagging when we lavished love all over him, and barking at intruders, and having his hair messed about by fond fingers. He had a touch of the Dalai Lamas, perhaps. You know, liked to detach himself from civilisation as we know it.' I reached the final word skilfully as the phone rang in a wild scream of abuse.

'Hullo darling,' I said carefully.

A faint voice murmured words that could have been a Dutchman telling his beads into a pint mug, but they ended, '. . . for the call?'

'Of course!' I cried heartily, 'delighted, lovely, splendid!' I found myself beaming as though I were being carefully watched.

When Pa came through he sounded as if he'd landed at Chesapeake Bay in mistake for Faggots' Halt and his voice kept surging on the tide.

'It took a hell of a time to get here,' he exploded, confirming my suspicions, 'but it's taken a damn sight longer to get through on the phone. What's happening there? What's going on?'

I began, 'Well, Charlie's rocking, Ben's eating, I'm chatting – all very much as . . .' But he interrupted, 'I've seen it. A snip, I tell you. A snip!'

They're all snips till we get down to the foundations or glance up at the roof that happens to be missing. However, I like to be co-operative, so I asked as if I really cared, 'What is it then? I mean, what sort of place, actually?' I was dead keen to know at that point.

'It's – well, it's a signal box, you might say,' he paused uneasily, then rushed on, 'not used now, of course.' Well, that was a comfort. Boring, I imagine, to live with those great clanking handles being drawn like The Incredible Hulk's half-pint every time an express is due to thunder past the bedroom. 'But there's bags of potential,' he ended weakly.

For a moment I thought he meant sacks of something like concrete. He once almost bought an offshore island (but what other kind is there?) because it grew good cauliflowers, and another time rang in great excitement to say the roof of the rotunda had collapsed but grapefruit were only sixpence in the village shop. He could find silver linings in the middle of a fall-out.

'Oh, yes?' I queried, cynically.

'The tunnel's thrown in, you see,' he began. I thought he said 'blown in' but I wasn't too bothered. Unless you're a mole, it's no fun tunnelling around for a bath or to do the sausage-and-mash for supper. He went on, 'You could grow mushrooms, there. We would build on to the box, of course. A few acres come with it. Rather isolated but a very amusing view. Plenty of scope.' I tried not to see a scene which would have me falling through the new curtains to admire the scope which grew like mad all over the wide grey yonder, a thousand miles from anywhere.

'Interesting,' I muttered, losing any attempt at enthusiasm.

'Better fly now. This can go on the bill and come off your expenses,' he suggested. He's under some peculiar impression that if we claim calls under 'Business Expenses', we just don't pay real money to anyone.

Then we both said goodbye and he said he'd ring again or be home before midnight. Exasperating men are always the most endearing. It's insufferable.

'A signal box,' I said to Ben who was waiting for news with his fingers in the biscuit tin, 'and tunnel. I'm to grow mushrooms. View of a busy sidings, I should think, plus industrial background. Should whittle down our dog population and keep callers away. Can't you imagine, 'Do pop in for a coffee, Doris. We're about five miles from the third bridge after you leave the shunting yards, heading north.'

'On the Up Line,' Ben filled in usefully.

'Bags of potential and plenty of scope, so we should be all right for the next strike.'

Treacle, a 'coloured' dog, as Emily referred to her when she first came to stay, slithered over and licked my hand. Treacle never fails to watch my metabolism rise and fall. At that moment, it was about as low as it could get. My Spirit Level is the way I think of it: a sort of emotional thermometer. Inside, the mercury dodges about in response to weather, prospects, people and the amount of sleep I can get. Just then, it was pretty inactive, and Treacle knew it. Treacle had come to us years before, sensitive, loving, domesticated and protective, a puppy abandoned in a ditch with her extrovert, swaggering, wilful sister Rosie. Rosie now lay under the table gnawing away at a smelly bone she'd dug up and brought in from the garden earlier. Rosie was one of those long-haired, scruffy dogs with a permanent grin and muddy feet. They didn't get on too well these days. Once devoted, they were now like relations who suspect one another of designs on the family silver. I never knew whether Treacle made a fuss of me for genuine reasons or to assert her virtues over Rosie's waywardness. Nevertheless, I stroked her long smooth head and she rolled over in a state of euphoria. How easy it is to be God. Does he, too, suspect all that praise and worship is just to get a place near the Aga?

On the wall, where I like to chalk inspiring sentiments, a recent one caught my eye. DON'T LET WORRY SCREW YOU FLAT: UNWIND AT ONCE AND KNOCK IT BACK! It was the only one Pa approved. He thought it meant a free hand with the bottle of Glenfiddich he kept among the vinegar, cooking oil and sauce bottles on the third shelf down in the larder, where stray callers couldn't detect it and expect to be offered a share. Theirs, a simpler Scotch, was with the medium-priced sherry, remains of gin and vodka from Christmas and a stray bottle of Martini, in the drawing-room where nobody ventured from September to April if they had any sense and were allergic to refrigeration. Occasionally I sneaked a bottle into the office for clients or friends, but thin ice formed over everything in the drawing-room, and just handling a bottle could cause frost-bite. Ben once said ours was the kind of house where you put on a coat to come *in*.

'Better than that multi-storey car park, though,' comforted Ben, after a silence between us full of heavy thought. Pa had seen that as a possible block of flats, filled in with 'a bit of breeze block' and promising me the penthouse with roofspace for the dogs. 'Nice income from the lower floors,' he anticipated, 'and very handy for the card shop next door.' He has vision, he says. He accuses me of lacking it. I badly need vision, he says, specially when I demurred at a lifeboat-house near Pevensey Bay or a disused sorting office up for grabs in Gwent. 'You don't have the *vision*,' he complained, like a tub-thumping Evangelist, 'Can't you see a home is a home wherever you choose to make it? Look at the birds, they're not fussy.' So when he comes up with the aviary at Colchester Zoo, I'll be ready with chirrups of delight.

'We'll do it up a bit here and there,' he once said airily, trying to win me into a desolate hotel with a hundred damp bedrooms on the edge of a Cornish cliff, 'and flog it off at enormous profit.' You see, that's his great super plan, if only I could be enthusiastic, too. I discovered the hotelier had given up after a bit of aggro through the loss of guests over a garden wall to the sheer drop beneath. When his cat vanished, it was the last straw and he walked out, leaving some eggs scrambling on the hotplate. The wretched dump had actually been knocked down to Pa at auction for a ridiculous price (though I thought any price would have been utterly ridiculous) and included palms in the dining-room and seating for multitudes in summer all wearing cotton frocks and shoes full of sand. Kitchens lavishly offered a selection of cooking equipment for my occasional tin of beans. I refused to risk *our* cat's life there, so Pa unloaded it on a couple who kept pigeons.

He rang back when we were having supper and said quickly, 'Built to last, you know. Signal boxes are like that. Tunnel happens to be all good London brick and a bit of slate. Stand a thousand years, I shouldn't wonder.' Such a relief. You don't want your signal box to fall down when you're making the beds, for heaven's sake.

'Nice,' I agreed, 'see *us* out anyway – with a bit of ivy to hold the drainpipes steady for the millenium.' You can say anything to a Man with A Mission. He stays starry-eyed in the face of downright ridicule. I liked to know he was having a good time, though nothing was going to coax me to go and live on the Brighton line.

He'd just announced that he'd be very late back when the pips joined in and cut me out again.

I had to be able to stake my claim *here* before he staked ours *there* – or anywhere else. Even if Lulu found a lover within the next twenty-four hours, it would still be nine weeks before I had proof positive that I was established in a flourishing business. After that, of course, I'd be winning on points and any coaxing to go and view 'a gardener's bothy in Bangor' would justifiably fall on deaf ears.

'I'll have to give Hetty a ring, I suppose,' I finally admitted. Ben gave a short laugh. We both knew all along it would come to that. Hetty had acted for the past year or more as vet, friend, adviser and general manager unasked, but usually with relief from me afterwards. Hetty was born organising. I would never be surprised to hear she stage-managed the whole scene in the Delivery Room. Hetty would know somebody, something, somewhere able to help. Then she'd box me smartly about the metaphorical ears and set the adrenalin at full ferment again. Hetty was very fond of Pa and though she would never do a thing to stand in the way of his plans, she was quite selfish enough to keep him around by making sure I did.

Ben said, 'In Imperial China, pekinese puppies were suckled by wet nurses. Female babies were, of course, drowned.'

'Naturally.' It seemed reasonable. For one litter of puppies at that very moment, I would have willingly drowned a handful of humans, provided I could choose which ones. Sometimes I do have vision, you see. Quite a lot of it.

# 2

Pa rang again just before I took out the dogs for their last run before bedtime: Charlie, Treacle, Mattie, Rosie, Sniff and Snuff (boarding while their owners were skiing), Lady (Adam's dog who was now practically permanent) and Lulu (on a lead and in her own exercise yard). Sniff was pure Cairn, but Snuff was somewhere related to a poodle which made for added interest in the leg-and-lamp-post area. Frilly came with us and a homing hen called Atilla, who lived in the old game larder, abandoned by me because it was even colder than the fridge. Atilla flew in and out through the small high window, perched on the game rails and had been known to lay the occasional egg in an empty gardening trug. We struggled against an icy wind, some of us disappearing discreetly into the rhododendrons and most of us wishing we were back by the fire. Rajah, the spaniel who belonged to Emily, hovered in the porch.

Pa had warned me he might have to stay overnight. 'There's quite a reasonable little hotel here,' he had said casually. 'Snooker table, carpeted loo, and a barman who knows all about axed railway lines.'

'Very useful,' I said.

'The only way I could get home would be by cab to the main line, then the 9.15 which means I wouldn't be back before midnight even if it was on time.'

'Very true,' I said.

'So I'll take a room and be back about midday. OK?'

'OK.'

'If I'd started earlier and got here sooner, I'd have been back quicker.'

'Look,' I said impatiently, 'you don't have to feel so guilty. It's common sense to stay overnight. What's more, you'll get a decent meal and a super breakfast. I'm just envious, that's all.' He hates travel – he says. Hates being away from home. Hates hotel bills and beds. Now I don't. Yet he's the one who always seems to be on the move while I'm static. It's just the way it goes but at times I

26

want to send a stern letter to God who does seem to get his lines crossed rather easily. It's my belief he's trying to do too much. He should learn to delegate.

When I got back to the kitchen with the dogs, the phone was ringing. I hoped it was Pa back on the line again so I could be nicer, wish him a happy time, say I'd miss him which I would. I'd do it warmly and sincerely, instead of with an edge to my voice which must have been only too obvious earlier. But it was my friend, Marsha.

'Darling,' she murmured huskily, 'I've something to ask you.' Marsha is a lady of some delight, often alone and palely loitering by someone else's phone to save on her own bill. Hence the late call, I guessed. Sometimes she silver-sat for friends, or Picasso-sat, or mink-and-sable-sat in summer. She charged the very highest rates and did rather well out of it. She only drew the line at babies or pets, and elderly relatives were definitely out. She had once fridge-sat for a friend who had to go out and leave a prepared dinner for six. And another time, script-sat because burglars nowadays know just where the true values lie, and food or ideas come pretty high above Grannie's pearl choker and the Aubusson.

I have to invent more excuses to outwit Marsha than I avoid raindrops. Marsha has been divorced several times, but regularly loses sight of all alimony and has to be helped by social services to pay her rent and living expenses. Marsha says she gets her solicitors mixed and writes to the wrong ones. I can only approve of her ethics reluctantly because in her time she's paid out so much in rates and taxes that however much she takes back now in handouts could never be more than a minute fraction of the total. Marsha considers, rightly or wrongly, that living for years in the top tax bracket was simply an insurance for falling on harder times, such as now. In fact, she complains, the Welfare State is a bloody sight meaner with her than she ever was with them. Marsha never, never borrows money from anyone. She usually wants something far more daunting, such as our spare room. Already I was on the alert.

'Go ahead,' I said, sharpening up what was left of my wits.

'Your meadow.' She paused. Perhaps she was beginning to recognise silent resistance. 'May we have it?'

'Have it? How do you mean, have it?'

'Use it, borrow it, be in it. We want to hold an Equinoxial Ablutive Antrada. It would be the ideal spot.'

That was all I needed. Marsha moving in was always a perfect argument for us to move on, preferably out of reach. If Pa knew she was coming, we'd be more than half way to the signal box, the bothy or the abandoned car park.

Marsha was very much into fringe religions. Gone the period of pop culture when she clamoured for the company of groups and gigs. Now it was all worship, worship, worship. First it had been Nature, pronounced as if just discovered, and represented by the simple Oak with much dancing around, bowing to, and planting of acorns where they would probably be a dreadful nuisance to future generations. Then it was what she called the Sense Scene. 'One incurs the ideology of extra-sensory interpretation,' she explained during a weekend with us when feelings ran high because she had discovered the Glenfiddich, 'It's very moving.' ('Very,' my husband had grumbled later when he found everything used up in the bathroom. 'I shall put a rev counter on the loo roll if she stays faithful to the Cause.') But she had gone on to other creeds and cultures, and God, who rarely got a look-in but probably watched it all with some amusement, glad to get away from all that cant and dogma in his gloomy Branch Offices, had no more ides than we did what the next and latest cult would be. I was always having to head her off from bringing it to us, too.

'It's very cold up here,' I warned her quickly. 'Very high we are, you see. Bitter winds from the sea. Snow. You'd never believe the ice on the pond!' I wasn't sure I did myself but I felt sure it was there.

'Cold?' queried Marsha, as if the word was new to her. 'What is Cold?' From one who had kept the fire on in our spare room night and day during a mild September, I did think she might have had a rough idea. 'You must learn to defy all senses but the One Great Awareness, darling.' She gave a little laugh, which was a reproof if ever I heard one. So the Sense Scene was over, and all that sniffing and tasting and touching was now past, and this was the other extreme. I remembered her taking in great deep breaths of fertiliser, the henhouse floor and even rotting greens with apparent ecstasy. But it wasn't unusual for Marsha to rush from one extreme to another. I was dying to ask if the latest faith cut her off from the continual indulgence of cigarettes, Bounty Bars, brandy and seed cake with which she seemed to surround herself by courtesy of the State.

'Manure, too,' I went on, urged by my dismay. 'Covered in pig manure. You would need tarpaulins to sit on and a supply of air fresheners or clothes' pegs. Smells frightful, and now it's all over the house.' I meant the smell but I believe she thought I meant the manure; probably reckoned on me introducing porker-boarding into the general scene. We never surprised one another, both secretly convinced the other was mad.

Marsha said, obviously shaken, 'Maybe spring?' and I, knowing by then she'd be on to Water Worship or the Cult of the Abdomen, which could be better carried on elsewhere, agreed whole-heartedly. Marsha and I shared a pleasant relationship, playing off one another's wits, and she did at least sharpen up mine when they were beginning to go a bit blunt. It's a fringe benefit of the less attractive religions. You can step back, relieved, that you anyway won't be called on to shave your head, hand over your life savings or get up at three in the morning because you have been told by someone less gullible than you are that it's going to get you membership into the Celestial Club. Which, on thinking about it, would probably end up as full of conditions as the one they're busy creating below.

When I put down the phone, Ben said, 'Did you know a certain tribe in south-east Asia during the third century worshipped rats?'

'Then Marsha might get round to me yet,' I said, wishing I'd been a bit more sympathetic, 'but it's no comfort. Tell me something I'd really like to hear, go on . . . ' I took milk from the fridge and began making cocoa.

Ben thumbed his way through the dog-eared paperback which he kept permanently in his pocket. Then he read out, 'A blue whale's testicles weigh a hundred pounds each?'

I shook my head gloomily and began with the tin-opener.

'Beef cattle have a lower sex drive than dairy hens?'

'*Hens?*'

'Sorry, herds. It's been dripped on.'

I shook my head again and sighed.

Ben read out desperately, 'The police got a lot of calls after a rat was seen in Chelmsford High Street with its head stuck in a yoghurt pot, then?'

I laughed. I laughed so much I had to sit down. 'It's rotten for the rat,' I gasped sympathetically, 'but it's much funnier than the whale's testicles!'

'They're not meant to be funny,' complained Ben irritably. 'They're a collection of strange and interesting animal facts, that's all. I think they're fascinating.'

'Does it say whether there's an AI Centre for sealyhams?' I asked despairingly. If we left it much longer, Lulu would be off the boil and I could reckon on a rapid rush to some bus shelter in Bridlington. During my married life, I'd lived in converted schools, an abbey, a castle, a Cathedral close, a London square, on a farm, in a folly and I felt I'd done enough adapting to call a halt.

'You were going to ring Hetty,' Ben reminded me.

I began to dial her number before putting down my mug of cocoa . . . I started again. Hetty was at home, between sherry and surgery, a very good time to get her really.

'How did the mating go?'

'It didn't. Her legs were too long. Anyway she's not keen on him any more and neither am I.'

'If you don't hurry, it'll be too late,' she warned me.

'I know. But where do I find a sealyham stud with approved leggage who won't be too fussy about ours? The Puddisey Pedigree was the only one for miles, you said so.'

'Ma Mince always gets her complaint in first when her boys can't make it. They're probably all gay dogs anyway. I often thought so before. Lulu's legs are lovely. Just right. You'll have to go a bit further afield and try one of the Tartan tribe. Robespierre would be best. A fine, upstanding randy beast. No trouble there. Sired more sealyhams than I've had pigs' pregnancies!' She gave a throaty laugh and I suddenly felt hopeful again.

'Where would that be?'

'Bunty Finch's. The Finch twins used to be a big name in the breed. Now they're happily retired. They do a bit of mating, but they don't show much.'

'Some girls get all the luck!'

'Tell them I recommended Robby. He must be six or seven now, but he's very reliable. Very reliable indeed! I've known him service four a day in his prime and then go out and find a couple of bitches in the village.' I wondered if *that* was anywhere in Ben's book. Hetty went on, 'Ring her tonight. If not Robespierre, Tartan Trespasser the Third would be OK.' But my heart was set on the dashing Casanova.

Hoping the Finch twins didn't go to bed early, I rang the number Hetty had given me. Bunty Finch sounded hale enough, not to mention hearty. She asked if Lulu had been 'out' before and, because she was so friendly I confessed about the morning's misalliance.

'Huh!' she snorted, 'he never was what you might call keen. Nice action though. Can't say I ever fancied him much myself. Never thought he got stuck in with the enthusiasm I like to see.' I was quite taken aback, but relieved she could confirm it hadn't just been lack of allure from Lulu.

'Frankly, I didn't care for the way he dug out a squeaky toy and played with that instead,' I said.

'Well, you can't go wrong with our Robby! Rarin' to go, he is. See you tomorrow morning, then, OK?' She suddenly rattled with laughter. 'Don't know where we are, I bet! Quite forgot. Easy enough to find if you keep on the Fenhill to Larkspur Rise road. Head north from Tussock's Edge till you come on a U-turn and follow down the river meadows to the humpty-backed bridge. Don't go over it for heaven's sake! Go round it. You'll see a sign which says 'No Through Road'. Take that. You'll come to a fork half way. Ignore it. Take the S-bend to the T-junction and . . .' but I stopped even trying to understand a word of it, interrupted, 'Thanks a lot: sounds straightforward enough to me,' and got out the Ordnance Survey map as soon as she'd gone.

Ben and I spread it all over the table and shut Frilly in the cupboard because she always sits on the bit you want to look at. We poured over the B roads and the river and all the humpty-back hillocks where our supper plates got in the way. Then Ben said, triumphantly, 'There! Where Emily spilt the coffee that time. That's it.' The house, Bunty had said, was called Molehills, and you could just see the final 'ls' next to a spot which might have been undulating territory but was really Em's elevenses.

'The village looks as if it's called Slappits Bottom!' shrieked Ben with delight. We got the magnifying glass and that's exactly what it was.

'I'll never dare ask for it if I get lost,' I said anxiously, 'and it looks terribly complicated. It's miles away, too. I wish they'd come here.'

'They never do,' said Ben wisely. 'You might sneak him off to serve another three bitches in a back room while she's sipping Madeira in the conservatory, you see.' It all grew more shocking by the moment. Still, if it would save me from a life condemned to a set of signals, I could shelve moral outrage.

'Did you put the van away?' asked Ben. But I'd left it round by the back door and I wasn't going to go outside again. Any wind was from the north and the frost had taken over. The ground crackled underfoot like walking on cornflakes. The air was like glass which splintered against one's eyes and brought tears. Breath wreathed a shroud for the foolhardy and snow frittered and faltered, waiting its chance.

31

The van had been left to me by the Priddle sisters when they gave up the village shop. 'Do have it,' the younger and prettier Priddle had pleaded, 'we shall be buying ourselves a little bounder. That's what I always call those small compact saloons.' So I took the gift of the van most gratefully. It had PRIDDLE SISTERS on the side, with 'Grocery & General Provisions delivered regularly' beneath. It was as clean, reliable and sturdy as its original owners, and not much younger. Ben kept suggesting we gave it a respray but I found it more comforting than strict anonymity.

Pa used the equally aged Triumph Herald which had been my pride and joy so long ago that I forgot what its original colour had been. It was now pink. All my cars end up pink. I once had a very old Rolls when it was still possible to find one left to rot in a barn, and this one wasn't even rotting. It had been carefully constructed with love and strict attention to detail in 1926 and it still had double-declutch mechanism, of course, and a hand-brake on the running board. I lacquered it pink myself, because no garage would consider such folly. It gave that Rolls a new lease of life and we plunged skittishly round the countryside together, striking terror into the hearts of local people in the West Country. I believe it's still remembered around firesides on dark nights when tales are told of past horrors. But it was the only car I ever made money on when I sold it.

'Shall we lock up and go to bed?' I suggested, yawning. It was ten o'clock but we did have to be up early and, anyway, I prefer the radio in bed to the television almost anywhere. There's true luxury lying in dark warmth lulled by music. And don't give me the womb simile. I always think that must have been a dreadfully boring place. Joggled and splashed around and never catching the entire conversation outside. No wonder babies look so terribly cross when they finally emerge. That first cry is definitely one of protest at being kept like a ferret in a damp sack and missing Christmas.

Ben was still thinking about the Rolls. 'I'd really like a Bugatti,' he said. 'When I'm marketing in a big way – I'm doing a Kosher section to the Menus and a separate chapter in the Recipe Book – I shall get a bronze repro. Custom-built, of course. Copied from the original. I ought to have some vans first, though, for daily deliveries, like Meals on Wheels, with 'From Door to Dog Daily on the Dot'. One or two courses and every plate with the name on – mine one side and the dog or cat's the other. I'd do budgies and tortoises too, only they're not so fussy about mealtimes. I aim at a complete mobile pet service eventually. Thousands of kids want to be vets and can't pass the exams: all girls want to work with animals. Think of the teams I could send out to groom, or exercise, or simply visit for daily conversations with parrots, ball games with labradors, walks with snakes. Did you know snakes like a stroll? It says so somewhere in my book. And snakes are very popular at the moment. We've a few adders at school.'

We stared at one another and then I said, 'Did you mean that to be funny?'

'No,' said Ben, rather pleased with himself. He was never madly witty, but he had a terrific sense of humour. Kids are funniest when they don't try. He went on, frowning a bit, 'I'm just worried about cats. I can't think of any personal service I can advertise for cats. They're really into the Do-It-Yourself thing. Daily feeding, of course, and grooming long-haireds, but your simple tabby doesn't demand much.'

I picked up Frilly and hugged her. She demanded nothing at all. She would have got by in any situation on mere charm, and other people's plates.

I said, 'Once I'm established as a breeder, I'll get a pedigree queen and include kittens – Persians, white perhaps. Or do you think Burmese or Siamese, Ben?'

But he was pondering something quite different. 'How would you feel about running the first Pets' Restaurant here? I thought we could advertise 'Owners Welcome'. Just through summer to start with, of course, and outside on the lawn; and later in the conservatory? No tables – just a few rugs and cushions. . . . '

'Maybe something really rare like Russian Blues or Tonkinese. There's an Egyptian Mau in Canada, I believe. And of course there's Devon Rex, Cornish Rex and Short-haired Stumpies.' Frilly leapt down and stalked away, her tail flicking with agitation.

'We'll both be in the Bugatti class at this rate!'

'We might serve coffee and cake, I suppose – no, why should we? If you go into an ordinary restaurant, nobody would hand Charlie a menu, would they?' But if they did it nicely, he'd eat that, too.

We locked up and fed the boilers and turned out the lights. On the way upstairs to bed, Ben said, 'Did you know giraffes get very bored making love? The female often walks away in the middle of it and the male falls over.'

I stood alone in the middle of my bedroom and began to undress. Opportunity's a fine thing.

# 3

I came down at seven, took out the dogs, tidied up a bit and was sitting with the toast when Ben came in. Our regular postman, Humphrey – who had one plastic eye and a wife who stirred a herb cauldron at home and sent out remedies which, miraculously (and to Hetty's irritation) often worked – usually joined us for a mug of coffee, but this morning had only time to call out, 'I'm not runnin' well. Don't like the look of me front suspension. Got something for you tomorrow!' and was gone. I carried in the handful of letters and said, 'He's having trouble with his front suspension but he's got something for us!'

Ben said quite seriously, 'Perhaps the two are connected,' and loaded up an orange grove of marmalade on his dairy herd of butter. Humphrey often tantalised us with gossip ahead. (' 'Eard about the trouble down Wayward's End? No? Tell you about it tomorrow when I've got more facts.')

'It's going to be foggy,' Ben went on, glancing out of the window. A thin mist hung over the reservoir lying far below us and defying the laws of nature by threatening to boil up for a giant's brew. But somehow I could sense the struggle of good over evil where the sun was struggling to break through, and I wasn't worried about the drive to Slappits Bottom.

'I've a feeling it's going to be all right today. I feel extremely positive this morning. I do think one has to take circumstances in hand and manipulate.' I scurried about from the porridge to the toaster, trying to see myself as the sort of person who made quick decisions and didn't dither between honey and lemon curd and then decide on marmalade. The News on the radio sounded like a replay from last week.

Ben said, 'And I've been thinking about the Pets' Restaurant, because if we could do that, I could find out what went down well before I get the Meals-on-Wheels service going and the recipes ready for publication.'

'Good thinking,' I said briskly but reeling a bit from the whole concept. 'I think I'll have an egg.'

'We don't have any,' said Ben, putting peach pickle on top of plum jam. 'I used the last in a trial run for the Spare Part Pudding. It's an idea for fussy dogs. Uses up the parson's nose, sheeps' brains, that sort of thing.'

'I've gone off the egg now, anyway,' I said faintly, 'or anything else. I'll just have coffee.'

It was eight-thirty. 'I'll help you start the van,' offered Ben. 'When are you going?' He got out the map and opened it up across the table. I watched peach pickle sink slowly into the English Channel.

'Half past nine. I'll do the kitchen. You do the dogs. I'll feed Connie and Tilla. You wipe the jam off the Ordnance Survey, the bread board and the Busy Lizzie.' I tried not to make it sound too obvious, but Ben got the message and hastily dabbed about with a dishcloth.

We made our own beds and put our own smalls in the washing machine. All housework was cut to a minimum. Dust lingered, harmlessly, until it was convenient to move it on. I have a theory about dust. It never vanishes. It's always with us, but it moves from place to place, pushed around by dusters and picked up by the vacuum but it's still there – somewhere. I really think it has a purpose and shouldn't be lightly dismissed. I rarely dismissed ours at all and we were none the worse. My mother used to say dust was 'clean dirt' and only the other kind was offensive.

'When I've made a fortune as the world centre for well-cared-for pedigree puppies, I shall buy a custom-built Railton, I think. Or perhaps I'll just design something myself, something unique, and they can stuff the engine somewhere inside where it's convenient,' I drooled over the dishes.

'I'm all for the Bugatti,' maintained Ben. The sun began to make a laboured attempt to scale the window and reach the room inside. The washing-up water was hot and the suds caressed my hands. I wished I could stay home all day and chatter with Ben.

'The Twelvetrees had a Bugatti. A genuine, early one. Their 'man', Twiggs, drove it to the Dorchester sometimes when I was there. I remember Lady Twelvetrees refusing to go to some charity affair in it because the new upholstery clashed with her hat.'

'What were you doing at the Dorchester?' asked Ben, probably expecting me to admit a humble start in life as chambermaid on the fifth floor.

'I was lady T's social secretary.'

35

Ben laughed so much he choked on the last of his coffee. He was back in the rocking-chair and three times Rosie got her toe caught underneath as he tipped back and forth. Mattie lumbered over, grumbling under her breath about the current generation who couldn't think to move a paw for themselves. I dragged Rosie away to stop Ben from amputating her leg altogether. Treacle licked Rosie's ears in sympathy and concern. Treacle would approve of acupuncture: she licks ears to comfort paws, and my hand when I've got a headache.

'It's not that funny,' I said indignantly. I threw Ben the tea towel and he began to gather himself together. I concentrated on getting the dogs' dinner out of the oven where it had been cooking slowly all night, like a cannibal stew. It smelled marvellous, however repulsive to contemplate.

'What did you have to do?' asked Ben, trying to keep a straight face. He whisked through drying knives with a flick of the wrist as if preparing to throw them. 'Let's have another quick coffee. . . . '

I agreed weakly. I drink oceans of coffee every day but I don't like it much. One doesn't expect to actually like beverages, whether strong Indians, weak Chinese, alcoholic or Brazilian. Every drink of any kind is an excuse for doing something else – standing in a pub, stopping for a chat, putting up the feet or sharing somebody's company. The Housewife's Seal of Approval or a break in the monotony. A man's alibi for skirting reality. This time, I excused myself by making-up at the same time. The eye-shadow had never been the same since I had dropped it in the dogs' water bowl, but it did have a more liquid effect. I can't see all that well at close quarters but as I aim at effect rather than detail, I'm usually satisfied. Cosmetics give confidence, and I was going to need a lot of that this morning.

Ben was reading the paper. 'This woman who won the Pools says she puts it all down to her lucky no-score draws,' he said. 'I thought you had to do the Magnificent Seven or the Famous Five or something?'

I ran the tap on my hair and shoved my fingers through it. That's all anyone could hope for with hair like mine. It's wilful and has a life of its own which has nothing whatever to do with me. I said, 'I'll tell you why I was at the Dorchester – if you'll put down the paper and listen – and how it happened I became a social secretary to the gentry.' The coffee was hot and black and bitter, like a soul singer in the early days of jazz. 'Do let Sniff out, Ben. He looks as if he's about to be sick. I saw him pinch Snuff's porridge.

*And* Rosie, or she'll think he's after her rabbit leg. She buried it yesterday under two dead leaves and a yoghurt carton round by the stables. Yes, well, the agency were getting desperate, you see. They thrust this job at me and more or less closed their doors. I was curious, I'll admit. I'm a bit of a snob, too. I wanted to see how a titled lady lived. You know, the grand and gracious bit? I saw myself swanning about at parties, looking quite stunning, chatting to diplomats as I kept the champagne flowing – that sort of thing. (Now let them in again – not Rosie! not if she's got that rabbit leg!) I knew I'd get the job if I tried, because of The Method.'

'What method?'

'How to win jobs and influence authority. I show a bright and eager enthusiasm and find a point of contact. I once got away with a terrible tax muddle by exclaiming about a framed photo on the Inland Revenue man's desk. It was of a young couple walking down those steep steps at Clovelly. Before he started the procedure to clap me in irons, I said, "Clovelly! I was there on my honeymoon!" and threw him a look of romantic nostalgia, with tragedy, ecstasy and appeal thrown in like you never saw.'

'Do it now. . . . ' I tried. Ben shrieked and spilt coffee all over Treacle.

I said indignantly, 'Well, it worked nicely then.'

'I bet he was terrified. He thought it was a threat.'

'Actually, he said, "that's *our* honeymoon picture." And how strange it was we should both have honeymoon memories of Clovelly. And I said, "Ah, how life has changed", and he looked sympathetic and a bit uneasy and offered me a cup of tea.'

'I see,' said Ben, knowingly.

'You don't. More men want to talk about their sentimental moments than make passes at tax-muddlers, so there. He showed me another picture of them outside the guest house and I said it looked very much like the one we were at, only his would have been more recent than mine and who was the lady in the felt hat? He said it was his mother, who went with them, and it was called Wellaway.'

'The felt hat?'

'The guest house, idiot. I caught my breath as if I recognised the name, and . . .'

'Did you?' asked Ben, directing Snuff to the cupboard where she had a small collection of half-chewed carrots that meant a lot to her.

'Did I what?'

'Recognise it?'

'My dear boy, I've never been near Clovelly but I've seen postcards, haven't I? And anyway I spent most of my childhood in Devon and know the beauty spots as well as I know my own bed. By the time I left, I knew all about his fading ambitions to be a landscape gardener, and he knew all mine about studying classical ballet, and he knew about the awful thing that happened to my cousin in Copenhagen, and I knew all about the ghastly tragedy which marred the marriage of his second wife's half-sister. What was far more interesting, of course, was that he tore up all my papers relating to the failure of a mail order business I once thought was going to make me a fortune, just after I closed the fruit juice bar which followed the amusing little shop, ("Capes & Cloaks") which took over from the disastrous little store ("Crocks and Clocks"), after I finished with the. . .' I stopped. I couldn't for the life of me remember what disaster preceded which. I got up and peered out of the window. I said with a sigh, 'I'll have to go.'

Ben stared after me, his mouth open. Time was when his back molars were as familiar a sight as the engaging grin, but maturity and a new awareness of the opposite sex had done wonders.

'The mail order business,' he began, but I said hastily, 'Another time, Ben. Do come and help me push,' and led the way out to the van. Warmer in the garage, the van might have started after the ninth try, but on the slope outside, it only needed a push. Before I got in, I said, 'Make notes of any calls. Emily should ring; she's due back in a day or two. If Pa phones, tell him I'll be home by lunchtime. Alternatively, *he* may be home by lunchtime and I may still be trying to find Molehills. Could you have a look for Dick's ducks? I let them out this morning but Rita looks as if she's having web trouble again, she was limping.'

Dick, who worked the smallholding a mile or so further on up the road, always boarded his ducks with us when he went away. He brought down the duck-house on the back of his van, and a bungalow bath because he said they might drown in our pond. He loved his ducks, did Dick. He had a girlfriend 'over Witsea way' he told us and he liked to visit her now and then, more to check on what she might be up to than for any more romantic reason. He once said to me, when he came to collect Cynthia, Rita, Dora, Sharon and Paul the drake, 'She do be fair 'nough. 'Er Dad be sick so 'er can't go scalliwaggin,' and he'd come back a day early, satisfied.

I switched on the engine. Ben said, 'How about the Dorchester, then? The social secretary to Lady Twelvetrees? How about the Bugatti?' His voice raised to a shrill squeak as I closed the window and let the car begin to roll. 'Push harder!' I shrieked back. Ben gave a mighty shove and we were away. 'I've forgotten the map . . .' but my cry never reached any ears but Lulu's, sitting beside me on a folded rug. I threw the gears into second and heard that delightful gasp and gurgle of the engine.

In a few minutes, I reached the motorway and a steady speed of fifty in the slow lane. Lulu curled up and slept. Lorries thundered alongside: great container trucks from the European markets cocked a snook at the lorries as they hurtled past. Lorries sneered as they passed vans. Vans hooted impatiently as they found me in their way. I began to sing to give myself courage. I felt like an earwig in a bus station. One of those long, threatening car-carriers came up behind me and swung round on to the middle lane. Along the side was chalked, 'It'll have to get better if you picket!' The driver leered down at me. I lowered my voice in spite of the closed window and broke into another song. 'Heart of oak, Leyland lad, Pass the buck, Union men. Our shop steward's ready: Anarchy's heady. We'll strike and we'll bluster again, and again!' As I flashed him a beaming smile, I saw I was coming up to the access road I wanted.

# 4

The frost had lost its sparkling freshness early and left an uncertain thickness about the air, like the cigar smoke of boring elderly guests after they've gone home. The car was draughty but I was used to draughts – in the house, in the car, even outside in summer when I lay in the sunshine and breezes got at me like gnats. I was wearing a thick sweater and leather jeans which narrowed all the way down and clung on to my boots like leg-irons. I'd bought them off a motor-cyclist I met in the village pub who had complained they were nipping into him. Betty, behind the bar at the Dun Cow, suggested the motor-cyclist should exchange them for my denims plus a pint of their strong ale, and we did a swop behind the pin-table. I only remembered later there was a £5-note in one pocket, but I still didn't regret it, and I don't suppose the motor-cyclist did either.

The roundabout I came to showed three or four roads off. Ben had said I was to take the second on the left. The mist completely blocked the sign-post and I was glad to have listened so carefully. One of the main hazards in motoring is snap decisions, like whether to pass the Sale at Redditch and Prettyman's or stop dead outside and check on the cost of their coloured tights. It's just no use hovering. My daughter accuses me of being a weaver: my son says I'm a wanderer. My husband never says anything any more, but his expression speaks every volume of the Highway Code since Mr Rolls met Mr Royce. So I try now to be very brisk, turning smartly at one-way streets and often vanishing into coal yards. Priding myself on instant recall from discussion at the breakfast table, I shot off down the relevant road, only to realise half-way that it headed straight back on to the motorway again.

I rained a few mild curses on Ben until I realised the approach road would hardly be shown on our ancient map which probably still had coaching-inns and cart tracks. I stopped short half-way down as other cars sped past. I sat, frozen with dismay. If I carried on – and it was, of course, one way – I would be back on the slow lane until the next access road which might easily be another twenty miles. I couldn't turn and drive back against oncoming traffic, occupying the whole width of the road as they rightfully were. I could only go into reverse and keep stopping as things raced past. It was risky, even dangerous, illegal and time-consuming, but what else could I do?

Seeing through the rear window of the van was almost impossible. The area was small and the glass badly blurred by weather. I stuck my head out of the window and began. If you've never tried going backwards through a heavy mist up an incline on a one-way lane, don't start now. Twice I ran into the verge. Six times I paused nervously and crossed my fingers as a few cars shot by. Finally I made a rush at it and leapt the last lap into the path of an oncoming police car.

Everything stopped. Their car, my car, their usual benevolence and my heart. For an instant the world joined a two minutes' silence, paying respect to all the rules of the road. Then they opened their doors, I opened mine, and Lulu, waking suddenly and under the impression her hour of glory had come and the groom awaited without, scrambled over my knee and bounced joyfully away.

I shouted, 'Lulu! Grab her, for God's sake!' Below, traffic thundered along the six-carriage motorway, around us cars swung and speeded up or slowed a little according to their individual reactions to the police car. One of the two men caught Lulu as she reached them with little cries of submission, overjoyed that we were about to consummate a long-awaited promise.

Both men advanced on me slowly. It was like 'High Noon'. I leant back against the van as though I expected to be beaten up. I managed a sickly smile and a croaked 'thank you' to the younger one who had picked up Lulu. The other said, 'And where do you think you're going?'

'The wrong way backwards up a one-way lane' sounded rather as if I might be being truthful but I would almost certainly be condemning myself before trial. Since I had hoped they might think I'd only just turned the corner, which would surely mitigate the crime, I said boldly, 'Slappits Bottom.' After all, that was my ultimate destination provided I could avoid Holloway en route.

The younger, who looked like Che Guevara with a touch of John Lennon, said, 'Why? What's 'e done?' and held up poor, disillusioned Lulu.

'I mean, that's where I'm going,' I explained. Then, remembering my boast to Ben about handling awkward situations, I added enthusiastically, 'I was just about to go wrong, you see. Now I'm sure you'll be able to help me!' I flashed one of my selection of smiles. It read 'Come on, you boys; I didn't actually hit anything!'

'Licence please, Miss,' demanded the other, an older, Yul Brynnerish one. The 'Miss' was comforting anyway. It gave me extra confidence. I wished he would display a picture of his mother-in-law in a felt hat outside 'Wellaway' or some other point of immediate contact between us. But they stood there, menacing and cold, like twin lemon ice lollies. It was up to me to melt the edges. I played for time. 'Half a jiff: it's here somewhere.' I rummaged in my basket, diving into the van to reach it on the floor in front of the passenger seat. I wished my leather trousers were less tight across the behind. I emerged triumphant, blushing and uneasy but noticed a slight thaw. Che Guevara hastily stroked Lulu. Yul Brynner glanced at his watch. I handed him my licence. He opened it as I stood smiling, but ruefully, to show a proper shame.

Several things dropped out of its little plastic case. The two men exchanged looks. He bent and picked them up, suspecting a fiver. If I had a fiver to spare, it wouldn't be in my licence. It would be in the hands of the local Rates office. I waited while they glanced at a credit note for £4 from Redditch and Prettyman's where I had once regretted the purchase of bikini briefs with scratchy bows. A picture of a pug I once boarded, with 'Kisses from Kupkake' written on it. A shopping list boldly headed, 'Pa's Parts' which referred to spare bits I had to pick up from the garage for the Herald, and an ancient love letter from a man called Joss which I still used like prayer beads, to restore my confidence when flagging. I could have done with a quick look at paragraph three right that minute.

Yul read it all. He did it very quickly but I could see from the twitch on his lips that he enjoyed para. three. Paragraph five slightly shocked him but all he said was, 'Who's Jess?' and raised his eyebrows.

'It's Joss!' I said indignantly. I may have a bit of a butch bottom but I'm straight as a ruler. 'We are now just good friends.' I let my eyes suggest a bit more than that.

He looked at Che. Then he nodded his head, almost imperceptibly and I knew Joss had helped me once again. Indirectly, of course, the Method had worked. Che handed over Lulu and Yul gave me a sharp lecture and a dire warning. I apologised, and halfway through the exchange, suddenly grasped my jaw, closed my eyes and appeared to be in the throes of anguish. Even Lulu, back

42

in her seat, looked anxious. 'Sorry,' I muttered, 'it's my nervous wisdom.' I'd wasted enough time.

'Your what?'

'It's a nervous tooth. Sensitive to atmosphere: the cold, you know.' It was a bit much to expect anyone to believe that it only ached when I didn't like the company I kept. Or that it had only just begun after having had my face exposed to an icy January day for ten minutes.

'I've one a bit like that,' said Che eagerly, 'Back there – can you see? Just past the gap. Gives me hell.' The cold air reached it and he uttered a moan. 'Keep twingeing,' he said to Yul.

Yul was unsympathetic, but he said a bit less severely, 'Better get back in, then. See you took over from the Priddles, did you?' I nodded. It was easier than explaining and it gave me some sort of respectability. The Priddle Sisters were remembered fondly by those who knew them.

I got in the van and they helped me reverse the final few yards on to the roundabout and showed me the probable road for Slappits Bottom. Neither of them knew it but they agreed it was somewhere in that direction. I would have agreed to anything. I apologised for the last time. 'I'll try and remember it's against the law to head the wrong way backwards on an uphill one-way lane,' I promised earnestly.

'Try neat alcohol!' Che shouted after me as I headed away from them. I think he meant for the tooth but it sounded like a good idea anyway.

A few miles further on, I recognised some place names which indicated that I was on the right road and if I went far enough, I should pick up the signs for Slappits. I felt extremely chuffed. But after another eight or nine miles with no sign of any kind at all, I began to wonder uneasily whether I'd passed all those S-bends and T-junctions, humpty-back bridges notwithstanding. I was about seventeen miles from the motorway when the van began to grow uneasy too. It coughed a bit, sighed twice and slowed down. I wondered if it might have spotted a signpost I'd missed. I was only surprised it's indicator hadn't signalled automatically but, when it did come to a halt, it was dead in the middle of the road. Very dead.

As roads go, this was a very quiet one. Nothing much wanted to get anywhere on it except me. I sat in the van and pondered. Then I got out and opened the bonnet, more to let in a bit of fresh air than actually do any good. I poked about and wished I could remember something about an article I'd once read entitled 'Your Car's Got the Gripes' which told you just what was best to do when it got stomach-ache. It compared the engine with intestines and I tried to reason out the fault along those lines, but apart from the pancreas being a bit oily and the kidneys rather shaky – which could happen to anyone – I couldn't for the life of me recall any medical advice. There were some knitty bits hanging loose, but I daresay we've all got some of those and I was just about to have a poke around the appendix when one of those much-maligned enormous container lorries drew up.

'Am I all right for Mischapel's End?' he shouted. I didn't know who Miss Chapel was, and it sounded as if I never would now, but I didn't want him to rush off and ask somebody else, so I said in a tiny voice, 'No, it's in the opposite direction.' He only got the drift from way up there so, somewhat alarmed, he got out and came over.

'Did you say opposite direction?' he asked, horrified.

'No. I said I honestly didn't know,' I lied, spreading smiles and charm like polyunsaturated fat on a dietician's diploma. 'My car won't go.'

It would hardly have been standing in the middle of the road for any other reason but he said, 'Oh dear, let's have a look at it.'

He had a nice woolly sort of hat with a bobble on it, curly hair and a plaid bomber jacket with a fur collar. Someone's Dad: some lucky woman's husband: my saviour, because he found the fault in moments without referring to anyone's indigestion. Then he set off in quest of Miss Chapel.

And about 100 yards further on I saw the sign. It said clearly, 'Slagpits Bottom' which explained evsrything, and pointed down over a small bridge towards the S-bend, the T-junction – and Molehills.

Molehills was a rather pretty house, pale pink and showing Flemish influence, unusual in that part of S.E. England. There was a lake in front with willows, but when I got closer I could see it looked a bit green and messy. Plaster was falling off round the front door and the house badly needed painting. Once I rang the bell, a great deal of barking at the back of the house confirmed I was in the right place. A thin shriek bawled above the din, and was completely ignored. 'Stop it, chaps!' wasn't going to make much impression on that lot anyway. 'Shut up, you silly bitch!' I find effective to quieten Daisy, the demented dachshund we board sometimes. Pa only tried it once because it scared off the owner of a pet turkey, being delivered for me to keep safe over Christmas; the man thought he'd walked in on a family row.

Bunty Finch opened the door to me with at least fourteen sealyhams crowding behind her. She was a fifty-year-old teenager. as teenagers were before they turned into urban guerillas and nightclub singers with satchels. Bunty still wore school knickers. I never actually saw them but you got the distinct impression they were there and I'd take a bet any time. She was just slightly everything, slightly plump, slightly pretty, slightly untidy and certainly slightly grubby. The house was exactly the same, and so was her twin who suddenly appeared in the background like a reflection of Bunty in a mirror. Time had stopped for the Finch twins in the Sixth Form.

'Super!' cried Bunty, spitting a little. 'You found the way! Jolly gee! Come in, come in: back, boys, back! This is my sister, Wendy, and this – no, *this*, is Tartan Tomahawk. Down, Roly, *down*! It was Tommy you wanted, wasn't it? Oh, Wendy says it was Robby. I believe he's out somewhere . . .' She gazed round vaguely, like a teacher resigned to pupils playing truant to the cinema during an art gallery visit.

The house smelled of wet dogs, like stale biscuits and cheese. There was a suggestion in the air of boiling lights and simmering fish. Bunty's jumper smelled of damp sheep. They took me to a room set up as an office, with a roll-top desk open to reveal old Christmas cards, sale catalogues, thermal underwear mailing lists, some rather withered grapes and innumerable bills. Letters, possibly about the bills, spilled through the gap at the bottom where the hinges were. Wendy slammed it shut so we could get past and a shoal of snaps, mostly sealyham, hit the deck. They joined an old Turkey carpet veiled in a fine weave of dog hairs and some shreds of chewed sponge rubber. I suspected bits of rat or rabbit under the cushions. It was very homely.

Bunty turfed out the rabble and I heard Wendy calling Robby somewhere at the end of the passage. I put down Lulu and watched her enjoy a good sniff round like a child inspecting the attractions of a sweet-shop. Bunty said, 'I say, what a super little bitch!' Lulu rolled with concentration on a bit of something not quite nice, using great determination and considerable effort. Then she got up and shook. The beautiful bridal coat looked somewhat less pure.

'She reminds me of Tessa Truelove's Montesuma Mary

45

Magdalene. I bet she's got some Montesuma in her. I suppose Mary wasn't her mother, was she?'

I reeled at the honour. But I said no, I was pretty sure she wasn't. I had begun to feel a bit itchy. No one admits a flea in their own parlour but we all suspect them in others. I was carrying the precious pedigree in one hand and passed it over for Bunty's approval.

'Crumbs!' she said reverently, then, 'Golly!' and then spoilt it with a little moan as she glanced back over the auspicious ancestry. 'Not Brambleseed of Brackenbury! I thought . . . maybe not, though. Oh, heck, poor little Awayday Doris! That woman should be goaled for life. I see there's some Bachelor's Buttons in her. . . . '

I glanced anxiously at Lulu but she was flirting with a chair leg, sort of getting up steam, I suppose.

Wendy came back carrying the bridegroom at that point. He had mud up to his ears and a bone in his mouth.

'He'd just dug it up and wouldn't let go,' she apologised breathlessly, dropping him close to Lulu. I hoped it wasn't the remains of an earlier affiliation because he looked rather big and fierce but, as a present to his new love, it was a dismal failure. Lulu had swung into action with all the fervour of a Soho pick-up, using every bit of her anatomy from eyes to tail to lure a real big spender. Robby ignored the audience completely and began to investigate the possibilities. I glanced aside, decently embarrassed, but Wendy and Bunty watched and chatted politely at the same time. It was like being at some blue film show with the Mothers' Union.

'Her first time, isn't it?' asked Wendy, politely. ('Get her comfy, Bun. Move the bone. I should hold her, I think. Hold her still. She's inclined to slip and he won't make it. That's better. That's nice. That's lovely . . . ')

'Yes, it is her first time,' I squeaked, desperately trying to appear nonchalant but feeling like a mother selling her virgin daughter to the only bidder. 'She's not quite two yet.' It sounded terrible.

'Does she show well?'

'Sorry?' What did she mean? Show what?

'You did put her up at the South Slough Sealyhams, didn't you? Wasn't she Reserve Puppy First Class?'

'That's Mrs Smelt, Wen. She's this afternoon.' How could they? Time after time, sitting through such intimacies, and all for money! I felt faint with shock. But we all stayed there complacently chatting as if we were at a vicarage tea party. Why couldn't we have withdrawn tactfully and left them in privacy? I said timidly, 'Would they be better on their own, do you think?' because Robby was being very vulgar and Lulu was looking a bit embarrassed. Maybe she would enjoy it more if we weren't there.

The twins looked at me in amazement. Their expressions said, 'What? Miss the best part of the show? You must be mad,' and Bunty said, 'If we did, *anything* might happen.' The mind boggled.

I was glad to see the bride get more and more accommodating and tried not to deplore her lack of discretion. No wonder she was uneasy when she met my eye. I looked the other way and admired the willows through the window.

'Tea or coffee?' asked Wen suddenly, and I turned to find, with some surprise, that the performers had taken up a position back to back. To my knowledge, nothing like it appeared in Alex Comfort's *Joy of Sex*. Maybe the author had something yet to learn. I was glad about that.

'Er, coffee I think, please,' I said, though I didn't fancy anything at all. It was all too much like a Roman orgy.

'We always enjoy a mating,' confided Bun, adjusting a small string of pearls at the round neck of her Orlon jumper, 'it gives us a chance to have a good old gossip about the others.' I was quite shocked again. Which others? What was she going to tell me?

'You know Mamie Fanning, of course? Well, were you at the Fastnet and Feathersea when she dropped her valium in Staggerend Surely Snowbound the Second's bread pudding?'

My head whirled. I said thickly, 'I don't go to shows. I've never shown anything. I wasn't even at Slough and I don't know Mamie Fanning or Snowbound the Second Bread Pudding.'

'Bread Pudding isn't his name, silly,' laughed Bunty to hide her disappointment with me, 'but he always has some to take to shows. He loves it, Mamie says. But Wen and I reckon it's full of uppers.'

I said, 'Uppers?' Charlie enjoyed a chew at my shoe any time, but I never had thought of putting the uppers in a pudding for him. I made a mental note to tell Ben.

'Stimulants. He wouldn't show well otherwise. But he ate all the pudding instead of half so she had to use the valium, didn't she? He's got a pretty foreleg, I'll give you that, but he's never really *brisk*. Sealyhams should be brisk, like Westies and Yorkies. Now just look at Robby, there –' I looked – and looked away again hastily. He was drooling with climactic lust. And *I* was paying *them*? 'He's always brisk and on the ball' (I thought she said 'boil' but he was that too) 'and it's well known Mamie Fanning takes the bread pudding to shows for only one reason . . . ' She nodded her head slowly. Then she turned to Robby. 'You don't need bread pudding, do you, darling?' she reminded him with pride. Robby needed nothing at that particular moment, though I noticed his nose was running and a tissue might have been welcome. His eyes regarded us with a mournful expression, like a dedicated monk at prayer.

The coffee, when it came, was surprisingly good. Bun and Wen had obviously been tutored in the arts of home-making but it's a charm that rarely attracts men until after the wedding, when it suddenly becomes all-important. The girls must have given up most of their efforts years ago, when lovers and suitors became rather thin on the ground. I remembered a friend who told me she made it very clear at the start of an affair that she would be happy to share her lover's flat but she was a lousy cook and hated housework. That was OK, he said. He believed in absolute equality. He only wanted to be with her, share everything, care for her for ever. She agreed, he shopped, they ate out and someone was paid to come in and clean. Then the silly things married. She said that from the moment she removed her veil, he was thrusting pans and brooms into her hand. I even believe he gave her a shopping trolley for a wedding present. 'All women do these things naturally once they're married,' he whined fretfully, just as if the ring at the altar had been a ring at the prison bell.

By the time the Oval Maries had gone round twice, conversation was growing a trifle laboured. I knew nothing of the deep mystique accorded the show ring, the groom was tottering off to the water bowl much as the pub calls after a demanding date with a new mistress and Lulu was having a shake and a good scratch. Then she climbed rather shame-facedly on my knee. Wendy said casually, 'She's got a good slope. No need to keep her tipped, I'd say. Wouldn't you, Bunce?'

Bunty shook her head. 'No. It was a lovely long tie, wasn't it?' She beamed at me. 'Tell you what, how's about a repeat performance tomorrow? It's OK, isn't it, Wence? We often give a second service free for a maiden bitch. Robby's got Mrs Smelt's Cabinet of Corsets this afternoon, but he'll be ready, willing and able by the morning.' I admit I may have misheard the name of the Smelt bitch but that's how it sounded to ears buzzing from the horror of going through all that again.

I thanked Wen and Bun and said that I felt sure all would be well and I drove away from Molehills, from Slappits Bottom and would have driven straight out of the entire breeding business only I was now committed up to my ears, and *had* to stay that way if I didn't mean to go and live in a GPO callbox or whatever Pa was probably inspecting at that precise moment.

That reminded me of home, so I rang Ben from a phone box just outside a drivers' roadside caff. The place seemed to be bristling with heavy vehicles and even heavier customers, all of them standing around in the doorway. I wished I'd gone a bit further and found more privacy. When Ben answered, I said in a hushed whisper,'I forgot to feed Connie.' There was a hum on the line from overhead cables and Ben shouted, 'What?' as if he were floating in space. I muttered, red-faced, 'Connie! I forgot her seed.' It almost sounded Old Testament stuff. The men were straining their ears. All conversation had stopped. I turned my back. They must have thought I was murmuring fond obscenities. Ben, coming suddenly to earth, shrieked, 'What? I can't hear a word you're saying?' There was no help for it. I bawled back, 'Feed the bloody parrot!' and because most of the glass was missing from the phone box, there was a roar of laughter from behind me. I escaped back to the van wearing a sickly smile and refusing a number of kindly invitations which followed me down the road.

I pulled up at another phone box further on and though the glass had been left by considerate vandals, the phone had been damaged beyond all hope. I spent a bit of time reading the graffiti. I liked 'Heavy breathing costs cash', though someone had added, 'Say something filthy and get your money's worth!' and someone else had put, 'Try a phone flash on your grannie!' It seemed the least harmful of the three so I ticked it with my lipstick and went on. At the next roundabout there was a small tearoom and although I was dying to get home, I was dying to go to the ladies' room too. I just hadn't fancied the inevitable odour of loofah and stale sponges that would undoubtedly join the cork mat in the Finches' bathroom.

For the third time, I stopped at a telephone box to ring Ben and remind him about the parrot's breakfast. This time, the line was clear and Ben, with an unusual economy of words, simply picked up the phone and said 'I did.' I pressed the money in and said, 'You did what?' 'Fed Connie: if you'd just listened, you could have saved the cost of the call. That's why I said 'I did' instead of who I was.'

'Gosh!' I said, rather like Bunty might. I could see their impact could be catching. Ben went on, 'She kept squawking at me. Then

she threw her cuttle-fish about. When she dropped her apple core in my mug, I knew she was trying to tell me something.'

'Is she making love to that grapefruit again?' I asked anxiously. Grapefruit really turned her on. It was noisy and rather embarrassing. Nature may be raw in tooth and claw but she's also a right randy romantic elsewhere.

'No. And Hetty thinks she's probably a 'he' after all. Perhaps we could call her Conway Twitty after that old pop star you liked. It suits her . . . him.'

'I didn't like him. I just remembered his name. Hetty's not there, is she?'

'Actually yes, she is. Oh, and Pa rang. He's seeing an old refrigeration plant this afternoon. Derelict but a bargain.'

'What's he doing that for? We've already got one!' I know because ours is the coldest house in south-east England.

'He'll ring back later. He sounded very excited.'

'I hope it keeps warm for him! What's Hetty doing?'

'Just a fun call. We're having a drink together.'

'A drink? A drink of what?' Hetty had been treating Ben lately as if he were eighteen. Ben had always adored Hetty. Men did. Women weren't so sure. Hetty was beautiful, intelligent, and even up to her knees in muck managed to look as if she was merely modelling for the casual country set about to lunch at some old moated mansion with other little dazzlers down for the weekend.

'Marmite,' said Ben innocently, and I heard Hetty's laugh behind him.

'Laced with Scotch, I bet,' I muttered. 'I'll be back in a minute.' I thought that might break it up. I'm not against the older woman syndrome – opportunity's a fine thing – but I did happen to feel some responsibility for Ben and I do happen to know Hetty rather well.

Mind you, she'd gone to lactate a cow's reluctant udder when I pulled up outside the back door half an hour later. Her new Mercedes convertible, so unsuitable for a country vet and so enviable, was no longer lording it well away from the trees where she resented birds using it for target practice. I went in the back door and dashed through to put Lulu in her basket. Charlie leapt after us, but I didn't flatter myself I was the attraction this time. Then the phone rang. Connie squawked, Frilly jumped, Rosie barked and I picked it up, cursing.

I might have guessed it would be Marsha. Marsha will be

ringing as I die, demanding that I should wait just a moment while she instructs me on the best way to get into God's good books.

'Darling,' she breathed huskily, 'I know you're fearfully rushed and probably terribly cross, but I must tell simply *everyone*. I've met Him, at last . . .'

The capital 'H' was so obviously emphasised, I thought she must mean God. 'How?' I asked, interested beyond my usual commonsense reasoning.

'At the Jacussi. You know we've got one in Hampstead, don't you? I go twice or three times a week. Sheerest heaven. Quite rejuvenated. Such divine bliss . . .' That figured, of course.

'But how much?'

'What?'

'How much does it cost?' Her frivolous extravagance outweighed even the holy intervention.

'Oh, darling, *much* cheaper than dinner for two at Clarrie's.' But I never did pay for dinner at Claridges so it wasn't the most informative answer. 'And anyway,' she went on as if it justified the expense, 'I met Him there.'

Now, by no stretch of the imagination could I see God appearing to Marsha in a Jacussi, so I supposed it had to be a new man after all.

'What's he like?' I asked wearily, 'come on, what's his name? Does he work? Has he any money?' because most of them prayed hard at sunset or wailed about eternity outside Woolworths, but few, if any, contributed towards the good of anything except their own souls and the regal upkeep of their leader. Fringe religions justify opting out of the boring business of being independent, even if you do have to wash up in the commune. Commerce, so sneered at by the spiritual, actually works for the good of the many as opposed to their own dedication which is mainly aimed at their own self-satisfaction.

'You'll absolutely adore him,' Marsha claimed confidently. 'His name's Polyflor. It means All Nature, you see.'

'Sounds like an aerosol parquet polish,' I said, irritated.

Marsha ignored me. 'We hope to be with you by midday,' she declared.

'What?'

'Midday, darling: just for a few blissful hours to get away from it all. Perhaps till Friday.' Marsha could make her voice as winning as a boxer's knock-out.

'When?'

'Tomorrow.' Her voice sharpened. It was another bout of the familiar contest. She, trying to get in. Me, trying to keep her out, like Churchill defying the Luftwaffe.

'Impossible,' I said firmly, 'Ben's got mumps.' Instant lies are the easy ones.

'Sorry, Ben,' I apologised when Marsha had dropped the phone as if it were one of the actual simmering mumps, 'but I was desperate and I knew she'd never risk Polyflor's manhood. Mumps would be hardly beautifying for her either.'

'You suspected me of mumps twice last year. She'll begin to think it a bit odd, won't she?'

'Marsha doesn't think. She acts on immediate Intuition. Memory doesn't come into that. But I do agree: next time it might be advisable to mump Charlie.'

'Did you know that impalas make love at the gallop? Sometimes at thirty miles an hour? They're nervous creatures.'

'Anyone would get nervous at that rate,' I said severely, trying to blot out the picture gradually forming. 'I wish you'd study something more useful for 'O' levels.'

Ben put the book back in his pocket. 'Hetty wants you to ring,' he said. 'She thought it rather interesting, actually.'

'Well, Hetty would,' I agreed. 'It's her profession, the study of wildlife.' And they wouldn't come much wilder than that!

'She'll be going straight back to Surgery. She said it was urgent. She's got an idea for you. I'm going to make a seedcake for budgies.' He got out a bowl and a bag of Swoosh (for Wildfowl in Winter) and began to beat things about. 'I shall call it Budgiebake.' I reckoned Ben would be the first entry in a sequel called *Dreadful Facts About Nature.*

The usual greetings over, Hetty said, 'Glad about Lulu. I knew you'd find Wen and Bun OK. They thrive out there on *Dog World* and mild content. I suppose any of us could be as single-minded as that if we tried, and didn't waste time looking for more. I mean, it's all there for the asking, beyond the end of our noses.'

'There's a few mixed aromas at the end of their's I wouldn't want,' I said grimly, and wondering how it is one rarely notices what lingers under one's own nose unless it's extraordinarily noxious. Houses all smell of who is in them. Artists smell of turps, soup and unmade beds. Writers of burnt toast and despair. The actor's house has a veneer of smelly luxury – scent and gin and pretending. I wondered about mine and had a quick sniff. Budgiebake and jacket potatoes with a trace of damp dog. What did that make me?

'I've been thinking,' said Hetty, 'you've a long time to wait for Lulu's first move – well, second – towards production.'

I broke in: 'That's just the trouble. Pa's going to come up with his Master Plan to make a million before then: he'll have architects drawing up plans for extensions, planning permission being hustled through for granny attics, and builders moving in to turn a wartime Nissen hut into a three-storey manor house. Or renovating a belfry in Bridlington to tempt some Arab with mosque-ito tendencies.' And I knew he'd have to sell what we were in to finance what we would be heading for.

'Listen,' said Hetty patiently, 'I've a very good idea. The answer to everything.' I waited warily. Hetty's ideas in the past had been a mixed blessing and ran from rearing a piglet I took in from sympathy and eventually lived with in terror. Bantams to keep us supplied with eggs who took up immediate residence in trees and provided us only with ready-mixed omelettes, and goats who grew beards and butted.

'Maternity!' said Hetty triumphantly as if I wasn't really trying.

'A Maternity Home for Whelping Bitches!'

'Go on,' I said wearily. It was no dottier than the time she enrolled me as Pets' Psychiatrist.

'Well, lots of my customers have really high-class bitches and they'd like to cash in on the puppy market, but because of other commitments – careers, travel, professions or just plain laziness – they don't want the trouble, the work and all the general attention necessary. No dogsbodying, you might call it.' She was pleased with her little joke. It did occur to me that Hetty had just about everything except a really ready wit. I was so glad to find a flaw in the diamond that I waited patiently for her to go on.

'They keep the bitch at home until, say, a week before whelping when she comes to you and makes herself at home in suitable quarters for the event. You will see her through, market the puppies, have me always on hand for emergencies and advice, and she returns home when she's ready. Owners can visit, of course: some may want her back directly after she whelps and do the extra work with the litter themselves. And believe me, it *is* work! You'll be able to ask fees, claim half the litter plus boarding or whatever we decide fair – it's no more than an annexe to what you've got, anyway!'

'The owners won't make a sausage out of that,' I protested. 'Who on earth would think it worthwhile?' Besides me, I meant.

'Look, Petal, you can't have any idea of the price asked these days for a really good puppy. People want the best. It's a status symbol to lead a pedigree around. Breeders seem very impersonal, however excellent. Customers would enjoy paying over the top for a puppy who had such an excellent start in life. No backyard scraps in the weaning bowl! As for owners, they'll just love telling their friends they took Blossom round to the Maternity Home yesterday. And they'll pop in to see her, bringing chocolate drops and munchies!'

'Not with me as Matron they won't,' I said grimly.

'Then you'll do it? You won't regret your luck, I tell you! With ten or eleven in a litter of dobermanns, at over £100 each, you can't lose.'

I hesitated. So she went rushing on, 'It's immediate, too. No waiting nine weeks while Pa settles for a smelly redundant brewery in Bow. I've got two bitches due almost right away. The owners have loads of cash but no time to spare, no patience to speak of and now it's about to happen, not a shred of nerve between them for the event. I've a number of others in the pipeline. You could be in business tomorrow if you liked. You can't start moving house with other people's puppies popping like peas out of a pod.' She stopped and waited. I never can make decisions. She knows that, so she makes mine for me. Then she dithers over her own. I know, because she dithered over her marriage and by the time she decided to do something about it, there wasn't one.

I said slowly, 'I'm not sure. I'm no expert. How about the bitch? Won't she hate being sent away to a strange place at a time like that? Couldn't she fret herself into a miscarriage?'

Hetty hooted. 'Such sentimental rubbish! By the time they come to you, all they're interested in is a private place to deliver the goods where it's quiet and warm and undisturbed. Owners get carried away with paternal pride and invite all their friends and neighbours to come and have a look. Kids are allowed to be in at the birth because 'it's good for them to learn the natural way' (so that they feel deprived when Mummy can only produce one) and the cat sneaks by and drinks the bitch's eggflip when she isn't looking. Now *you* can invite owners to call at stated visiting times for short periods and make it clear no kids or cats. Treat it as a proper, well-run, rather strict and definitely snooty Maternity Home. They'll love it. So will you and the patient. You can stipulate a minimum three-week stay but preferably six, to get the weaning established, with full nine weeks to distribution preferred. Think of all those fluffy, cuddly darlings!'

I still paused. It sounded very commercial. 'I don't know . . .' I began, but she interrupted crossly, 'Well, you've no alternative. The first one comes tomorrow because I've made all the arrangements. I'll drop in later this evening, after Surgery, and we'll tie up the loose ends.'

'Ben,' I said dramatically, as I put down the phone, 'Hetty's cornered me again. This time I may as well sail at midnight on the rising tide.'

'It wouldn't be rising and you can't even paddle a canoe. You wouldn't have the energy to escape. You'd have stayed on in Colditz, having an early night, and been the one to push the wooden horse at Troy.'

'It was going in,' I muttered.

'Exactly. Anyway, whatever you do can't be much dafter than what you've done. Here, have a swig of cocoa.' He passed me his mug. The cocoa had the beginning of a skin forming on top. I pushed the mug back.

'It's a time for Ginseng,' I said bravely. There were small packets in the back of the cupboard, to be made into tea. It doesn't do a thing for me, however much it made the Koreans hop 5,000 years ago. But I'm not allergic to self-persuasion and I try to react to the challenge of 20p a cup. It tasted, as always, like stale cabbage water, but after knocking it back with an attempt at relish, I said, 'Well, now you can turn your talents to invalid dietry,' and began to outline the idea.

By the time Humphrey arrived with the second post, his false eye swirling with the promised gossip, Ben and I had turned out all the floor-level cupboards running beneath the Victorian dresser in the table-tennis room for use as private wards. I could accommodate four, with an annexe for two in the morning-room. Luckily, the old house was a warren of small rooms and big cupboards, and my only expense would be extra heating. Ben found four large cartons, and took half a side out of each. I scrubbed the cupboards, he lined the boxes with newspapers and I made sure each door swung easily. Our wards could be absolutely private.

Charlie came round with us and sniffed out the mouse-holes which we stuffed up with newspapers, me feeling pangs of guilt about the mice. Humphrey, his mission somewhat thwarted, had dropped the mail and restarted the engine. He was looking decidedly glum, so I said, 'Sorry, Humphrey. Ben and I were busy, but we're stopping for a drink. Do come back in and have one with us.'

At that moment, Ben passed us and shouted something about going up to the field with more hay for Bubbles so I said, in all innocence, 'Now you must come in. I shall be alone.'

But with all that scandal around, Humphrey suspects designs from everyone. He had once warned me he was allergic to romance. It made him cough. Since then I've sometimes hinted at bouts of it we could share if only Ben was out of the way, and he took me quite seriously. I can just imagine the sort of scandal about me he took back on his rounds.

Now he cleared his throat twice and muttered, 'Got me extras on.' His plastic eye was fixed far beyond me.

'We'll soon have those off,' I said quietly but with meaning.

The mail van carried things from farm to farm, or from doctor to patient and vice versa. It was probably against Post Office rules, but in a community where transport is limited to twice a week, friends help one another. Several times a week, Humphrey picked up his 'extras'. I was never quite sure what they were but suspected bottles of urine samples for the surgery jostling Mrs Pye's Soggy Cake for her old mother at the alms' houses, and Samantha Chuddy's birthday present with a big bow alongside a cooped hen.

Humphrey looked as if he was about to have a fit of coughing, so I let him go. I was too interested in the letters he left behind, anyway. One was in a long thick white envelope addressed to Pa, but across the back, in neat blue dye-stamp, were the words I didn't want to hear again. 'Friends of Beowulf'. I stared at it for a long time. Then I hid it behind the khaki ones and stuffed them all behind the food mixer.

'Ben,' I said as he came back in kitchen, 'who was Beowulf?'

'It's colder than ever out there in the field. I've strawed down the stable. Don't you think Bubbles ought to come in later?'

'She hates being in. The lean-to shelter in the field's OK unless it gets really bad out there. Who was Beowulf?'

He was washing his hands at the sink. The running water made such a noise he probably didn't hear me, because he said over the top of it, 'Did you know there's a clairvoyant in Clacton who reads paws?'

'Don't tell Hetty, for God's sake. She'll have me throwing crystal balls or seeing their future in the bones.'

He came over to the table. I realised suddenly how much he had grown up in the past six months. He had filled out, his voice was less strident and he was having his hair properly shaped.

'But she's really smart, isn't she? I mean this maternity thing –

it's a very original idea. Could be very successful. Could be stretched to all pets, budgies on eggs and pregnant snakes, tortoises and goldfish and Shire horses and . . . '

'Dogs'll do for a start and I'm not even sure about *them*!'

'Cobra mating lasts anything from two minutes to twenty-four hours.'

'Nice,' I said weakly. Nice to be a cobra: they don't have to catch the corner shop before it shuts, answer the phone, or let out the cat.

'And a Mrs Maw-Strabbington in Canada reared a pet eagle, but it laid eggs and wanted her to sit on them.' Women are like that, Ben. At the command of men, children and livestock. We're too nice, that's what. Boils down to human nature again. No amount of sex indiscrimination will change that. We even resist opening letters when we're almost unbearably curious. We may be our own worst enemies but we do stay friends with ourselves, which is nice. Why does the winter bring the worst things? Or do they just bode ill when the weather does? I went over to the food mixer and shuffled through the stacked envelopes. I'd hardly glanced at them once I'd seen the Beowulf one.

The big square envelope was addressed to me. I took it out and stared at it, feeling that the blush in my cheeks must be so obvious I dared not turn and face Ben. Just sometimes the sun shines, I thought – and goes on shining through storms and the very thickest of fogs even if you can't quite see it.

There was one short page in the envelope, but the writing was easily recognised. I hardly saw the words but all my confidence came flooding back, and Beowulf receded into the background until he was out of sight. Until he was completely obliterated by possibilities and promises and pleasures from the past.

Ben's voice went on, '. . . and do you know the length of a whale's penis compared to a pig's?' I put the letter in my pocket and smiled at him. 'Yes,' I said. I went out of the room and into the office. Lulu leapt on my knee. I crouched over the remains of the fire but I was warm right through. I'd always known I'd hear from Ross Washington again.

# 5

'Eighteen feet. Pigs' are eighteen inches.'

'Ben,' I said earnestly, 'have you no romance in your soul?'

I had a lot in mine. It had shot me rapidly through a tepid bath, faced with the courage of my convictions, and into clean jeans, fresh make-up and an entirely revised outlook. The letter was in my back pocket, a mere boomerang from my heart.

'Facts,' said Ben, pronouncing it 'fax', 'thats what I like. Fax.'

'Aren't there any girls at school you're keen on?' I sounded like Wen or Bun, but I refused to use the word 'fancy' because it wasn't what I meant.

'It's not a feature of our place,' said Ben seriously, as if he were discussing Rugby football, 'not now. Used to be. We're rather off that sort of thing this year. We're doing a nuclear reactor in Science Class.' He sounded shockingly cool and clinical. But then I suppose you tend to be when you get 'Your Body As A Precious Tool' for homework. We're developing into a nation with silicone chips on our shoulders. It has to be Instant Coupling, streamlined with remote control. Except for the few of us who still remember what it was like to fall in love – and still keep on doing it.

I carried on tidying up, the urge extending from myself to the kitchen, as if Ross might follow the letter and appear any moment at the back door, white charger hitched to the gatepost.

'I wouldn't say Sex is Fax myself. If you believe that you believe anything. Anyway, I wasn't talking about sex at all. (In years past the word 'sex' only meant 'gender' anyway. I'm not sure it's ever officially become a verb.) *I rarely do.*' I emphasised the last three words to indicate he too often did, and it wasn't the only subject left in the world. I went on, sounding like Barbara Cartland, 'I'm thinking of love and romance, not practicalities.'

I went down to the game larder and dumped some newspapers. It was icy cold down there. I leapt back up the steps two at a time. The door had a latch instead of a handle and always made me feel as the cook, in distant days, must have felt as she came back into the warm kitchen from the cool marble slabs loaded with dishes of setting cream, pigeon pies and partridges imprisoned in aspic, with sides of beef and pork and bacon swinging from the huge heavy hooks still there in the ceiling. And every time I was jolly glad to have a fridge full of easy eating.

Ben gave me a rather odd look. 'Well,' he said defiantly, 'I take your point. And I can be like that too – only *I* don't talk about it . . .'

Embarrassment had changed sides suddenly, from me to Ben and from the physical to the emotional. Ben's generation, unlike my own, shied away from any hint of romantic vulnerability, while quite openly discussing the nuts, bolts and what might be referred to as the screws of love.

I said briskly, 'Move your elbows. I'm going to shake the cloth,' and whipped it off the table in a gesture of finality.

Silence settled between us. I wondered if Ben was skirting round something he couldn't bring himself to admit openly. I didn't want to discomfort him, so I chattered on. 'I never did tell you about the Twelvetrees' Bugatti, did I?' The cloth settled back on the table like a drift of cloud, the dogs slept, the moment passed.

'Go on,' said Ben wearily, 'nothing's going to stop you now.'

'It was a showpiece, Ben. Stopped traffic in Park Lane the day it drove up for Lady T. I'll never forget the row on the pavement about changing her hat either. Quite mad. But then she was a bit dotty, dear thing. They all were, though I really grew to love every one of them in the end.'

'Was her chauffeur really called Twiggs?'

'All her chauffeurs had to be called Twiggs, the same way her butlers were called Branch, the cooks, Mrs Trunk, and the house-maids . . .'

'But why?'

'Oh, Ben, don't you see? They were all part of the Twelve Trees! It was the sort of thing the Family revelled in. A sort of personal tradition, a hierarchy. The staff were very proud of their assumed names. Gardeners were called Root, of course, all five of them.'

'What did she call you?'

I stood with my back to the Aga and recalled those less fraught days and wondered where I had developed all my current muddles. In those days, I seemed to be forever on the fringe of magic and unreason and nobody ever tried to be profound. 'Well, that did present a problem. You see, she'd had lady's maids all her life, but never a social secretary. I only came into it because she found her sight failing so that letter writing – and even reading – became difficult. In the end she called me Sprig. Blossom was her personal maid and there wasn't much left.' That delightful, kind, wise, often autocratic and impossible old bird, spreading her wealth, like wings, over staff and charities and needy friends as quietly as shedding feathers. Hurrah for the bad old days! All those sour revelations of below-stairs deprivation risk losing sympathy in contrast with the many unspoken assets.

'What else did you have to do?' Even Ben was eager for the whine of slavery.

I couldn't oblige. 'Not much at all. I was only part-time, remember, but I stayed with her quite a long while. All her staff did. They were part of the family, you see. I was offered the job through that despairing agency. I suppose I was the only one they could think of who might accept what *they*, in their ignorance, thought of as a menial job. I'm sure I was the only one who applied, anyway. Lady Twelvetrees simply said, 'My dear, you have such a pretty face. I like happy people round me, and you smile easily,' and I was in. I did think it would lead me into high society, perhaps. You know, gambling with dukes, Ascot with earls, that sort of thing. I remember telling the woman in the agency that I'd like an appointment for the interview and wondering at the same time what to wear when I joined the Queen at Windsor for the Christmas house-party!'

Charlie came over and rubbed his head against my knee. Ben said, 'He can tell from the tone of your voice that you were disappointed. Dogs respond to inflection. They have a wonderful selective response, you know.' I could hear Hetty behind all that. She really was making an impression.

'This one's got a bit of canker, too. It's his ear he's rubbing against me. I'll have a puff with The Stuff.' We were always being given travellers' samples by Hetty and I never could remember the newest fancy names. I'm sure some were intended for thickening stews or starching collars, but it's amazing how often they worked. The latest was an aerosol marked, 'Ears' and I diligently pumped it into Charlie. Charlie rolled his eyes and adopted a sickly grin. He revelled in any kind of attention. He would have welcomed a tooth extraction for a birthday treat.

'Well, you never did say what you had to do at Lady Twelvetrees.'

'Besides the correspondence? Walk de la Rue – her peke. Rather

60

fat, he was. Had one eye that kept falling out. Had to be scooped up and put back all the time.'

Ben shuddered. 'Ugh!'

'Oh, one got used to it. Never fell far. A bit like Humphrey's, really, only his is plastic. Twiggs was supposed to walk de la Rue, but he was squeamish about the eye. Anyway, I never met so much as a diplomat. Mostly a few old cronies of Lady T who drifted in and out for her Tuesday Teas. Most of them were deaf, dear things. They shouted at one another but none of them ever heard a word. It was quite funny, actually. Lady T's great friend, the Marchioness, kept a hearing aid in her crocodile handbag and could never understand why it didn't work. Lady T screamed at her to put the thing in her ear, but the Marchioness insisted the young man had merely told her to carry it with her always, and she was doing that. Still, they were all very sweet to me and we did have a lot of fun really. Lady Helmett gave me a sequinned stole I admired, and the Duchess of Croydon sent me some velvet slippers presented to her by the Shah of Shamazabad. They were size 3 and I'm a 6 so I keep my beads in them.'

'What made you leave?'

I stopped to look at Sniff's paw. He was parading a very obvious limp. It was in competition with Charlie's ear, but I inspected it simply to please him. He stood carefully on three legs and looked up at me anxiously, affecting mild despair, until Rosie leapt for a passing fly and knocked him over. He shot after Rosie, using all four paws, but I grabbed him back by the tail and gave him a quick hug of sympathy. Treacle weighed up the situation, sidled over and licked his ear and my hand. The Good Dogkeeping Seal of Approval. Mattie grunted. Cynically.

'I left Lady T's when she went to Monte Carlo for a few weeks. I'd been with her two and a half years. She had a stroke out there and died. I was left with de la Rue and the official announcements, letters to distant friends etc. I'd grown to know so much about her life that none of it was difficult, just shattering. I cried all the time, and so did Twiggs and Blossom. You see, she was so good. Right from the start – well after the first week or two, when we knew we were going to be friends – she asked me to do all her correspondence myself. She wouldn't dictate anything at all. She wanted her sons and her daughter, who all lived abroad, to think of her as she always had been when they were living at home – active and energetic and busy. So we made up places to say she went to and people to say she'd met. And theatres and parties and balls and so

61

on. It was thoroughtly dishonest but the family were happy to think she was so well, even into her eighties. Sometimes I put things like 'danced with darling Charles all night: such a sweet boy', or 'Philip and I had a long and serious talk about carriage horses'. They could draw what conclusions they liked. I always read them aloud to her and she would laugh and clap her hands and say how clever I was. But it wasn't clever. It was easy with just a little imagination and so much better than wingeing about her arthritis or the miserable diet her doctor insisted would help a severe kidney condition.' I paused, tears waiting to well up and overflow. A lump rising in my throat. She had been such a courageous lady.

'So what happened when they all came back for the funeral? Did they find out?'

'Well, it was a bit awkward at first. Her reputedly glittering wardrobe had little but warm underwear and M & S cardigans in it. All her jewels ('Wore my diamond dog collar and the emeralds your father gave me on our tenth anniversary') had been sold long ago. There was very little money left because she'd given it all away to people in need. Never ostentatiously, so nobody realised. People like the hotel chambermaid who couldn't afford a holiday and the waiter who brought her trays to her room and longed to see Naples again. And the Children's Home she had always supported – they got thousands – and an animal sanctuary run by two lovely pensioners who found a new lease of life giving their time and love to innumerable unwanted pets. Sometimes we drove down there to see them, and sometimes to the Children's Home. It was the only time she ever went out.' She had once said to me, 'Children and animals are much the same. Only in those first few early years can we claim to be on the same level, and equal. After that, we deteriorate, I'm afraid, but the animals never do.'

'Were they furious?'

'Who? the family? Heavens, no! We hadn't deceived them at all. They knew, of course, all along how she was and what was happening. I wasn't the only one to write – there were solicitors and accountants and bank managers and old friends and relatives. But her children knew it would keep *her* happier. I really think it was one of the reasons they never came back to see her in the last five years. She would have been completely shattered if they found out. One of the sons did come over regularly, but stayed away from her, yet they all rang her every week and wrote to her often, commenting with admiration on her new clothes and her social life and her wonderful health. They thanked me such a lot for keeping the illusions going, and asked me to take anything I liked from her personal things as a memento.'

'What did you choose?'

'de la Rue.'

'de la Rue? You must have been mad! What about those M&S cardigans?' I was glad he could joke about it. Many would have said, 'What about her gold watch? the silver photoframes? her feather fans?'

'He needed me and I'd learned enough from Lady T to know that the most precious thing in the world is to be needed. She'd been so happy knowing her family needed her reassurances. All boils down to love, of course, and I did love de la Rue because he'd been precious to her.'

'One thing puzzles me,' said Ben. 'If she was such a lovely lady and so kind and sympathetic and all, why didn't *she* put back de la Rue's eye when it fell out?' I sighed. Behind the words was the current snipe at privilege and paid lackeys.

'Didn't I tell you she went blind? That's why she needed me to do her letters in the first place. She called me her Social Secretary to keep up the pretence of her social life to the family. They never let on they knew her sight had completely gone, of course.'

'Weird old bird,' but he sounded impressed.

'de la Rue lived on for another four or five years. In the end, he wore an eye patch and a surgical stocking. He liked that. He used to strut around like that character from Treasure Island. He was even welcomed in Harrods where he'd been known for years, of course. They like you to carry dogs if you take them in. A friend once carried her enormous silver afghan hound up to the Book Department rather than leave her in the kennels provided, where she used to scream like a furious commuter on the Northern Line.'

But Ben was still with the illustrious peke. 'Why a surgical sock?' he asked.

'Varicose veins, dear,' I said yawning. I was suddenly worn out with nostalgia. The past looks unreal when investigated and you wonder what special reserves you had then to survive it. Or bear to see it go.

I slept alone, with Ross's letter under my pillow that night. Some people take senna pods, others go for Vitamin E but all I ask is a bit of romance. Without our own individual crutches to steady faltering fortunes, life would be a lot less endurable. Talismen come in strange shapes and unexpected places and not all are bottled or packaged.

# 6

Falling in love has nothing whatever to do with marriage – it's a natural therapy provided to improve health and promote ego and id. It was only when one thing led to the other, disaster set in. Marriages are basically successful if they are practical partnerships: they should be arranged, with the mutual respect for one another's personal happiness which precludes possible disillusion. Nothing should get in the way of love of any kind, but the deep love between people in marriage is very much stronger, or should be, than the way a lighter attitude exists when falling in love. 'Falling' denotes losing one's balance and slipping off a normal course, which is quite unavoidable from time to time. There is no earthly reason why it should cease to happen after marriage, but you don't *stay* down if you fall. You explore the environment and then get back up again when you find your feet.

Ross Washington had arrived unexpectedly that first summer, to leave his two afghans for boarding while he was away in America. We both felt the instant flicker of interest over and above natural curiosity and though no verbal confirmation was ever made and no physical approach ever made either, the falling in love process had probably solidified during four brief meetings (he had come the following autumn to leave the dogs again) and since then we had exchanged a few phone calls and a very occasional letter. Always concerning business, but with an undercurrent which was far from impersonal.

The best kinds of affair happen mentally and emotionally and often at a distance, without risk of disappointments and disillusion. Fantasy affairs perhaps, although if both sides are involved it's not entirely fantasy. The whole thing boils down to a whirl of romance, which at any age can't be bad.

Ross may have flirted with Hetty and probably had other women elsewhere in his life, but this didn't detract from the special, tenuous link existing between us. I always knew I'd hear from Ross again – and again. He knew that I knew, and he knew

64

that I knew that he knew and that was enough for the moment.

Hetty arrived next morning while I was reading the gossip columns over breakfast. Gossip columnists are the fairy godparents of our age. It's my belief that Cinderella dreamed all that stuff about pumpkins and mice and glass slippers after reading Nigel Dempster. By the time she woke up and began to black-lead the grate, she was planning a similar escape into fantasy the following night. It does save a lot of trouble, and you don't have to go to the hairdresser so often. The only orgies I was likely to get in a boarding kennels would be strictly canine.

Hetty's car was a lesson in understatement – silent, to remind me what success could achieve, and beautiful to remind me I'd never achieve it. I threw the remains of my toast to Rosie who was guarding an old beak from her collection of interesting discoveries, under the table. I heard Hetty demand less demonstrative adulation from Charlie, who had been shut outside until I could remove the beak of contention, and, while Rosie was otherwise occupied managed to edge it firmly under the rug and place my chair on it. Once Hetty appeared, I wished I'd thrown all four slices of toast to the winds before I began loading them with butter and calories.

She brought in a bite of the air from outside. The wind, skidding over icy surfaces, stormed in as a warning. Then, as the door closed again, it settled for an instant before rattling the bones of dying trees and the pathetic covering of defenceless bushes and tearing off down the valley. Hetty was the only woman I ever knew who seemed impervious to weather instead of sheltering from, or playing up to, whatever it was doing. Her summer tan, always deeper than others and more tactile, suddenly vanished in early October and gave way to a wonderfully opalescent surface on her perfect complexion. Her hair seemed to grow suddenly and take on the colour of washed conkers. Her eyes became slightly more exaggerated by smudgey shadows. She was like an animal who adapts naturally and without effort.

This morning, instead of huddling into a thick coat and under an unflattering head scarf, she wore suede jeans, a cashmere sweater that matched exactly, and a very long scarf more for effect than comfort. Over one shoulder swung a sleeveless mock-lambswool jacket with a huge collar and loose belt. The jacket was, of course, white but the rest was soft pink. Her high cream leather boots were, naturally, an 'A' fitting. Only Hetty would wear summer colours in mid-winter and manage to look utterly ethereal on her way to castrate a horse. Farmers called her in out of curiosity – and then refused to have anyone else from sheer admiration of her efficiency and expertise. The nicest compliment I ever heard was from a sceptical old mysoginist pig-breeder who said, 'I forget 'ers prettier'n Mary Pickford when I sees 'er with 'er 'and inside me farrowing sows.'

Hetty gave Rosie a quelling look as she spoke to me. Rosie gave up her search for the beak and leapt on to a chair, then slid off and vanished when Hetty decided that was the one she wanted. I rushed over to shake the cushion like a lavatory attendant in a top-shop loo. 'Coffee?' I asked respectfully, watching Rosie sneak back to have her ears fondled.

'No, thanks. I've had quarts this morning. That absurd man on the Weather Forecast warned me it was several degrees below in the south of England, and that the roads were bad. It's trying to snow but I can't see it's all that cold, unless you hover. It's my belief the Met. Office operates from Alaska – one of those programmes we import, like "Dallas". Highly exaggerated.'

Perfect health and well-being, she intimated, were a matter of simple commonsense and attitude of mind together with hard work and a sensible diet. She was probably right, but it was a bit daunting all the same. Pitting her wits against prevailing conditions – which included germs, virus infections, bugs of all kinds and the united forces of nature and man – was something she enjoyed with the same relish as her occasional challenges with clients. Hetty always came out on top because she was skilful, informed and, above all, caring. She made me feel like an earthworm with measles.

Time had been when I suspected her secret was in the surgery drug cupboard, but over the years I realised that she actually did dominate her health with as much severity as she would dictate to a shepherd who ignored her instructions. She was more truly devoted to animals than most other vets because she was strictly vegetarian and abhorred the wearing of furs. Or was it because of a self-imposed fitness diet which excluded meat, and the fact that furs are so terribly un-smart and ageing? Her housekeeper told me she ate only one meal a day, usually salad, and topped this up occasionally with a plate of bran and slimming powder. Looking at her, I swore to myself I'd try it too some day. To enjoy my last moments, however, I cut a corner off the loaf and another off a new half pound of butter. They went together like heavenly twins and I felt my zip bulge with ecstasy.

She shot me a glance of despair. 'You'll be here at lunchtime?'

'God willing,' I countered, wishing for once I could answer 'No, as a matter of fact I'm lunching with Rod Stewart at Smith's Bay' – a notorious hotel with its own private bit of coastline. But what would Rod Stewart be doing down here? and would I even want to be doing it with him? I discovered, not for the first time, that reality is sometimes more enjoyable than flights of fancy.

'Then I'll be up with the Bolsovers and Demelza.'

'You'll be where with who and what?'

'You *do* have the whelping quarters ready?'

Hetty, with her leather-topped desk clear of all but immediate work, her filing cabinets, part-time secretary, her devious accountant and her fawning bank manager, could never understand my own methods – the encyclopaedias, Snoopy notebooks, newspaper edges, old envelopes and reliance on a blocked-up drain of memory. 'Well, I've got it all in my head, but I thought we were going to talk about it first?' I hesitated. 'I could make a proper start this morning, though.'

'I should do that,' said Hetty. She sounded quite chilly, but this was the side of Hetty I knew best. It was when she grew more human I began to worry.

She instantly grew more human. 'Where's Ben?' She smiled suddenly and her voice softened.

'In bed,' I said. And then added quickly, 'doing his homework,' to establish at once that he was a mere lad and discourage any ideas about popping up to say hullo.

'Ah,' she murmured, "The Body As A Precious Tool". He showed me.'

'Showed you what?' I demanded quickly, if not downright suspiciously.

Her eyebrows arched. 'I said I thought I could help him with it, that's all.'

I was being ridiculous but I heard myself saying, 'How? How do you mean?'

'*The Mill on the Floss.* I was a devotee of Hardy as a girl. *The Mill* is as familiar to me as a sheep's tick.' She was teasing and I knew it.

I said, 'He goes back in a day or two. Emily's due this week. She's mad about him, you know.' Emily spent every term with us, attending the village school, and stayed for part of the holidays, too. She had been nine when she first came to stay with her old spaniel, Rajah, and the two intervening years had done so much for her that I saw a difference, with a catch in my throat, every time she returned. From a rather sad little girl with a withered leg,

67

further hampered by wearing long Laura Ashley dresses all the time, she had turned into an active and unselfconscious kid in jeans, like the others. Treatment on the leg had lifted certain limitations and awkward appearance beyond belief, although it had taken some persuasion to get her parents to agree to what they feared might make matters even worse. Emily had finally taken the matter into her own hands and demanded the right of decision. She was never going to regret it. Her parents had only been, if anything, over-protective and were at last realising their mistake.

'I thought Emily fancied Adam,' said Hetty.

'Adam adores Emily, but Emily's mad about Ben.'

'Very Mills and Boon,' observed Hetty tartly, 'and Ben . . .?'

'Ben's into nuclear physics this term. He says girls were last year.'

'Ah, yes, *girls* . . .' Her voice indicated that the older woman was quite a different plate of parsnips.

I said defiantly, 'Anyway, he wants a Bugatti next year, so if he's interested in anyone they'll have to have one of those!'

'That's odd,' commented Hetty dryly, 'because I'm sure I've told you about Tony?'

I picked up a brush and began to groom Snuff: any of Hetty's amorous indiscretions could take time. Since a trial separation from her husband, she had gone overboard a dozen times but always surfaced long enough to tell me about it when she felt herself to be safe from the need for salvage.

'There was someone, I believe you said,' I agreed cautiously. But there would always be someone for Hetty. It was admiration she needed, more than romance. Beneath the surface Hetty was as insecure as a floating voter. Her ego had a leak in the bottom and needed topping up daily with dollops of reassurance.

'Mind the flying pickets!' She brushed an imaginary flea off her sleeve and went on, 'He's half Italian, loaded, bought that estate near Willowfield – the one up for auction last summer, remember? Taken over five farms and called me in for a consultation with his manager and veterinary adviser. We've been out to dinner a few times and I've promised to go to Italy in April and have a look at his farming there. He's really rather dishy.'

I sighed with relief. What had Ben to offer in comparison, except his youth? But wasn't that just what intrigued Hetty? And, great heavens! weren't Bugattis Italian? I stopped brushing Snuff's chin which she adored and went hard at her legs, which annoyed her. Charlie began pawing my arm to remind me of a few knots he could offer, and he promised not to move an inch or mind a bit if I pulled. On the other hand, Snuff had vanished behind the rocking-chair and Rosie was asking to be let out quickly. I suddenly remembered George Eliot wrote *The Mill*, not Hardy . . .

As if reading my suspicions, Hetty smiled benignly. 'He's got a genuine, original, reconditioned Bugatti,' she said smoothly. 'I'll take Ben over to see it sometime.'

I was very glad Pa rang at that precise moment or I might have said something Hetty would have regretted. As it was, she went on wearing a maddening grin and swung her elegant legs, which would have been even more welcome to the Playboy Club than they were on Midden's pig patch, and blew a gentle kiss to the phone.

'I can't get her going,' Pa said crossly. I glanced at Hetty. She would have come in with a crushing bit of advice, but she was turning her jacket pockets out to find some piece of cosmetic equipment with which to refuel her own ignition.

'Oh Lor',' I sympathised, 'I'll come and pick you up if you like.' I dreaded the boring miles to the station, and subsequent dreary efforts to jump .start a sullen engine from mine. Or the chancy towing with the inevitable cries of, '*Now!* I said "into second" didn't I?' (No, you didn't.) 'You've got the brake on!' (No, I haven't.) 'We almost had it then but you let it go!' Always my fault, you see. I once got out at that point and said, 'I feel ill. I'm going to faint.' I leant against the bonnet and closed my eyes. I was pregnant. I should have been cherished. I was furious. Instead of being helped back inside the car and advised to put my feet up on the back seat, I was acidly requested to go and faint in the boot or how could he get to the battery leads? I wish now I'd turned and been sick in the manifold, or whatever pompous name the pundits use for squiggly innards. But I *have* often wondered if the occasion accounted for my son's aversion to travel.

'No, it's OK, only I'll be later than I thought. I've got a marvellous mechanic from Crocks. I shall stay till it's done. Just thought I'd let you know. Didn't want to worry you. OK?'

'OK,' I said. Worry? How amazing they are, men. They please themselves all the time and then think you actually worry about them! I put down the phone.

'I'll have to go,' said Hetty, getting up, 'I'm working all morning on Midden's sows and I've a couple of goats to sterilise before lunch. Do you take *The Times*?'

'Not often. Why?' Was she now writing their leader column?

Composing the crossword? Taking over from Bernard Levin? 'Then order it right away. And the *Financial Times* as well.' She smoothed Mattie's muddled coat. Mattie grumbled under her breath. '. . . Never leave you alone to nap a bit. Always having a pat or tickle or stroke. Bloody people . . .'

'You see us *that* successful?'

'All the bigger Sundays too.' Publicity, promotion, pictures. I would give up chocolate cheesecake, forego peanut butter and bananas, stick to scraped carrot and wear zebra-striped catsuits. Cut my hair short, put in platinum streaks, get some teeth capped. I began to strut about. 'How about *The Economist? The Wall Street Journal? City News?*'

'No tabloids,' said Hetty firmly, 'just the full-sizers. And very large cartons from Dennis and Ralph. Easily disposable. Wicker beddy-byes are no good for this lot, you know.' I put away the zebra catsuits, I never could stand carrot. And look at the cost of capping nowadays?'

Ben came in just as Hetty's car vanished down the drive. Nice timing, I thought smugly. He said, yawning, 'That Hetty?' I was glad she was gone. He wore a velvet bath robe, a Christmas extravagance from his mother. Signs of maternal guilt were everywhere, from the gold digital watch to the 50% cashmere socks. His hair was a mess but his smile would have been the delight of a toothpaste commercial.

'We've got our first customer arriving soon,' I warned him, 'and she'll need the *Observer*. When you've had breakfast, be a love and dredge up what you can from the cellar. There's a load of old newspapers down there Pa kept for the Property pages. I'm going to get the whole place looking hygienic. I wish I'd remembered to ask Hetty about fees and what I'm meant to say to clients. We only discussed the wonderful world of Fleet Street, and farming in Italy.'

'Sounds pretty good stuff. Is there any more Marmite? Have you ever tried honey and peanut butter together? Did you know ostriches won't mate . . .'

'. . . on a Monday?' I finished tartly, 'Of course, I did. It's a well-known fact and accounts for them putting their heads in the sand. Honestly, Ben, I could get very bored with all these highly personal whims of the wild, couldn't you?'

Ben sighed and shook his head. Then he hit the toaster a rather unfair blow and it spat two slices of toast at him. He shrugged, piled half a pot of honey between them and somehow got his mouth round it. Through the Great Barrier Reef, he muttered, 'Your generation treats sex as if it's a secret family recipe, passed down behind closed doors through the years. The ingredients kept strictly for home consumption but anyone at liberty to share the meal. Well, this generation's not that bothered.' He made himself some coffee and sat down. 'Strictly for the birds,' he said loftily, just as if he'd passed through one phase, found it wanting and decided on another. I dreaded what that was going to be.

I said weakly, 'Well, that's the way I like it,' and began running hot water into a bucket at the sink.

Ben muttered, 'Whatever turns you on, I suppose,' and began to read the morning paper. I looked over at him and he glanced up and gave a short laugh. It was easy then to see what turned Hetty on. Ben was like the ripples at the edge of the tide. Only much later does it sometimes turn into nasty great breakers that toss you around and leave you flat.

We scrubbed out the dresser cupboards and lined them with newspapers. Then we found large cartons to go in each. Ben named them 'Bisto Ward', 'Chappie Ward' and our luxury suite, The 'Mother's Pride' apartment. We walked away quite pleased with our efforts. I found a clean white overall unused since the start of my career in kennelling when I wore it for two days in an attempt to look the part, and I tidied my hair. I do try.

Wen – or Bun – rang up just as I was about to make some soup.

'How is she?' one or the other cried down the phone.

'How's who?'

'Lucy? Loopy? What was her name now?'

'Oh, Lulu. She's fine, fine. I'm sure it worked. How soon can I tell?'

'You'll notice a change where she keeps the milk-shakes!' There was hearty laughter at the euphemism. The Finch twins veered between coy digs with sandpit spades, to great heaves with bloody shovels. 'Oh, ages yet, dear. Tell you what, though. We'll pop over sometime and Wensy will have a feel for you.' So I was talking to Bun. 'She's frightfully good at it.'

I said faintly, 'What does she, er, feel?'

'The bitch's ears. She says they swell a bit at the base. She says she can always tell. It's the way she carries her tail, too, of course.'

I said, 'Wen?' attempting to be funny, but Bun said seriously, 'Oh, in a day or two if that's all right?'

Abashed, I said I would be very grateful any time, but around four in the afternoon would be best. I'm wary of people who arrive in the morning. For some reason, any place within a dozen miles of the sea is considered fair game for a day out, so it's never just a coffee and off, but lunch, tea and 'Nationwide'. As darkness falls, they begin to hanker for city streets. They accept 'just a few sandwiches and some of that game soup, and perhaps finish the cheesecake' and leave at eight o'clock with apologies, 'only you know how bad the roads get later' and you're left with forty-seven pieces of unwashed china, tomorrow's dinner demolished as well as today's scratch cauliflower cheese and a plan to circulate news of your sudden emigration.

Mrs Bolsover was an egg-shaped lady with a narrow belt round her coat to indicate where her waist had been, like a Plimsoll line round a beached tanker. She wore a headscarf with pictures of poodles and she had broad feet spread into shapeless shoes. Poodles on headscarves indicate a gentle, if not entirely simple, mind, and her angora gloves in pink with embroidered daisies in the scallops would never have been worn by a master spy. She staggered under the load of a large dog as shapeless as herself, but with reasonable cause.

'This is Mrs Bolsover,' introduced Hetty unnecessarily, 'and this is Demelza.'

Hullo – she looks ter-rific!' which could have applied to either of them. I led the way into the office, Hetty helping Mrs Bolsover through the doors. Lulu dived under the sofa, but the moment Mrs Bolsover collapsed on it, she shot out again with a high-pitched squeal. 'Shall I take Demelza?' I suggested, but the lady shook her head.

'No dear, thank you. She's very nervous. Can you see her eyes from where you are?' I couldn't have seen them within a distance of three inches full frontal. Demelza had a coat like astrakhan in their natural habitat. I shook my head. 'If you could,' announced Mrs Bolsover with pride, 'you would see they were anguished. Anguished! She knows we have to be separated and it's breaking her heart.' Demelza yawned and tried to get down. Mrs Bolsover's voice faltered and she sniffed back a sob. The pink angora brushed away a tear.

I put out a hand. 'Don't worry,' I said seriously, trying to ignore Hetty's expression, 'she's going to be all right, I promise. You're doing the right thing. I'll look after her personally.' (As if I had a staff of twenty). 'Have a sherry.' I got up and went to the drinks cupboard where I'd carefully planted what was left of the Christmas Bristol Cream. I hoped she wouldn't think I was an alcoholic. I poured two glasses and enough into a third to cover embarrassment. We nodded soberly to one another, glasses at bay, and drank a silent toast. Then I sat down again and left Hetty staring mournfully at the bottle.

'I just hate leaving our little mother,' murmured Mrs Bolsover. The description was somewhat inept but I couldn't help feeling sorry for her. I made soothing noises and tried to find Demelza's chin for a quick tickle.

'I would have seen her through her trouble,' insisted Mrs Bolsover, 'rather looked forward to it, in fact. Mr Bolsover and I were never blessed, you see. I would so have liked a little girl. Still, I'm lucky to have Demelza, bless her, and when my friend Hilda came to see us with her boy, Chirpy, and the two fell in love – well, we hadn't the heart to keep them apart. I mean, you don't do you?'

Well, you do, actually, if you know what's good for you, I thought, but instead I asked, 'What exactly is the breed?' I felt sure there wasn't one in the canine calendar I didn't know unless it was Demelza's.

I was right. 'She's a Scottish Shag,' said Mrs Bolsover, brightening up a bit, 'they're very rare. Not recognised by the Kennel Club yet. We bought Demelza at a farm outside Inverness. Mr McDougal had a litter of four. We were very lucky to get her. Mr Bolsover would never have agreed to a dog only Mr McDougal assured us that once the breed had been officially acknowledged, it's value would soar.' She beamed proudly.

There was a moment's silence. I watched Hetty's face. It registered nothing. 'So where did your friend get Chirpy?' I asked.

'She recognised another Scottish Shag when she saw him in a pet shop in Scunthorpe. And do you know the pet shop owner didn't even know he was a Shag? *We* paid £40, and that was only because my husband managed to beat down Mr McDougal. He's good at bargaining, Mr Bolsover is. But Hilda only gave £3 for Chirps. Of course, we expect to get at least £60 for each of the puppies because of inflation. How do we stand for pedigrees?'

She was looking hopefully at Hetty but Hetty shook her head.

'Well, I suppose Normie will be disappointed, but frankly it's just Demelza I care about. I did so want to keep her at home, didn't I, Littlekins? But Normie didn't fancy the domestic upset. You know what men are?' He hates my attention to be divided. And then there's the Ladies Kitchen Club. I'm President this year. It might have been a bit risky when I'm away at meetings or when I have the girls home and perhaps Littlekins felt her time had come.' It sounded terribly biblical. 'Anyway, we want to do our best for her, so we were thrilled to know you could see us through the Happy Event.' She laid a pudgey hand on mine, pink scallops and all. I could feel thick and heavy diamond rings beneath and rallied.

'She'll be just fine with us,' I promised briskly. Remembering my role, I stiffened a little. 'But we do have to maintain certain rules, of course.' Mrs Bolsover sat up straight and even Hetty began to look interested. 'Yes,' I went on, 'I must ask you to limit phone enquiries to once a day and visits must be by arrangement. This is because I don't wish to have my mothers constantly disturbed. Perfect quiet before and after birth is my rule number one, I do owe it to all to give of the best, and owner's curiosity and concern *must* come second.' I fixed her with a steely glare. I was growing heady with unaccustomed authority. 'Gifts are, of course, welcome. The odd tit-bit, an occasional packet of doggy chocs, the simple chew for leisure moments. But no bones, of course. We are happy to accept nourishing treats such as small fillet steaks – or even large ones' (Ben's appetite!) 'new laid eggs or very fresh white fish off the bone. Many bitches enjoy smoked salmon, too' (I was one of them) 'or just a sip of champagne to celebrate.' I stopped suddenly, seeing vistas of hitherto undreamed-of luxury ahead. It had been ages since salmon – smoked, fresh or even tinned for that matter – had appeared on our kitchen table. And as for champagne, why, the last bottle bought for my birthday three years ago had bounced off the pavement outside the off-licence in Pa's excitement to prove his amazing generosity and I had had to be content with the thought that counted.

I was suddenly aware of Hetty's eyebrows, so I finished meekly, 'And we do insist no chidren or other pets, however friendly at home. But I'm sure that's understood. Now, do you have her dates with you? Splendid. And your phone number? Thaaaank you. We will notify you the moment labour is under way and when the litter is complete (unless in the middle of the night, of course). You can see them all after she has had some rest, and the puppies are well established.'

I wore the impersonal smile traditional to matrons all over the world. The one that says, 'No argument: unwavering obedience: absolute control.' It got rid of poor Mrs Bolsover and I'm not sure which of us, Demelza or me, was the more relieved. Demelza took to her new quarters like a duck to a drake and settled down with a sigh of satisfaction. Those hot arms and lush bosom had been slowly stifling her, I'm sure. She had a drink of water and then rolled over on her side showing acres of under-carriage stretched into bountiful teats, already bursting to overflowing.

'It was all very impressive,' said Hetty on the phone later. 'I'm just hoping it hasn't terrified La Bolsover into snatching her precious Littlekins back tomorrow.'

'Nonsense. Being bossed inspires confidence. She'll boast about my draconian attitude to all her friends.'

'She asked me on the way back just how many bitches you could take at a time. She had so hoped to see the others and their babies, but she didn't like to ask.'

'You see? Just as well I did intimidate her a bit.'

'Well, I've another one for the production line coming along this evening. She's a Dane. She wandered off and mated somewhere down the Fulham Road where she was seen with an impetuous but persistent Maltese. A real optimist. I can't see how he can possibly be to blame unless she grew tired and her legs sagged at the knee, because . . .'

'Thank you,' I cut her short crisply, 'but I would be glad if you could keep all scandal and gossip to yourself. I prefer to treat my patients with respect, if you don't mind. I'm sure her intentions were charitable even if her morals are suspect.' I was starting to see enough business at my end to put a stop to any silly nonsense about moving, from Pa's. 'But I'll take 'em all, any number, anytime. We Never Close. Day and Night Service.' ('That's what the Scottie said,' Hetty interrupted.) 'What was all that about a Scottish Shag?'

'It's the oldest story in the book. You get a litter of crossbreds, then try and pass them off as Tewkesbury Terriers or Red-headed Ratters or something, and you can ask the innocent a fortune for them as novelty value. I've had all sorts through my hands and the owners never believe they haven't got something rather special. They have, anyway. Any dog's special, individual, unique in its way. No point disillusioning anyone. I just make it clear they can't expect to get a pedigree, show anywhere under a breed name, or mate with a similar strain because there isn't going to be one. Then they can call it what they like.'

'What about Chirpy, though?'

'Lots of crossbreds around look alike, even the astrakhan kind.'

I sighed. 'Do you have any purebreds lined up? I seem to be getting all the riff-raff.'

75

'They pay the same rates,' protested Hetty, 'and royalty always expects exclusive attention and often get away without paying. But I do have a certain little lady Schnauzer in mind, actually.'

'Lady Who?' Shades of my days with the Duchess.

'A Schnauzer of the very highest class, bred to a champion in the same breed. Now she's going to elevate your status a bit.' I bridled, but she added, 'Just don't forget the added responsibility of puppies worth a ton a time!'

I went in and tucked a clean blanket round Demelza. I was glad I'd given her the *Sunday Telegraph*. She was resting her wet nose on Peregrine Worsthorne and seemed quite unruffled by the words, apart from an occasional snort as she shifted position. She appeared to be perfectly content but she lumbered to sit upright when I poked the blanket under her, and I caught a glimpse of resentment through her thick fringe. She was probably as furious about her condition as I would have been. I gave her little bits of ginger snaps while I talked to her. Every animal I ever had took comfort from a ginger snap, even Baby, a household domestic pig, or Constance, our superior parrot. Eric, the kinkajou, had once gone through half a packet before he could be stopped and even a snake known as Jim, during a past period of Government, went through gingers as if there was no tomorrow. There hadn't been for the other Jim, either.

Demelza tucked the final crumbs under the blanket, successfully scratching it up, shoving it into a corner and lying back on the newspaper with obvious relief. Then she gave a gigantic sigh, heaved over like a whale in the wake of a liner, and fell asleep again. Her snores followed me out of the room.

'We'll have to keep the Maternity Wing out of bounds,' I said to Ben when I got back to the kitchen. He was stirring a strange mixture in a large bowl. I sniffed the air and hoped it was for the dogs and not us.

'Magic Moments,' he said. It told me nothing. Anyone can hope for a few of those. But it reminded me of Ross's letter and I went upstairs and took it from under my pillow and put it behind the moisturiser on my dressing table. I keep my bills there. It's part of my filing system and very effective. I'd never see them again if they were filed but I dust once a week (in winter), clear the area and am reminded to take them all down to the office and write the cheques. Why don't I put them on a spike? on my desk? up the chimney? Well, if I did, I doubt if I'd see them again until they were joined by an equal number of summonses. Pa never went near them. He found them as depressing as a flat tyre. To me, they're a fact of life and a cheque is never real money, anyway.

I heard him come in as I started down the stairs. His voice boomed through the house as he fell over a dog. I heard Ben laugh, Connie trill, and Rosie's wild bark of excitement. Frilly would have leapt into line and be flirting her tail as the cupboard door was opened for the Glenfiddich. She'd get a bit of cheese as it was shared among them all. The House was Home again, the way it never really is when he's not in it, and I knew I'd go and live in a coalmine on Alcatraz if that's where he was.

# 7

After the Priddles left the village shop, a couple called Dennis and Ralph had taken over. A couple of young men, I mean. The Priddles had brought them to meet me, and then had a little Hullo and Farewell party after hours among the huge collection of seaside souvenirs in their small sitting-room. I always loved it there. Ribbon plates, showing a view of Blackpool or Yarmouth with the words in gilt underneath, lined the walls. Cups, saucers, teapots, plates, candlesticks and jugs represented every corner of the British Isles decorated with piers, cathedrals, promenades, cliffs, town halls and tabernacles. I knew how much the china was cherished. The sisters had been collectors from childhood and though its value wasn't in the range of Doulton or Minton, to the Priddles it meant as much as Ming meant to a dealer.

One of the main reasons Dennis and Ralph had been accepted as right for the place (many others would have agreed the asking price) was because of their intimate and admiring knowledge of Edwardiana. On their second visit, Dennis had brought the Priddles a soap-dish with a picture of fishermen's huts on the lid and 'A Present From Hastings' in Gothic gilt print underneath. It had quite won the Priddle hearts.

The shop had changed. Everyone was fascinated. It was, for a start, a little more artistically arranged. 'The Bicky Bit,' as Ralph explained to me when I commented, 'is really better in baskets held suspended from the ceiling instead of on the shelves where they got handled and crumbled.' The huge apple-pickers' baskets on the floor held potatoes and sprouts instead of being in old crumpled cartons. the short counter was enamelled bright pink to match the ceiling. Music played gently in the background – but Sibelius and Dvorak or the classical ballets. Special Offers were called Top Pops and though they were often on things one would never have thought of otherwise buying, their pink ribbon bows were an irresistible temptation. Through the summer, Dennis served real lemonade with ice while getting your order together – and the cost per glass slid unnoticed on to your bill. In winter, he kept his own French onion soup simmering to serve in mugs as we chose between Back and Streaky and took down his Recipe of the Week suggestions pinned up on a bright pink callboard. Shopping was even more fun than before, and over the pretty pink front door between the bow windows hung a sign which read, 'Just drop in and say Hullo. We like to see our friends, you know.' What's more, they meant it. People might laugh, but they flocked away from the town supermarkets while Dennis and Ralph blew kisses all their way to the bank.

'Hi!' called Dennis when I dropped in and said Hullo that afternoon. He was making up Mrs Patel's order. As I drank my soup, I watched the popadoms being fitted in between sardines and soap flakes and wondered at the way people adapt to circumstances, even in small villages where thatch and beehives were rampant. Ralph usually served in the Post Office (known as PO Corner). Both he and Dennis wore pink shirts and white ties and very clean, well-pressed jeans. They were always happy, never talked politics, and would do anything to help anyone. If we had to have a substitute for the Priddle Sisters, they were the best we could have wished for.

Mrs Patel took little Indira's hand and pulled her away from the basket of bananas. Dennis said, 'Oh, go on, *do* give her one, Mrs Patel! No, I didn't mean a slap, I meant a banana. The big one at the end. She really is quite hooked, isn't she? No, "hooked". It means, well, mad about them.' He made a face at me but the child was looking at him gratefully and with those enormous brown eyes that make the most Wedgwood blue of the western world look like a lost cause in comparison.

When they'd gone, I said, 'That's a fine way to kill the profits.'

'I believe in rewarding the ones who don't pinch. It's all you can do now. I mean, they're in the minority, the honest ones. A struggling minority group, you might say. Those Obadunga boys now, they never leave here without something slipped in their pockets. I've caught them at it often enough. I just add extra to the bacon on the bill or overcharge on the fags in the order. No, I know it's not strictly ethical, but I've warned them and their parents again and again. It's a case of survival and if it's going to be the shop or the shoplifter, I'll jolly well see it's the shop.' Then he said, 'What can I do for Florence Nightingale, then?'

'Hetty's been in,' I accused. How could they have heard about my Maternity Home otherwise? Dennis and Ralph (whom she called Tennis and Golf) were very special friends of hers. All three gossiped and giggled and cared about one another's colds. Hetty really could relax with the boys, she said, because she never felt a need to challenge with feminine guile as she so often did with men, nor try to assert her authority or equality. And, of course, there was no undercurrent of competition with other women. I daresay they were the best friends she ever had.

Ralph said, coming in from the back of the shop with a basket of grapes, 'It was Hosanna actually. She told us you'd started a Horse Hospital or something. She said you had a Catsualty Ward and Snakes' Surgical, I know!'

'Thank you,' I said. The soup finished, he offered me a grape. Dennis was filling cartons with my order. 'Big cartons, please,' I remembered. 'She's got it all wrong, of course.' God only knew what else she was spreading round the village – indeed, how she'd got hold of the news. Hosanna indulged in idle words though her tongue was never still.

Hosanna lived at the Gate House, lodge and one-time entrance to the manor, but long since sold off, together with outbuildings, estate farms and cottages so that the big house could be kept going with a few flowerbeds, a dilapidated range of greenhouses and the shared drive complete with pot-holes like moon craters. Hosanna's mother had lived most of of her life in one of the cottages but Hosanna had left home hurriedly when she was sixteen and only returned when her mother died eight years later. Harry had come with her. They had sold the cottage, bought the lodge, and settled down together for a lifetime of bickering. I liked Hosanna. She made boredom into a country craft, and her fraught relationship with Harry into an occupational hazard. Hosanna was wasted on the rural air, and she knew it. She had long dark ringlets, a high complexion and defiant, flashing brown eyes. She was short but slim and her teeth were startlingly white. She told me once she cleaned them with rhubarb. I tried it myself and it did nothing but put them on edge.

Hosanna and I were Jumble Sale Addicts. Together we ransacked every Rummage, charged through Charity shops and stormed summer Sales, but our deepest dedication was to the humble Jumble. Between Saturdays, we rarely saw one another but from 2 p.m. on that day we were as united as Bonnie and Clyde and quite as ruthless. Apart from that, we were poles apart. I was work-wild and she was work-shy. But that's a clash of metabolism rather than character, and circumstances rather, perhaps, than choice. Some people prefer ping-pong to Grand Opera. It doesn't make them anything but different.

'A maternity home for bitches,' I explained to Dennis and Ralph, 'and my first patient arrived this morning. It was all Hetty's idea.'

'She's fantastic,' murmured Dennis. Then he said, 'Darling, don't for God's sake ask me for the Cheshire. It's really leathery this week. Leathery . . . I'm thinking of sending it back. We do have some rather special Brie, though. I'll put that in at a special price for you – or the strong Cheddar's good.' He reached past me for cornflour. 'Large or small?'

'Small, please. Brie and Cheddar. Make it a large cornflour, after all.'

'There's a Rummage at St Tristram's over at Barleybridge on Saturday,' said Ralph, tying a top-pop bow on an announcement for 2p off dill pickle. 'Hosanna asked me to tell you when you came in. She'll ring, anyway.'

'I don't see how I can get there,' I began. With a houseful of pregnancy, I was going to be needed at my post every moment of the day. And night, I suddenly realised, appalled.

'Ah, but they do say it's rampant with Priddle originals.' I saw the wink he gave Dennis but I was rooted with dismay just the same. When the Priddle Sisters left the village, they sent much of their discarded wardrobes to local charities for their bazaars and sales, including some beautiful hand-woven tweed capes from the early Thirties, pure silk blouses worn by their mother, heavily embroidered and of superb Edwardian elegance, and their late father's army trench coat from World War 1. Colonel Priddle was a tall slim and fastidious man who had taken great care of his clothes during his life-time. The coat was in perfect condition for it's age, still boasting the original cashmere lining. It fitted Hosanna or me without a hitch and looked all the better for being a bit on the generous side, we told one another. It came to the lower calf, was festooned with important-looking buckles and pockets and weather capes, and dramatically belted had an air of dash and panache reminiscent of ace reporters on monochrome films about American newspaper life. Hosanna and I longed to achieve such an effect in a world of M & S serviceables and mass-marketed mediocrity. We had been allowed to try on the coat during accounts of the Colonel's exploits, over 'strong Indians' among the seaside souvenirs, and when we heard it had gone with the rest of the coveted memorabilia for the Church Restoration Summer Scramble, Hosanna and I had gone along and lined up early.

It had started the Quest. No Holy Grail nor Sword of Excalibur was ever sought so eagerly, dauntlessly and energetically, yet we never quite caught up with any of it. Either the industrious workers kept back the best bits, justifiably, for themselves, or goods got re-sorted and passed elsewhere when there was an overflow. Sometimes we suspected we were just not quick enough, someone in front reaching the right stall before us. Once we actually saw one of the capes being carried away with a damaged umbrella, two rusty cake tins and a pair of Harry's discarded jeans. Our faith was pinned to the fact that everything had to be some-where and even when bought, would eventually get passed back into the stream that flowed continuously from village to village, scout hut to church hall in winter, and vicarage garden party to cricket ground fête in summer. The same old crochet cloche hat with daisies reappeared often enough, and so did the dressmaker suit with the stained lapel – and it was merely a matter of time and luck before the reappearance of the capes, the blouses and, most cherished of all, Colonel Priddle's trench coat.

Hosanna reasoned that anyone acquiring it for 20p would in-evitably find it too posh, too long, and too reminiscent of regi-mental parades in 1918 to be any good for ploughing or feeding the pigs. In the meantime, rumours ran ahead of us, rumours of sightings at Bring and Buys, or Nearly New's in the town or distant village, and Hosanna and I would hare off early and queue opti-mistically. I used to wonder what would be left in life once the trench coat was triumphantly borne away, and which of us would have it. We were both secretly doubtful about wearing it since skirt lengths had changed and eagerly-digested fashion pages told us the Military look was passing. The search had now become more a raison d'être than a means to an end. The entire village followed our fortunes and would have been as disappointed as either of us if we ever gave up.

We came back home every Saturday afternoon, through the dank mists and the bitter cold, loaded with cracked goldfish bowls, balding bristle brushes, and plus fours smelling of mothballs which usually ended up as a dog blanket. Hosanna had once bought a tapestry waistcoat for 5p and found a scandalous letter in the pocket. We looked at the churchwarden's wife with added respect after that. We turned scarves into cushion covers and big cotton curtains at 5p each into anything – tablecloth, skirt, bed-spread, caftan or chaircover. We bought pictures with good frames and strong glass and turfed out Auntie's attempt at York Minster in watercolours, replacing it with embroidery, photographs or one of Harry's caricatures. It was never so much the discovery as the re-creation of the discovery, even if we simply threw it back to the scrimmage in aid of the Cubs' Christmas Carol Concert later.

I went straight round to Hosanna's and parked outside. She was lying on the kitchen floor with her head on a cushion and her feet stuck up on the rail of the Rayburn. She wore a woolly wrapper I recognised from last autumn's Liberal Party Supporters' Fund-raising Jumble Sale at the Town Hall. It had been worth the trip because political charities bring out the best from fanatics' ward-robes and you can tell way ahead of time the sort of stuff you'll be offered. Liberal meant earnest, imaginative but rarely stylish. Conservative was tweedy quality, dated, in excellent condition and well cut, if dull. Labour would be jeans and nylon shirts, toys and discarded spin-driers which would only be last year's model badly used. Electrical equipment at either of the others would be of an age practically antique but still in immaculate running order.

I let myself in at the back door. Hosanna was reading a paper-back with a lurid cover. I could hear Harry's radio going in the studio. The sink was full of unwashed crocks and there was another pile on the draining-board. The room was in chaos. Chester, the tame cockatiel, sat on the edge of the lidless mar-malade jar trimming his claws with his beak. The cat sat bolt upright on the bread board. I'm not saying I couldn't get just as disorganised. I'm just thinking I'd have put the lid on the mar-malade.

'Zanna,' I said mildly, 'why the floor? Shall I make some coffee? Has Harry had his?' I knew Harry operated on black coffee all day and strong beer all evening. Both looked and acted on him like sump oil.

'Harry can make his own. I'm on the floor because it's better for the chin and exercises the neck muscles as well as doing something I forget to the pectorals. And it's warm here which it isn't any-where else in this whole damn house except the bloody studio. And I'm not doing a thing I don't want to do today or ever again because Harry doesn't *work*. He enjoys himself.'

I must have come in at the tail end of an argument. 'He's painting. Isn't he painting?'

'Of course he's painting. But he enjoys it and that's not fair. I don't enjoy housework.' I picked up a tea towel pulled down by the cat, a Siamese who seemed to live on a diet of detergent-washed fabric. All about me was well-sucked and nibbled – the tablecloth,

Harry's socks, Hosanna's bra and the other scant underwear airing round the boiler. I watched the cat stretch out a slender leg, more elegant than a human's could ever be, and eye me disdainfully as he drew the serrated side of his tongue the full length. Hosanna said he was Bolshie, and she called him Trot. Harry called him Omega because he said he was the very end. The cat answered to nothing and was impervious to both. Harry said names were superfluous anyway and we should all be registered with number plates like cars. We could earn our names from what we became. I think he was envious of Hosanna having one which made people curious. The truth was that her father had been suffering from a hangover when he wrote the baby's name on the birth certificate and his 'R' for Rosanna looked more like an 'H'. His religious mother-in-law had seen this as a sign of recognition from on high and made sure it stayed that way. She herself handed out the names over the font, all printed clearly – Hosanna! Gloria! Victoria!' It was a pity they were originally of gypsy stock and their surname was, inevitably, Smith. . . .

'You're crazy. If I were Harry, I'd beat you.' Hosanna said, 'Yummy!' so I put on the kettle and washed up some mugs. I liked Harry. I felt sorry for him, too. Zanna lived in a state of perpetual resentment because she felt she wasn't appreciated for her true worth. No one with her looks could fail to see in the mirror that she was as out of place as a disco in the desert. The music thumped on, even though the dance floor was too sandy to be used. She once told me she reckoned she was having to bury her talents in order to release Harry's. Her talents were mainly visual but she would have made a sensational stripper.

As the vicar once said to my mother, when she cast her violet eyes demurely away from his lustful lips, 'Many a flower is born to blush unseen and waste its sweetness . . .' Whereupon, she confided, he added, 'waste not, want not,' and led her to the organ loft. I once told the story to Zanna and she burst into tears. Vicars, alas, are not what they were. Ours had a part-time job as a cinema projectionist, four kids and a steely wife who ran a successful domestic agency from the vicarage.

Hosanna put down her book and began on the exercises. 'No coffee for me,' she said, swinging her legs above her head. 'I'm on the Three Day Clearance Diet again.' Periodically, Hosanna said she lived on water and nuts to tidy up her inside. It could have accounted for her perfect skin if she really did, but I suspected the nuts came in chocolate bars and the water in thick soup – or whisky.

'Right. You told Dennis about the Rummage. I'll be in touch before Saturday but I've got these pregnant bitches now and I may not be able to make it. Not if they all start popping at the weekend.' We had never discussed which of us was actually to have the trench coat if we found it. The aim was to get it. You don't discuss where to keep the gold medal while you're still training for the Olympics.

I took a mug of coffee to the studio and left Hosanna doing press-ups with the paperback still at eye level. Chester had left the marmalade and was feather-picking on the edge of the milk jug. Trot-Omega was sampling a pair of Y-fronts with 'Y.M.C.A.' stamped across the back in red. The studio smelled of paraffin from the stove and turps from the brushes. Very Paris attic-y and much better than the kitchen which merely smelled of detergent steam and parsnips.

There was a wistful view of some lonely river taking shape on the easel. I stood a moment, just looking. I never knew quite what to say to Harry but I didn't have to dredge up some suitable comment because he muttered, 'I know who it is. Come in, shut the bloody door and shut up.' I did all three, waited a few moments till he turned and then said, 'Nice to get a welcome somewhere in this house.'

Harry grinned. He was broad, bearded and had a lazy grin which he used to get what he wanted. 'Glad to see you, actually. Zanna won't cook, clean, speak, shop or sleep with me. You know how she is. Gets a bit boring though.' He cleaned the brush in his hand and squinted back at the canvas.

I said formally 'That's a really fantastic view. Which bit?' The river runs south of the village, lots of it round the housing estate where the bluebell woods were demolished for concrete adventure playgrounds nobody uses, and high wire fences put up to stop paddling. People throw old mattresses over the top – even old prams and bikes. It's a kind of local sport. Soon be traditional, I daresay, like pub skittles.

'Any bit.' He shrugged. 'All imagination. Too cold to go out and sketch something. I thought, this morning when I got up, Why Not A Bit of River, I thought. I did a cornfield yesterday.' Harry could do a picture a day when he felt like it. He often felt like it. That's what annoyed Hosanna. He made mincemeat of the 'starving artist' theory, sweating it out in anguish never applied to anyone so highly successful in modern times. Harry had left art school and worked on a building site and made so much money that he took six months off to paint and never looked back. His

85

work was always in demand commercially. He scorned exhibitions. He said art existed in advertising, packets, printed matter – it was all around us these days and there should be no need whatsoever to gather it together in small pretentious groups for the intellectually initiated. He wanted his own work to be seen and enjoyed in everyday life. Maybe his standards weren't that high but I do think he had a point.

'Nice coffee,' he said gratefully. He ate vast sandwiches packed with cheese and stuffed with pickle, or stopped the fish and chip van before it reached the village. When Hosanna was in one of her moods, he often tucked in at the local where Betty Tidy's steaks were as luscious as her boobs. Zanna had some serious opposition from Betty Tidy, who adored Harry.

'What's it for?' I asked, watching him dash in two willows and a cow.

'A calendar called "Remember Britain?". It's for sending to all those lucky bastards settled in the sunshine on tax escape routes. A bit of nostalgia for something never really there. We ought to be honest and show bus queues in pouring rain or pickets keeping food from the docks. Old people besieged in strike-ridden hospitals and eventual mass suicide.' He struck savagely at the cow and eliminated it. Then he put in a flight of geese with tender fingers and incredible delicacy. 'Pays well, though.'

'Do you call it something? The picture, I mean.' I didn't want a lecture about anarchy.

'I thought "Pastures at Pengellen"? Perhaps even "Peaceful Pastures at Pengellen"? Or perhaps "River near Crappits Farm" or "Cannabis Fields, Early Spring"? Whatever I put, they'll recognise it as the bit where they had their youthful gambols with Doreen. I get letters all the time from people who recognise things from my imagination as areas of their childhood. I suppose one river's much like another and one field could be any. Even Doreen was probably a sniffing Cynthia.'

I sighed. Life was an illusion, after all. 'I'll have to go. I've started a Maternity Home for Dogs.'

'Dogs?'

'Bitches.'

'Nice one,' he said absently, adding, 'Hosanna needs a job, a baby or both.'

'But she wouldn't like either. Neither would you.'

'We can't have just what we like. Sometimes it takes a whole bottle of medicine to get rid of the pain.' That was very profound for Harry. He had said often enough that he didn't like children. They had such a boring sense of humour: they couldn't discuss the relative merits of expressive media, and they couldn't draw. Harry was one of the few people I ever met who thankfully failed to fall into hysterical excitement at the sight of a lop-sided cottage with square pigs outside, and no attempt at perspective, just because it was scribbled by a four-year-old.

I left him putting in a cloud, symbolically black, and muttering under his breath. Trot-Omega followed me up the path, tail tip quivering. I'll swear he was trying to tell me something.

# 8

Charlie bounded down the drive to meet me when I got home and I could see Rosie stalking through the thin covering of snow in the orchard, tracking fantasy rabbits. For a brief moment, the sun had come out and rhinestones hung in the bushes like gems in a dowager's wig. The reservoir in the valley laughed in great ripples after days of still greyness and a massive sulk. I opened the back door and called out the rest of the dogs to admire it. They hovered round the table legs like kids reluctant to go to school. Mattie didn't stir, just a low mumble told me it was no weather for the aged. She played on her advancing years in the same way perfectly hearty pensioners feel compelled to conform by finding twinges. I left them all there and went through to check on Demelza but I could hear her snores even before I opened the door. I went to the bottom of the stairs and bawled, 'Ben!', went back, put on the kettle, sank into a chair – and saw the note on the table.

Most notes on tables are weighed down by milk jugs and say 'I'm leaving. God knows I've been trying' and that's usually very true. This one said much the same thing but the intent was less clear. 'Sorry darling, Auk phoned. He's got something!' (swamp fever?) 'Have to see it right away. Must have a proper talk when I get back. Will ring. Love & XXXX Pa.' Underneath he'd added, 'Rang the Knicker woman about offer for house. Very keen!' I wasn't sure if he meant he was, or she was, or both were. I only knew I wasn't.

I was just pouring out two mugs of the inevitable pacifier and feeling pretty shattered, when Humphrey let himself in the back door. The dogs glanced up at him and then turned over and went to sleep again. I felt like doing something similar myself.

'Got me extras on,' he announced, the joke having suddenly registered just as it was over.

I said, 'Do shut the door. Here . . .' I pushed a mug over. It was the one marked FAT GIRL which is supposed to warn me off drinking chocolate liqueur with top of the milk.

'Something for you,' he said, as if he were giving me my Christmas present eleven months early.

"Thanks. What is it?'

'Flowers. It's flowers. A great box. Proper 'ot 'ouse stuff. From a place in London by way of Mrs Cherub. Come to the pub, they did, for me to bring on.' We had this complicated system of Interflora whereby most red roses were as dead as the love that prompted them by the time both arrived.

He went back out and brought in a Florist's box tied with blue ribbon. 'There,' he said as if he'd picked them himself. ''Oo sent them, then?'

'Kevin Keegan?' I suggested, but I was beginning to blush a bit. The flowers lay like gentle words in the wind, delicate, ethereal, soon to be gone for ever. I opened the tiny envelope and brought out a card. It read, 'Because . . .' and the signature was 'Rose'. Trust Mrs Cherub to drop a spider in the syllabub! She never does get things right. I once sent a wreath to a place near Nottingham called Burton Joyce. It arrived from 'Bert and Joyce' and mystified the mourners.

Ben came in and said, 'Phew!' in amazement, picked up the card and asked, 'Who's Rose?'

I merely replied, 'There's your coffee. The one in the blue mug.' It said HOME IS WHERE THE FOOD'S FREE and was a sharp reminder to Pa that a poached egg with me is worth two at the Metropole. But that was the furthest thing from my mind at the moment. Even the words on the wall above the cooker, TODAY IS TOMORROW GONE WRONG AND A YESTERDAY BETTER FOR- GOTTEN couldn't lower my spirit level. I offered round some of Ben's Bottle Biscuits which he completes with a few splashes of rum and really aren't half bad. His canine snacks, known as Old Sows' Tails, steamed evilly as they cooled on the game larder shelf.

'Rose is the name of a friend,' I said truthfully. I was suddenly quite grateful to Mrs Cherub. I could keep it a secret that the flowers were from Ross.

They both stared at me, waiting. Neither said a thing. Both tried to find a way to ask me outright for more information. Neither could do it. In the end Humphrey tipped back his mug, dripping coffee all over the table-cloth, wiped his mouth with the back of his hand and said, 'I 'ear as 'ers got 'erself in a right barney.' His information was often cryptic. This gave him the satisfaction of arousing curiosity without suffering the guilt of actual gossip.

'Oh?'

'Aye!'

'Who?'

"Er.'

Ben said impatiently, 'Who's done what and why and when and where?' I glanced at him gratefully. He took another Bottle Biscuit and leant back in his chair. Maturity was bringing an air of masculine authority I admired and deplored at the same time.

"Er at the lodge. The gate'ouse, like. Bet says 'ers taken them pills and can't get orf the floor. An' I saw 'er through 'er window. There she was lyin' in a stupor . . .'

I interrupted, 'Humphrey, that's a load of rubbish and you know it. Hosanna gets fed up sometimes, we all do, come to that. She gets rid of it by indulging herself for a few days with a book and a packet of wine gums or something. She's into diet and exercise, too, and the floor's very good for one's spine: Irene should be able to confirm that. It's one of nature's basic remedies. My God, it's a lot better than Harry who rushes off to the Dun Cow and wallows in gin!'

Ben said calmly, 'Swedish vets have perfected a contraceptive device for weasels.'

I shot him a venomous look, gratitude gone. Goodness knows what Humphrey would say about that down the village. He could twist anything. What he said to me was, 'Irene swears by Maiden's Prayer.'

'And a lot of help that's going to be,' I muttered darkly. I'm sure a lot of maidens have done a bit of extra praying in their time, to minimal effect.

'Better than them pills,' grumbled Humphrey, but we were talking at cross purposes so I got up, put the florist's card in my pocket and the flowers in a bucket of water.

'What do you propose to do with that lot? Stew them with butter?' asked Ben.

'You really would rather it was spinach,' I accused him savagely. Ben had the eye of a commis chef when it came to floral grandeur. I was a tiny bit against cut flowers myself, or had been until these arrived. It's not so much on the Rape of Nature principle, but because they're such a bore to arrange. For me, anyway. All those large, hard vases to handle, unsympathetic glass and intractible china, the cold, repellent water, reluctant, protesting stems. The plunging in hot water first and the beating with a rolling pin. None of it seems to have any relation to those wonderful, delicate things, once taken prisoner. Nothing shows it's dislike of being tamed more than a tulip.

Humphrey said, 'Aye, an' them cost a bit'n all!' His words

rarely expressed what he really meant, but the way they were spoken certainly did. Humphrey, it was clear, suspected gifts of any kind and a bucket of blooms out of season spelled bribery – or worse. Nevertheless, he added that Ireen was having a bad time just now. His eyes were on the gladioli but nothing would have persuaded me to part with anything from Ross. I hoped Humphrey got the message when I folded the wrapping paper and put it in the linen drawer, smoothing it with fond caresses. But he merely went on, 'Likes a glad eye, does Ireen.'

I knew what he meant. I couldn't be caught out by Humphrey. Not after he'd mentioned our high drains near the stable block. It took me several days, some borrowed rods, a lot of time and sniffing before it became clear they were hydrangeas he was talking about. Ireen's bad time could have been anything from menstruation to morgue fever, so I wasn't going to ask.

Ben went to feed Guy, a salamander Hetty had given him when Eric, his kinkajou, died suddenly from a surfeit of silk tassell. Guy was far less trouble. He lived in a glass-sided terrarium with small boulders, plants, pebbles and ferns which looked quite attractive, instead of shredding the pelmet the way Eric preferred. There was a rather repellent dried-insect-based food Hetty provided, which saved Ben the trouble of catching flies or spiders to satisfy the monster's cannibal appetite. If Guy had been mine, he would have learned to enjoy toast and marmalade in record time.

Humphrey could see the show was over. He got up and left, mumbling about the Tidys' bunker knobs. I presumed these were a part of his 'extras' and he would be imbibing further at the Dun Cow. I was glad I came early on the round. Mrs Widdow's pregnancy test would probably get confused with Arthur Bonnocks' home-made Hogbean Cider before it reached its destination.

When he'd gone, I asked Ben if Pa had said where he was going, exactly. 'No idea. He got this phone call and was so excited he just grabbed his things, scribbled you a note and left. He did ask whether he ought to take some clean socks and a hat, so maybe he's viewing a mosque or a Cathedral. He also said would you be back soon and I said I didn't know and he said he wouldn't.'

'Wouldn't what?'

'Be back soon. He's going to ring later.' You leave a man reading his newspaper and next minute he's vanished into the blue wearing a hat and clean socks. I said, suddenly realising, 'He hasn't got a hat.' You could discount the topper, bowler, straw and stetson –

all from jumbles and irresistible in moments of nostalgia.

I rushed to the phone when it rang an hour later, but it was Hosanna.

'There's a trench coat, lined, full length, right colour, similar detail, in the 'Help!' shop in Eastbury. It's on the theatrical rail together with directoire knickers and a wimple. I'm going over right away. Can you come?'

'Who told you?'

'Posy. She heard it from Betty. It's priced at £2 but I can get it down a bit I expect, specially if that pretty blonde woman's there – the one with the devastating husband.'

This was the third time Betty Tidy had reported a sighting, this time via a third party thus avoiding suspicion. I strongly suspected it was to get Hosanna out of the way while Betty rang Harry and got him down to the Dun Cow for a meal in her parlour. Harry could never resist food, and Betty took a bit of resisting too. She was a rollicking dolly and once extolled the joys of their new juke box to me across the village shop, to the utter delight of Dennis behind the delicatessen counter. 'It's not so much the current pops on it,' she cried, her vast bosoms brushing crumbs off the patisserie platters, 'but for 5p and perched on the right bit, you get ever such a thrill!' It was probably more than she ever got from Wilf, her soccer-mad husband, who lurked permanently in the shadows, waiting until he could blossom out in his club colours on Saturday to find his own – and only – thrill of the week as life and soul of the Supporters' Club coach.

I told Hosanna I couldn't possibly make it and she promised to ring me when she got back. She agreed to keep an eye open for boiler suits, plumbers' for preference. At Charity shop prices and dyed a good strong colour to hide the oily marks, they were the most marvellous investment. Hosanna and I were very keen on boiler suits worn with jerseys in winter or shirts in spring, or nothing at all underneath in summer. Like the devil getting all the best tunes, we reckoned men had evolved all the most practical and comfortable ideas for themselves and we were working on a single-garment all-season style which would combine both easy-fit and ultimate allure. We were confident that as soon as we got it right, we would make a killing. We often discussed it although neither of us quite knew what we really had in mind.

Ben and I shared a pot of tea, both of us pensive. Ben was putting off the evil hour dedicated to final packing. His mother would be ringing any time to coo at him uneasily. Term would start and the real and awful pressures of education would become dominant. What a way to start life! If it wasn't for the promise of the following forty years, the first gruelling twenty would hardly be worth bothering about. Parents shouldn't be allowed to have children without prior warning at conception that they were going to find school obligatory.

For me, Emily was coming back to start the term again. This would be her last at the village school and from September she would have to travel daily into the nearest town. Adam would be coming to spend the last few days of his holiday with us as usual before going back to board at his Prep School. His beloved dog, Lady, had spent a lot of time lately lying with her nose near the back door, or tearing up to his bedroom to check he hadn't sneaked in without being observed. She could be seen expectantly sniffing the air outside. She had always reacted violently to sneezing but now hardly noticed, and her mad rushes round the duckpond were strictly limited. It was like living with a sensitive volcano. Because of his divorced parents, Lady lived with us all the time and Adam came to stay whenever he could, but she knew quite well when he was expected.

I was just putting a few of Ross's flowers in the Maternity Wing and checking on water bowls, heating and draughts, when Pa rang. He said he was speaking from West Niblick.

'That sounded like West Niblick!' I laughed, showing how magnaminous I could be. I was still feeling like a cold sausage put back in the fridge.

'That's what I *said*. It's a little further on than East Niblick and much nicer.' He went on to say he was sorry to have rushed off to the Niblicks but I did seem to be ages in the village and he supposed I'd been gossiping as usual! There was a touch of the ha-has about it, which went with the mysterious hat. Older men like to think of their women being all frills and scandal, when they're actually lugging heavy baskets from supermarkets, wearing boiler suits and only hesitating as lethal container lorries run over their wellies. Younger men simply see a second wage packet.

'I called in on Zanna,' I said tartly, 'and she was flat on the floor. She's having one of her no-work weeks.' I hoped that would underline my continual all-work ones.

'Was she in her knickers?' he asked with sudden interest.

'I expect so, but it's nice of you to care. I'll tell her you enquired.'

'Well, you know the last time I dropped in she was wearing

nothing but those pink spotted panties. Remember?'

'You obviously do,' I said with feeling. 'That was midsummer. Everyone was in knickers.'

He changed the subject as he recalled the minutes ticking away. 'I'll be up here a day or two, I think, staying with Auk. He told me about this place I'm going to see. Honest to God, it's such a site!

'Don't doubt it,' I said.

'SITE,' he spelled out crossly. 'Magnificent, acres of it, edge of town, bang opposite the local comprehensive and two doors down from the hospital.'

'Don't doubt that either.' It figured. In future, all hospitals would be built next to Comprehensives and the firearms factory down the road.

'But don't you see? The ground it stands on alone must be worth a fortune! So far, it's not on the open market. I might just be able to creep in on the ground floor.'

'Best place to start,' I agreed.

'You'll love the roof. Spanish influence, and the mezzanine tiles are pure Italian, I'm sure.'

'Very cosmopolitan. What exactly is it?'

Pa hesitated. I said quickly, 'You better make it fast. Your time is almost up. Just speak with your hands over your ears and then go away. I'll pick myself up and have a strong shot of the Glenfiddich.'

'Use some imagination, for God's sake!' (How often we think of Him teetering on the edge of anguish about some potty decision. I bet he doesn't care either way.) 'It's a – well . . .'

'*A well?*'

'. . . I'm sure you'll laugh,' (anything but) 'only it's a . . .' the pips began, ran through their repertoire and stopped, but in the space they leave for you to say 'for ever' to a 'goodbye', or 'I poisoned him' to 'the sad death of Uncle Ned', Pa managed to get out, '. . . a roller rink.' Then there was a high-pitched squeal and he was safe. Any laughter from me was short and slightly bitter.

It wasn't that he had any wish to run a business. The very idea appalled him now. Money was to be made from speculating, himself being smarter than the few dozen others in the know. So any proposition was temporarily going to be for us to live in, pending slight alteration. Oh, well, I tried to comfort myself, I always did like a nice, big hall, and at least there should be plenty of seating accommodation for casual callers. I wasn't sure yet what we could adapt for sleeping quarters but at least there would be a

94

handy snack bar I could use for a kitchen, and the tiles on the mezzanine were going to be a rare comfort since the vacuum wheel had fallen off.

Luckily Hetty's voice could be heard outside, and I stopped my mounting blood pressure with the reminder that I was getting far too established now to be moved easily towards Niblicks North, South, East or West. Visions of having to do a double toe axle jump to reach the loo vanished as I opened the door and was met head on by a beautiful cream-coloured pony. On closer inspection, I could see it was actually an enormous dog – possibly from the painting of Diana, wind-blown on the Uplands. Golden and beautiful and heavily pregnant and next to her an extraordinarily narrow-looking girl. Short, thin hair, small absent eyes, no expression. She wore a drab blue mac and a headscarf. Behind them stood Hetty.

'This is Killarney Green,' she said brightly. I reached out a hand and stroked the dog's head. It turned away and stared at a withered wallflower. 'She's lovely,' I murmured with sincere admiration.

'No,' said Hetty sharply, 'this is Miss Green.' she indicated the wan woman. 'And *this*,' indicating the dog, 'is Miss Phillidore Stossen.'

The girl muttered, '*Mrs*, now, for God's sake,' without the ghost of a smile.

I laughed. The girl glared at me and Hetty shot me a warning look. It said, 'Keep your levity to cool your porridge!' so I went on hastily. 'Do come in, won't you? I think we can give her the Mother's Pride suite and I'm sure you'll want to see it.'

But the girl handed me the lead without the slightest flicker of interest. 'I've left my numbers,' she said gruffly, 'just ring when she's had them, that's all,' and she turned to go.

'Numbers?' I queried. I was staggered and enraged that anyone could act in such a cold and detached way at such a time. Hetty said quickly, 'Miss Green has left various numbers where she can be contacted by phone on tour. I'm sure you realise she's the well-known Blues Singer and Irish Folk Dancer.' It sounded as if she were reading from a publicity handout.

'Of course,' I said, as if I hadn't needed telling. But did you ever hear of anyone singing the Blues while dancing a Jig? Entertainment nowadays is so complicated. You have to be right up there with the cynics and satirists. It's no longer enough to sing like Bing or train like Fonteyn. You have to be better than the next guy by snapping iron girders with your elbows while you do it, or break into a political impersonisation. Otherwise your Equity Card isn't worth a spent match.

I watched them go without a backward glance, closed the door quickly, knelt down and put my arms round the dog's thick proud neck, rested my cheek against hers and muttered, 'Rotten bitch!' meaning Miss Green, of course. 'She can go and jig among traffic for all we care.'

None of us had mentioned anything about disposing of the half-breed puppies to good homes. Hetty had simply intimated that in every case I could sit back and make a fortune from the fees. I could leave it all to her and simply decide where to invest and in which tax haven to retire in eternal luxury. But Hetty had said it all before.

Mrs Stossen stumbled heavily behind me into the Maternity Ward. We stopped together and surveyed the hitherto seemingly spacious Mother's Pride quarters. A border collie might have fitted quite nicely: even an afghan or borzoi might have been persuaded to fold its feet neatly to accommodate itself, but a Great Dane – an extra great Dane – was different. Demelza peered out of her cupboard and gave a low warning that she would stand for no squatting *her* end. It was quite obvious that our latest patient needed a private room rather than a share. She glanced at me anxiously. 'Don't worry, darling,' I muttered uneasily, 'I shan't send you to the stables, I promise.'

Lulu wouldn't welcome company in the office, so we trudged up to the small spare room over the front door, which was just Mrs Stossen's size, really. It was about right – cosy, not cramped, a low divan and plenty of reading matter. There was a wall heater and a fitted handbasin. I could have been quite happy there myself. It made me wonder why we didn't move into igloos all winter.

I went back downstairs determined to take my typewriter back to the loo in the cloakroom which had a pleasant view of the garden and beyond, adequate seating, instant warmth from a high-powered ceiling fitting and merely required a small table. During the previous winter when Pa had been using the office, and the morning-room was turned into a base for stripping, clipping and grooming, I'd spent some very quiet and pleasant hours working there, even if it had meant the rest of the household having to go upstairs whenever they needed to go to the lavatory.

'She's here,' I said to Ben who was pushing some of his cookery notes in the drawer for safe keeping while he was away. 'Up in the small front spare. She won't fit anywhere else. Her name is Phillidore Stossen, (Mrs, of course). But we'll soon see about that. I suggest we call her Phyllis. She's quite adorable. I'll take her some water. She can have a meal later when she's settled down a bit.'

'Is this a dog we're talking about or a visiting relative?'

'A bitch.'

'But is it a dog or a visiting –'

'Very funny. It's Hetty's next. She's the Great Expectant Dane and she's gorgeous. Her mistress is a cold unemotional fish and looks like one. Her ridiculous name's Killarney Green, would you believe?' I got a large casserole out of the cupboard where I keep cracked crocks which might just come in handy for something else, like large dogs dishes, and filled it at the tap.

'Not *the* Killarney Green? With Custard Corpse and the Cadavers?'

'The very same, I'm sure. Well, it seems highly likely.'

'God!'

'No,' I said crisply, 'dog.' Help me find something large enough for a brontosaurus to whelp in, but first take this up and meet her.' I passed him the bowl and the phone rang.

'Sorry about the cool customer,' said Hetty, back at the surgery, 'she can be a bit odd. But she's devoted to the dog. It's just that when she's working up for a concert tour, she has to detach herself from emotion to get in the right mood.'

'That's nice,' I said sarcastically.

'And anyway, I'd given her such a glowing report about you, she knew she had simply no need to worry. She's very nice really.'

'You and Ben should join her fan club,' I said, regretting it the minute it was out. Hetty leapt at the coupling of their names. 'Ben likes her, too? that's terrific. She's given me tickets for her show. The two of us could go together. Make a night of it, perhaps.'

'While I sit at home minding the babies?'

Hetty laughed. 'I'll be round tomorrow with the Pawleys' pug.'

'Oh, no,' I protested, 'not Pearlie-girl?'

'Oh, yes,' said Hetty gleefully, 'Priscilla P took Pearl off on one of her weekends and was, of course, too preoccupied to notice what was going on elsewhere.'

'Not another mixed marriage?'

'Who knows? There did happen to be a perfect pug stud at the same hotel, but there was also a dobermann, a ginger pom, two scotties and an alsatian guard dog. I think we might eliminate the alsatian and the dobermann, and one of the scotties was sixteen, blind and rheumatic, but that still leaves an even chance between the last two.'

97

The Pawleys lived in a modern bungalow in the village which they called a 'bungalette' because it had a room in the roof behind twin gables. It also had fibre glass beams, and cons that were so mod they had yet to appear in *Good Housekeeping*. Everything was immaculate, including the blue Rover car with the plaid rug for Mrs Pawley's bad leg. They were both privately paid-up card-carrying hypochondriacs. In contrast, their daughter Priscilla, shortened to Pretty, was as wild as a daisy in a hot-house of orchids. The Pawleys talked sternly about 'the permissive society' as if it were a group wearing badges dedicated to being a personal affront to them both, little realising that Pretty practically stood alone as its local representative. We were all waiting for the day she left home and appeared on page 3, en route for the Sunday sexationals.

For obvious reasons, we called them the Proper Pawleys. Mrs P called the pug her Pearlie-girl and Priscilla called her parents The Prudes. They were all about as typical of East Anglian village life as our curate represents leather-bound Hell's Angels.

'Three bitches seem enough for now,' I warned Hetty, my professional feet at freezing point, 'but I do want your advice about a cat. I thought it might be a good idea to breed Persians or Siamese. I mean, in for a penny . . .'

'And a pretty penny they'll cost you. Do they call them Persians and Siamese now? Shouldn't we be saying Iranians and whatever it is they've decided to rename Siam?'

'If we do that we'll never sell any. Ayatollahs instead of Eastern Promise? Ugh!'

'I'll sound out the market for you.' I didn't want to be mercenary and I really do adore cats. Cats are not just different from dogs; cats belong in an enclosed Order of their own. Often the most dedicated of owners like to think they've been allowed in but they only get a glimpse through veils of mystery. Cats can never be analysed, and books about cats only reveal more about humans. Dogs grew alongside men, but cats wisely stayed well apart.

'Lovely,' I said warmly. Time was when Hetty had been the best friend I ever had. Time was when I looked back wistfully and wished she hadn't.

'I'll take the customers out now,' I said to Ben as he came back through the kitchen door.

'You're a bit late for Mrs Stossen. She's pee'd all over the spare room rug.'

I do try to make it understood by visiting dogs, as well as our

98

own, that the shrubberies are handiest for all purposes, but should there be a mistake, an accident or even a brief lapse of manners, I clear up as I would a dropped casserole and refuse to get hysterical. I went upstairs and gave the rug a nice scrub all over. I believe in turning disasters to my advantage, however downright inconvenient originally.

'Why "Phillidore Stossen" anyway?' asked Ben at last. It was nice to have the answer ready and I'd have been disappointed if he hadn't asked.

'A character from a Saki short story, of course,' I said loftily. 'Killarney Green played her on radio a few years ago.'

'I didn't know she could act as well,' said Ben, impressed.

'She couldn't. That's why she jigs now instead.'

Luckily Em phoned at that sharp point and said, excitedly, that she'd be with us in the morning and could she say Hullo to Ben. I left them at it and went into my office. It was very cold because Demelza had my electric fire. The Old Wrecktory didn't run to central heating and we froze or scorched in pockets of resistance everywhere. I dragged out the old Aladdin oil stove and decided to Get Organised.

I usually decide to Get Organised as from next week, which is the same day I plan a Sensible Diet and begin Regular Exercises. But Next Week is always the one with an Instant Blizzard or something so that the chosen bran-and-baked-bean routine has to be put off through non-delivery; exercise in fresh air is out of the question and somebody brings me a box of cream eclairs, home-made, and stays to share them, during which time the roof caves in, the washing-machine blows up and I break a leg. It's quite obvious God doesn't think much of being organised. Otherwise he'd do more about it himself.

So I made A List. When I make A List, I feel half the work on it is done. The List was very familiar. It always begins with 'Things I Must Do' and goes on the other side of the paper with 'Things I Must Get' to do the 'Things I Must Do.' I get right down to basics, beginning Paint, Brush Restorer, Stripper and meandering on through Early Nights, Alarm Calls, and finishing desperately with More Time and, pitifully, A Holiday . . .

But this time, I added a smaller List because I noticed a piece of lilac paper about as big as a visiting card which had been torn off something else and wanted writing on. I wrote this List with loving care, quite slowly, enjoying the way my ballpoint was running. It was a cheap one from the village shop and said 'Happy

Christmas' on the plastic surface in gold letters. It was my current favourite in spite of the gold one, still in its box, from Adam's mother on my birthday. That one was spiky and firm and only expensively reliable and efficient, unlike my favourite which seemed ready to write anything with a flourish. With it now, in bold flowing letters, I put 'Write to Ross' on the lilac paper, admiring the way I was doing the 'R's. I wished I could actually do the letter as easily as the List but I'm a very late developer and most of my maturing seemed to draw to its conclusion around the age of twenty-two. Writing his name reminded me he would be calling to leave his afghans with me in due course, and I rushed back to List No. 1 and put an exclamation mark after 'Thoroughly Clean House'. I pondered about that a bit and added down the side 'Make New Loose Covers?' 'How About Pretty Rag Rugs?'

Well, how *about* pretty rag rugs? I'd enough rags, goodness knows. I saw this feature in a magazine I read at the checkpoint in the supermarket. It was called 'Lots of Ways to Brighter Days' and showed pictures of 'little things which can be done to greet the spring.' I rushed home and ripped up a dozen discarded dresses and began pulling strips through an old sack (just like they said) and it looked terrible. Nothing like the picture. If it had only worked. I'd been thinking about going in for a small home industry making rag rugs for cottage floors. Hosanna had been interested in a co-directorship: we were going to buy up all the left-overs from jumbles, at a takeaway price, offer to relieve farmers of all their old sacks, enrol the help of anyone willing to make a fortune with us, and become rich and famous. I'm not sure what went wrong, except I didn't have enough time to get organised and Hosanna really prefers lying on the floor with her feet in the air and sulking at Harry. It's hard to watch opportunity pass so close you feel the touch of its feathers. I comfort myself with the reminder that sacks are mostly plastic now, anyway.

I did put (and underline) 'Follicle Food' on my shopping list, though I was very doubtful that it would be on sale in the village. They prefer things for the hair like Misty Magic or Passing Cloud. But the follicle food was being highly recommended by a serious man in an overall on TV commercials. He came right up to the screen (glasses didn't seem to help his kind of short-sightedness) and asked you if you had any idea what was happening to your follicles *Right This Minute*? He suggested you thought about it. A pause and then he turned and walked away leaving you so ashamed you put down your knitting and ran a hand through your hair. You could almost feel those old follicles starving and begging for food. Then this girl came on, in one of those slow-motion takes, leaping across mountains, as if the food had got down to her feet as well, with her follicle-fed hair streaming out over what looked like the map of Italy, with Barcelona in the background, and you wished you could do the same. The commercial hinted that you could if you fed your poor, rotten, miserable hair with Follicle Food. Insidious, it was. I didn't want to jump about over Italy, but I did want to look nice for Ross when he came.

I put away the lilac paper and tore up the others. Then I began a new List. It read briskly, with no nonsense about rag rugs and new chair covers, 'Emily's Room, Sort Drawers, LARDER! (*Wash!* chair covers?) Bed-spread (mend), Attic roofspace, KNEES!!! Cellar safe, Ring re TV aerial, Zanna's aunt (picture), Ireen re Sticky Willie, Hips and Bogbean.' I knew I'd be querying the 'Hips' eventually (and possibly the KNEES) so put 'rose' over the top which was OK because it ran into Zanna's aunt who's name is Rosiebelle. I stopped, satisfied, looked back over it, added 'Make More Effort' like a headmistress glancing over the term's report for a third-former, put the list in a library book on pigeon-fancying, and never saw it again.

By the time I finally reached Demelza for Things She Must Do, she'd done them.

Pa rang just before I went to bed. 'Darling,' he said penitently, 'I'm a pig. I've been thinking about it all day. I do wish I'd waited for you. We could have had a Talk.' (We're always going to have a Talk, but neither of us ever knows what to say.) 'Now I'll have to stay on a bit. I really am sorry and I do promise I'll be back the very soonest I can!'

You'd think I had nothing better to do than sit wringing my hands and plaiting my hair until he got home. He never took *my* work seriously, any more than I took his.

'That's OK,' I said comfortingly. 'You have your pursuits and I have mine.' I couldn't say 'work' because neither of us had any kind of work at all we hadn't brought on ourselves, right down on our own heads knocking us senseless.

'I left the car with that smart mechanic,' he went on, 'and she said –'

'She?'

'Didn't I say? She's marvellous. Knew just where to look. Put her finger right on the spot!'

'Goodness!'

'Thorough knowledge of basics.' I wished he'd stop being so patronising. 'I took her for a drink and she was telling me she much prefers the older ones. They may have done a lot of mileage but they're always more reliable when it comes to the crunch.'

He was teasing me and I knew it. So I said, 'Nuts: anyone would go for a younger model when they see some chassis after a shower!'

'Well, she's giving me a thorough going over when I get back so you'll be getting a souped-up accelerator and a real fancy action.'

I tried to think up something about 'needing a new gear-box' but was afraid he'd tear off and buy a gent's compactum full of stylish suits, so I told him about the Pawleys' pug and we made a few indecent comments and blew kisses. I admitted I missed him terribly. He made soothing but complacent noises and said Auk was boring. He said he was hungry. He was always hungry away from home. It was the nearest to a confession of love and dependence I needed.

Joan Pawley had once told me that Clarence was a perfect husband. He hadn't 'bothered' her for sixteen years. I must have looked horrified because she added, 'Do I shock you?' meaning, of course, by speaking of anything so intimate. I'd never been more shocked, but only because the poor lady had been 'un-bothered' all that time. She said she hoped for a nice professional husband for Priscilla, 'one who doesn't indulge himself without restraint,' she said, 'if you understand.' I hadn't understood at all about her aims. She intimated that 'a professional husband' would have a mind above such things as sex. What she didn't know was that Priscilla was 'indulging' herself all over the place and it had become a local cry of "Ware, Cilla!" as people on country walks stepped over clinched couples, with Priscilla initiating the local lads.

Pa and I had said goodnight and goodbye when I remembered Em's room. I'd replaced the sprigged muslin curtains with a bold red and orange Cubist cotton print from a bale on sale at a Christmas bazaar. A great roll of it someone had probably got rid of after a change of heart, for just £2. I reckoned Emily had grown bored to the teeth with her innumerable Laura Ashley prints, provided by a caring but unrealistic mother over the years to hide the withered leg Em had suffered from birth. We had persuaded her into jeans and shorts and swimsuits and the sea – and freedom. Everyone downgraded the importance of the handicap which had hitherto ruled her life. It was my private belief that her mother subconsciously felt a child slightly immobilised would be less trouble than seeking treatment which might result in adolescent problems as the child, almost literally, found her feet. I'm quite sure she never actually reasoned along those lines but we all operate by instinct and not always for general good. First in all our impulses is self-preservation.

But recently Emily's leg had received treatment. A Dr Harvey, leaving his English setter with us during the previous summer, had suggested that Emily should attend his clinic and already there was less of a limp and a far more sightly limb. An operation was suggested for later, but in the meantime the sheer force of hope had helped Emily grow up and establish a new and stronger identity.

So the room with her name on the door now reflected that. Pictures were of horses and buildings. It had been Emily that I encouraged to exercise Bubbles, the lumbering grey in our meadow. Bubbles was safe, and a comfortable ride, like Grannie's old sofa. He shared his days with Jody, a donkey Hetty had introduced when it was left homeless. Emily adored both.

Yet, confined in youth and often housebound, Emily had an eager yearning to create cities. All her drawings were of houses, streets, high public buildings, open spaces between office blocks and adventure playgrounds. It was easy to find exciting pictures to cut from magazines, or posters from travel agencies and she made towering skyscrapers from cooking foil which she pinned to a blue background. While she was away, I made an enormous collage from brightly-coloured jumble rubbish, machine stitched to a felt backing, and representing the New York city skyline in cottons and tweeds. None of us had ever seen New York, and Ben said my Statue of Liberty looked like an iced lolly, but it had a certain magnificence, and took up almost all the inside wall.

I went to bed highly satisfied with everything – until 2 a.m. when I woke suddenly and said aloud, 'Not Saturday!' because Hetty had warned me it was probably going to be Delivery Day for Demelza and Phyllidore Stossen, and it was also the possible Rainbow's End on the Trail of the Priddle trench coat. I couldn't possibly be in two places at once.

That's the worst of leading a full life. Too often it overflows.

'Rubbish!' I said crisply to the taxi driver who had brought Emily from the station the next day. 'It's never more than £2!' The trouble with cabs outside London is their lack of principles and a meter.

'An' isn't three phwat it always is to this place?' he protested, trying out an Irish accent but so badly it made me lose my temper.

'All right. Three then, but you won't get a tip!' I gave him the notes, 'and good afternoon.' If they were cowboys, I could be an Indian any time.

After an ecstatic reunion with Rajah who had been trembling with excitement all day, Emily had taken her small case and gone into the house. Ben was staggering after her carrying the rest of the luggage. I was amazed at his immaculate Levis, the new pink sweater scorned at Christmas, and neat new ankle boots. I rarely saw Ben in anything but old jeans and rude tee shirts with maybe an old anorak or jumble jersey on top. The mind boggled at his possible choice for the Killarney Green concert with Hetty.

The driver said, 'Isn't he lovely?' I turned back surprised, but he was making a fuss of Rosie. Charlie stood behind me, barking, and Sniff was preoccupied with the cabman's boots. He said, 'You board, don't you?' His accent was back to East Anglian. I nodded and turned to go inside, but he called, 'Would you take our Chummie come summer? We usually go to Ibiza for a month and he ate the canary last time he went to the wife's mother. She won't 'ave 'im again!'

I couldn't say I blamed her, but I said shortly, 'Well, only if he signs a statement to say he'll leave my parrot alone. He'd get the worst of it anyway if he tried any rough stuff. It's just that I don't need any aggro.' And if he went on overcharging, I reckoned Chummie would be able to live on canaries for the rest of his life.

Emily was sitting on her bed admiring the room. 'It's sensational,' she said, putting her arms round me and kissing my cheek. She had grown during the holidays and her hair was cut shorter. She looked gamine and chic. French words for Gallic assets. She wore jeans and a very lovely soft blue lambswool sweater. There was never any lack of money at home, only shortage of companionship and difficulty in communication. Career parents often mean well but don't do so good.

'I'm wild about the mural.'

'I thought it was just a collage on some roofing felt! Recognise that bit of Ben's check shirt? The one he lost when we went to the river that time. Rosie brought it home filthy just before Christmas. The sun's rays are strips from my gold shirt, the one from the Guide's Autumn Give-and-Take. The red bits were from some of the fabric left over after I did the curtains and the orange windows are all that was left from the picnic cloth made out of the kitchen curtain I got at the Pensioners' Party-Fund Fête. You'll recognise lots more. It represents all that was going on round here last year. It was fun doing it.' I tried not to feel smug about my sketchy efforts and wished I could have done one for Adam, as well.

'The bedspread, too . . .' Em fingered the patchwork effect from enormous triangles put together on the machine, 'and the chair cover!'

They're a bit jazzy taken all at once.'

'I adore them. Oh, I'm so glad to be back. I've a letter for you from Daddy and a pressie from Mummy. She gave me a heavenly satin bomber jacket for Christmas with 'Solid State' printed on the back. I've got a book for Ben about food. It's called *Food's a Fad* and says eating's unnecesary. It's just a form of self-indulgence.'

'Tell that to the starving natives in Bangladesh,' I suggested.

'Have a *J'aime Chocolat* bar. They're very popular in Paris. Much nicer than fishnet tights and Charles Aznavour. We spent Christmas in the Georges Cinq with friends of Daddy's. They had a dismal daughter called Chloe, who wore stiletto heels and plum eyeshadow.'

'Why not?' I countered. I don't like intolerant children, putting themselves above others. But Emily added, 'She was seven.' So I let it go.

'I'll go and see Bubbles and Jody now,' said Emily, grabbing a jacket from her cupboard, 'coming Ben?' I was glad he went, albeit reluctantly. I hoped he would change the boots. He was fond of Emily, liked pleasing her but was very big-brother and it wasn't quite what Emily wanted. Not now. Not any more.

# 9

On Saturday, Hosanna rang early. 'We'll have to leave the village at half past one,' she warned me. 'It starts at two and takes twenty minutes to get there. I've organised a couple of Scouts, of course, but you can't rely on them the way you could in Baden-Powell's day.' She added that there were two oil stoves and a motor boat propeller there. Her cousin in the WVS had seen them when she was doing Meals-on-Wheels. I wasn't exactly lyrical about the chance of acquiring two oil stoves and a motor boat propeller, but it was a distinct sign that the Jumble Sale wasn't going to be a last-minute collection with nothing more spectacular than a cracked washing-up bowl in blue plastic with a few unmatched plates to fill out the piles of discarded jumpers.

I asked after Harry. 'He's lovely,' she murmured, so I knew they'd made it up again and were probably planning to cross the Atlantic on the oil stoves and propeller. Every reconciliation brought a planned safari or desert caravanserai or something, only to have it all fizzle out when they quarrelled again over how many tubes of toothpaste to take.

I said I'd be at her gate by 1.30. Then I went to look at the dogs. Phyllis was a nice simple name and I prayed hers would be a nice simple case. She had taken very well to the small spare room, slept a lot, dawdled out for walks, entertained Frilly (who always flirted with newcomers in the hope of sharing their dinners) and looked highly unlikely to do anything dramatic for the next twenty-four hours. Demelza seemed completely unaware of new surroundings, routine, diet, exercise and company. Perhaps that was a characteristic of Scottish Shags.

I rang Hetty for reassurance. She was off in a hurry to a woman who'd trodden on her budgie. '*Trodden!*' I shrieked in horror, 'On a *budgie?*'

'For heaven's sake,' said Hetty irritably, 'lots of people do. They let the thing out, come back suddenly, don't look what they're doing and – bingo!' You'd think to hear her that it was a national pastime.

'Isn't it dead?'

'Of course it's dead. They always are. One of my clients had her chihuahua sat on. Now that was very dead. The sitter weighed eighteen stone. He was just visiting, lowered himself into a chair without looking and only realised a lot later it wasn't a lumpy cushion.' I tried hard not to think about it. 'He just dared not get up and go home. He just sat there glumly for ages. The dog's owner grew desperate. Kept dropping hints, but he sat on firmly for five hours while half the household searched for the chihuahua and the other half brought him drinks. It was only when they all went in for dinner (which he refused) that he dared get up and disappear, out of the chair and off the corpse and into his car and, next day, so the story goes, out of the country. My client got herself a mastiff after that.'

I said did she think it safe for me to go out for an hour or so and leave the pregnant bitches?

'Why?' she asked suspiciously. 'What's so urgent?'

I felt my whole professional image was at stake if I admitted I was putting a Jumble Sale before my new calling. So I hinted at a rendezvous with some lover who must be nameless and she practically gave me her blessing.

In Ben's room the bags were packed ready. Adam's room was coming to life – Emily had already put out her Christmas present for him, an enlargement of Lady, his dog, in a red frame. It overpowered the miniature of his mother in silver. I noticed Emily had rearranged the furniture a bit and added patchwork cushions to the wicker chair. She had left me very little to do. The drawers were almost empty but under some of his summer tee shirts, neatly folded, I found a crumpled picture of Emily. It was dog-eared, tea-dripped, much-handled. It showed her being pulled by two Pyrrenean Mountain dogs, Troilus and Cressida, boarded through the previous August. Emily was laughing and her hair, then long and stringy, was falling over her face but the small pretty nose and wide eyes were clear. Also clear was the fact that Adam had treasured it, kept it in a pocket, looked at it lovingly and often. Falling in love happens all the time, thank God, from age one to one hundred.

I went downstairs and said, 'Adam's room looks lovely.'

She replied absently, 'Well, I like rooms to be all right,' but she suddenly looked anxiously towards Ben.

Ben was sorting his books at the table – homework and leisure. He said, without looking at either of us, 'Will Hetty be here in the morning?'

107

I nodded, but I was thinking in terms of the typical romantic serial: 'Emily, young/lame/beautiful is in love with Ben. But Ben young/ginger-haired/but into-nuclear-physics-this-term is interested in Hetty. Hetty. late thirties/well-off/devastatingly attractive/successful career woman is amusing herself with Ben but is in love with an Italian multi-millionaire. Adam, brown-eyed/sweet-natured/lonely is in love with Emily and . . .' But what could I say about myself to complete 'The Story So Far'? Except that I was sitting on the edge of a few pregnant volcanoes and dying to get off to a jumble sale?

It's love that makes the world go round but no one ever added what happens to the world when love isn't returned. Still, it all goes to prove romantic serials have far more than a grain of truth behind them.

Phyllis, perhaps, represented love at its least devastating. The casual encounter, the detached relationship, the temporary family. So why did I feel sorry for her? I went in and looked at her. She was sitting up on the divan and when she saw me, she lumbered off, wagging her tail. The wag sent the bedside lamp flying. I reached out to stroke her head and she turned so that a whole pile of paperbacks, idly chewed at the edges while she rested, scattered like autumn leaves. A small framed painting of Rye Harbour lay face down on its broken glass. The edge of the rug was wet where she'd nibbled on it earlier. Pregnancy is a very boring pastime even for the enthusiast. It's the one thing they've never managed to get speeded up at all.

I sat holding her paw and stroking her head and telling her how lovely she was for quite a long time while I thought about different things. Then I cleared up the room, gave her a kiss and went away to write my letter to Ross.

The water in the reservoir was like frozen mercury: the motorway like a despairing soul, as I walked with Charlie to the pillar-box. And only such a short time ago they had been tinsel and fairy lights respectively. Frost had gripped bushes and trees, now reaching out to fondle my ears and nose and taunt my finger-tips. I turned and ran back to the house, leaving a trail of breath behind me. Phyllis and Demelza – one mad, shared, generous moment and then, for them, complete independence again next time. Whoever first said 'lucky dog' must have been feeling all the undefined rebellion of every human being.

Pa rang early. He said he was going to view a Fishery.

'A Fishery?' I queried. 'Do you mean a Chippery kind of Fishery? Or a Herring-guttery one or what?'

The line was terrible. Half way along it, someone was telling someone else that this was the last time. The *very* last time. She had had enough. She had, not to put too fine a point on it, had more than enough! I shouted 'So have I! Would you please get off my line!' But she went on, 'I've told him, this is the very end: the very end I told him.' So I said loudly, 'I'm a heavy-breather and I'm going to start any minute . . .' and by the time she'd slammed down the phone, so had Pa.

'He's skated off the roller rink,' I told the other two. 'He's into fish.' Emily was wearing a zippy towelling flying-suit in bright yellow. I wondered how it was going to be now that everyone round me was flashing their tail feathers like peacocks and I was still huddled into a couple of jerseys and a heavy-duty oil-rig boiler-suit. She poured herself black coffee and ignored the toast. 'What sort of fish?' she asked. She could even defy grapefruit.

'Skate?' suggested Ben, 'Or the plaice where you live . . .'

'Oh, very witty, dear. He didn't say. Could be a folly on some ornamental lake in a stately home – or Billingsgate.' Then the phone rang again and I said, 'I'll ask him.' But it was Hosanna.

'We meet as arranged 1.30 sharp,' she informed me as if rallying troops. I felt briefed for surprise attack. 'Would it be best to go separately, do you think? In case the van packs up or breaks down?' Her voice held the ring of the easily defeated. Too many battles lost already.

An hour before I was due to leave, Phyllis brought up her breakfast on a copy of *Vogue* dated July 1971. She looked very apologetic. I wondered whether it heralded further action during the day and began to feel uneasy about leaving her. But it was obvious the lampshade fringe had disagreed with the porridge, so I cleared up and cheered up and went to check on Demelza. She hadn't even eaten hers. I felt they might be ganging up on me and decided to make the jumble a rush job. I certainly wouldn't wait for the 'Everything A Penny!' offer ten minutes before closing, which helped to clear the hall.

I put on my jumbling gear (jeans, jersey, wellies, raincoat, scarf, wool gloves – though a suit of armour with helmet and visor would have been more useful) and went back to the kitchen to give final instructions, only to discover Hetty standing there, holding the Pawleys' Pearl. She handed the barrel-shaped bitch over to me with some relief, dusting her hands as if they were covered in contaminated fall-out. The pug was like nothing more than a pig-shaped balloon. A lot of unfortunate words begin with 'Pug'. Pugilist, pugnacious and even pugger which they tell me is a small shunting-engine and could have applied equally well to Pearl. 'Pug' itself is also a kind of clay and this one looked like the lot.

'You didn't say —' I began, appalled, and trying to keep the latest patient from bouncing away.

But Hetty interrupted, 'I didn't know until Pretty P brought it over just before I left home. She said the Pawley parents refuse to believe Pearl could do anything so vulgar as get herself in trouble and put the extra weight down to over-eating, so they've been cutting down her food in this hope, I suppose, that it's going to go away when she's thinner.'

I began to feel the usual stirrings of agonised compassion. 'She shall have our most luxury suite!' I cried, trying to keep a tight hold of the smoothly rounded bits of Pearl. She was squealing like a pig as well as feeling and looking like one, trying to get down and run to save her bacon. I introduced her to the Mothers' Pride corner hastily, while Demelza lumbered upright and watched us warily. Each cupboard under the long dresser was completely self-contained and, with the doors half-closed, every bed was private. Not for us the distinctions between National Health and BUPA. I went across and tidied Demelza's carton. I noticed the newspapers had been turned over a bit, but I thought it was because she found the City pages depressing and decided to cheer herself up with Clive James. She still had a blanket, but preferred it to stay screwed up in a corner to keep her paws warm.

I went back and said to Ben, 'I'm going.'

'We'll keep an eye on everything,' promised Emily, almost pushing me to the door.

'You sure you'll both be all right?' I asked anxiously. I only meant if anything happened, but Emily said obscurely, 'It's going to be fun!'

I looked at Ben. He was sitting with his feet up on the edge of the table, chair tipped back. He was reading that wretched paperback again.

'Did you know pug puppies are only born . . .'

'. . . when there's an 'r' in the month,' I finished. Mattie warned me from the corner that no good would come of it. I should have listened.

Even then I was called back from stirring the van into action by the phone bell ringing inside. I hastily scrambled out again. Emily called, 'It's OK. It was Pa. He says he's got it!' Nevertheless, I rushed back in, grabbed the receiver from Ben and shouted, 'Got what?' but at the same moment Constance fell off her perch and woke up with a shriek, which woke all the dogs and created a universal bark-in. I couldn't even hear the dialling tone. Not for the first time I wondered why I bother with a phone in the kitchen. It was like being in a school playground with low-flying planes.

'What d'you think he's got?' I asked anyone who'd help.

'He sounded pleased,' Ben said, 'so it's not scabies, herpes or pox. It could be a fish shop, of course.'

Only the jumble sale could comfort me now.

The scout hut stood on a piece of ground that no funds had so far been found to change from corn to concrete. The mud, which had frozen overnight, thawed miserably and reluctantly during the day. Now a weak sun had coaxed it into slush, slowly seeping over the row of patient wellies.

Hosanna and I walked boldly to the front of the queue, where two boy scouts, early risen from the cubs, chewed lengths of liquorice and peered sullenly from anorak hoods sparsely edged with nylon fur. Resentful muttering from the rest of the queue was studiously ignored as money changed hands. 'Ten pee each, I think?' Hosanna said in a low voice, but with a note of authority. 'It's not yet —' She displayed her digital watch, 'ah – 2.15. In fact it's just changing now. The microchip cannot lie.' It was, in point of fact, about four minutes slow, but no one, least of all a Scout, argues with the wonders of modern science. They sloped off to try and wangle a fag from the assistant Scoutmaster, an eager young man anxious to demonstrate his tolerance and understanding.

I waved to a woman in a red felt hat and thick glasses, five couples back, and through my beam of brotherhood muttered, 'Old jampot's here.'

Zanna said, 'And the Snake. Did you notice Lizzie Chizzler coming up the lane, full steam behind the pram?' We knew all the regulars, named for their characteristics. What they called us, I hate to think. I know they were indignant we turned up every time and considered Boy-Scout-bribing a blatant cheat. They felt the same way about several others, too, such as the Major, who collected old military manuals or anything connected with World War 1, and Mrs Frisby, one of several heavily disguised dealers, who often hung about at the door and bought from those returning triumphant from battle. The urge to make fifteen pence on a deal which would probably net her a couple of pounds, was even so, irresistible. But we were social side-steppers and they didn't like it. We should have been the benevolent and lordly givers of jumble, not the eager and enthusiastic purchasers.

Equality sounds good in the ears of socialist fanatics and left-wing aristocracy, but in the ranks it will never catch on. Your true blue villager doesn't want to recognise a turn in the tide of fortunes. Even now it was happening at the edges, and they were uneasy about having their perks taken away in exchange for nebulous advantages. In any case, it was now the housing estates which glowed with imitation electric log fires competing with their underfloor central heating, while we were ready and willing and only just able to pay the 50p for their simple, discarded oil stoves. They were the ones posting off for new mauve nylon fitted sheets, while we eagerly treasured their grandmother's steadfast linen gradually finding its way on to stalls every weekend at villages all over the country.

We stood in a sullen, suspicious group, as alien from the townsman's idea of a happy rural scene as Balmoral from Balham. Behind the locked doors ahead, lying between us and Treasure Trove within, could be heard the sound of tables being pushed about, chattering and laughing. It was warm in there and the queue grew restive. 'A picture gone!' muttered Hosanna crossly as a crash of glass was followed by, 'Sorry Mrs Pound!' A china mug fell and was rescued minus its handle. 'Never mind, dear, it's a set of three from Rene Ribb's up at Sparrows. The two left will make a pair so we can ask more that way.'

Hosanna and I exchanged looks. The group behind us muttered. The wind blew like small screams of anger off the sea and threatened snow later. We shivered and stamped and blinked and knew that it would take very little to arouse the anarchy, the storming of temples, the Charge of our Rights Brigade, which would bring down the door and wreck all within. Coughs rose to a crescendo. The woman in a balaclava sneezed violently down my neck. Somebody went round the side to peer through the window by standing on a pile of old boxes. I tried not to think about home, about Demelza and Phyllis, Ben and Emily. The Aga and a teapot.

To distract myself, I asked Hosanna about Harry. 'We made it up, but he wants to go on a walking tour and I don't, so we're withholding contract again.' She was a one-woman union of her own.

'You quite enjoyed walking the Wine District,' I pointed out, sniffing a bit. Laughter burst out from inside, faces behind us grew more menacing. Angry muttering and an exchange of opinions about the time passed down the line. Was it all worth it, I asked myself, to go home with Mrs Ackerly's old underwear, or someone's discarded strapless summer sandals?

'That's because we drank so much on the first day that we spent the rest in bed at the hotel!'

'Do the same this time,' I suggested. No walking tour should fail to recognise the real priorities.

'In the London Dock area?' Hosanna said witheringly, adding that Harry felt he needed sharp contrast as stimulation to the recent rurality of his painting.

'Why not let *him* do the Docks while *you* do the West End shops and meet up every night in Soho, say, or . . .' We were still discussing possibilities when the doors were flung open.

The rush of freed political prisoners from newly liberated Third World gaols was nothing like the cut and thrust from forty women wanting to be first at the White Elephants. Stampeding like bulls at Pamplona, they scrambled over one another to get at the egg whisks, old electric razors, and castanets brought back from Benidorm. Forgotten the outstanding rent demands, Jim's redundancy and the twins' teething troubles. Forgotten the dismal weather, the stone-cold feet, the toothache, the temper, the temperature and the tiredness as they all rushed together towards Nirvana, signified by Old Joe Hatchett's darned long johns, and Maisie Frolic's 42" bikini, broken buckles and all. Hosanna forgot Harry and the docks, I forgot Demelza and Pearl and Phyllis and Ben and Em and even what Ben called Pa's 'Castles in Vain' as, by tacit consent and prior agreement, I covered the men's stall and Hosanna the Nearly-New rail. Then, as if signalled, we changed places to check the other's possible failure in the scrum to recognise what we were looking for. But there was no Priddle trench coat. Had it at some point surfaced from the Pakamacs and Gannex we would have felt triumph, followed rather quickly by sharp regret that the glorious chase was over, the kill made, the day finished for ever. What did Arthur do after Excalibur? And St George when the dragon was slain? I daresay even the Holy Grail sat on the sideboard and everybody forgot to polish it after the first hullabaloo died down.

'Capes,' I muttered swiftly to Hosanna, pushing my way through a horde of battling women towards Coats & Skirts. I was after the lesser Priddlewear, but Zanna was heading for the hitherto besieged White Elephants and I lost sight of her under a flail of fists waving chipped enamel pie-dishes and tattered paperbacks.

At the opposite trestle, silent women worked more menacingly, using elbows and shopping baskets and moving eagle-eyed and efficient, grappling, trampling, digging and throwing aside like demented checkers on a fast-moving factory belt.

'I'm going,' I said wearily when I caught sight of Hosanna again ten minutes later. The feverish activity had abated a little, but the energy expended would have run Cape Canaveral for a couple of years. Zanna said she was staying on for the auction. Any bigger items, such as armchairs without bottoms and old bikes, carpets or depleted vacuum cleaners, were kept for the highest bid (usually 50p) at the end of the first half-hour. This was a subtle move which kept the public on its toes and its toes inside the hall, while its fingers continued buying until the time was up. Some West Country Jumbles auction everything, from a bundle of old socks upwards. Bids of a penny are taken seriously and I once got five plastic raincoats for tuppence which I made into Christmas presents for twelve people.

'What for?' I asked, meaning 'For what?'

'The red rug with the burn hole, and that footstool. It only needs another leg. May go for the splintered spice rack too.'

'You've got one.'

She glared. 'Do for hanging other things.' Her defiance made me hope she didn't mean Harry. I wished her luck and staggered to the van with a pile of old Punch periodicals, some agricultural boots size 8, a tweed hat with a feather, some torn velvet curtains in faded blue. (I grab anything faded. First because they go so cheap and second because they date from days when dyes weren't 'fast', and thirdly because they're so much more attractive than current designs and prints.) And two hand-worked cushion-covers with crinoline ladies in gardens rioting with flowers. I have a perverse admiration for what is termed 'kitsch' and gets the cold shoulder from contemporary taste.

I was just starting the engine of the van when a woman banged on the window. 'Can you give me a lift?' she mouthed, eyebrows raised, through the glass.

I opened the door, the window being the kind that sticks for ever after the first few weeks' use. 'Sorry,' I said impatiently because she might have lived anywhere, 'but I'm in a tearing hurry to get home,' and to show I meant it, I let off the brake and began to move forward. She ran after me trailing jumble and calling, 'I'm new at Swallows Farm! We met in the village shop one day. Just drop me at your gate and I'll walk the rest!'

I hesitated, turned and then, as she lumbered towards me, I saw the Priddle blouse. There were two of them somewhere, so far undiscovered by Zanna and me. I felt the blood rush to my head. How on earth had we missed it? Silk, of course, can be far too dignified to display itself brazenly among Bri-Nylon and Courtelle. Somewhere lurking among that mound of moving rubbish, it must have hovered, uneasily dominated by the more flamboyant checks and stripes and floral prints.

I now had to play my cards carefully to score at last over Hosanna. There was no question about which of us would have it. Only the trench coat was for sharing. Smaller Priddle trophies became the prerogative of she who was smart enough to find one! The blouse, creamy-rich in colour, slightly deepened by age, was bundled with the rest of her stuff into the back of the van, but I could see the high neck, the beautiful embroidery and the edge of a frilled cuff. My heart sang with excitement.

The woman was chattering. 'I wanted plants. You know, cuttings and that?' Everyone makes excuses for jumbling: with some it's books, others home-made cakes (and I once knew a woman who went in the hope of finding a Bokhara rug – she's still hoping). 'Having moved into this new farm, you see, we need a nice lot to cheer things up a bit. Them corsets, of course, I want for the whalebone. You know why?' I shook my head although a single glance at her rolling acres would have been enough to justify killing any whale.

'Make good flexible supports for the more fleshy ones.'

Well, she was certainly one of those. The little van sagged with protest. I asked how she'd got to the village in the first place.

'Bob Fossett's Funerals,' she said dismissively, leaving me wondering whether she'd gone as a mourner and dropped off half way. Some people will do anything for a bargain. 'Busy Lizzie.' For a moment I thought she meant . . . but though I saw her as a member of the deceased's family, in a black felt hat, bunion-broad shoes, tutting with disapproval and probably taking her knitting to the crematorium, I realised she meant what *we* call Fussy Fred, because we believe in sex equality. I tried to show a lively interest and almost hit a woman with a wheelbarrow, which proves sex equality in rural areas is unfortunately happening all the time.

Plant people always imagine they alone know a cineraria from a symposium, the way a lot of perfectly ordinary domestic cooks nurse the secret opinion they alone can make a scone. And if one happens to be noted for doing other things, even boarding dogs, one has to be inflicted, quite regularly, on how to go about producing lumps of dough stuck with currants. But my passenger was vague about any interested enquiries concerning her Wandering Sailors, and it's my belief she wouldn't have recognised one if it had leapt from its plastic pot and belted her. Nevertheless, we chatted amicably – and on my part with positive enthusiasm – coaxing and begging responses that might eventually, by default and indirect enquiries, somehow win me the Priddle blouse.

'I'll run you to your door,' I promised wildly at one point. Swallows Farm was beyond the old wrecktory. Considering the collection in the back of the van, it was the least I could do. She said her gate would be far enough, and I knew it was less for my sake than to keep me out of her kitchen. We had passed my own gate, and I was just about to advance the subject of the blouse when she hissed, '*Stop!*'

For one awful moment, I thought she might be a bandit and would whip out a gun from her ample bra and hold me to ransom for the tweed hat. She could have kept a machine gun in there without it being obvious, but she had half-turned away from me and I could have knocked her senseless with her own goods, then strangled her with the limp frills of a rather dreadful party dress. I could then have made off with the blouse if I'd had the wit to do it. But she turned back as I was weighing up the chances, and said, as if announcing the Day of Judgement, 'It's my husband!'

A weary-looking man was pushing a very old bicycle through a field just ahead of us. He looked utterly harmless. To start with, he was half her size in all directions, and to go on with, he looked completely worn out. 'Would he like a lift?' I asked sympathetically. 'We can get his bike in the back if we pile up a bit: on top of everything.'

She looked at me as if I were mad. 'He mustn't see me,' she muttered, trying to vanish by the effort of simple necessity. She shrank towards me, face down, apparently hoping we might merge into the illusion of one enormous driver with two heads. She closed her eyes to mere slits as if this might help. I continued to sit bolt upright, feeling awkward. Her hair smelled of parsnips and her breath of onions. It was like being forced into a stale stew. I tried to look straight ahead and hum. I wanted to ask why she was scared of seeing him or him seeing her, but I didn't want her to be upset in any way. I wanted the blouse.

The man closed the farm gate behind him and for one awful moment I thought he was coming our way and we should have to

116

rush forward and mow him down as they do all the time in seemingly civilised communities on TV. But he crossed the road, opened the gate opposite, and proceeded to carry on over the fields towards a footpath. When he was almost out of sight, the woman sat upright suddenly and beamed at me.

'He disapproves of jumbling,' she explained calmly.

There was something familiar about the man. Something I couldn't name. Had I seen him before? and, if so, where? We climbed the hill and the farmhouse came in sight up a long, muddy track. I stopped at the gate and jumped out of the van. Then I opened up the back as she was still lumbering out of the door on her side into a well-chosen frozen puddle. I slipped the blouse under the tweed hat and carried the rest of the things to her gate and handed them over. She thanked me in an offhand way, her mind on getting in before her husband, and hurried up the drive without even glancing at the goodies, her eyes too occupied in watching the distant figure of her husband. Measuring up the chances, I would have taken a bet at them both arriving on the back doorstep within seconds of one another, awarding the Gold to the Jumble competitor.

I would like to have stayed. I was dying to know what happened next. The corset strings were trailing in the mud as she scooted away and the frilly dress flew out behind as she made for safety. Did she leave her hoard secure behind the pig-bins before facing and embracing her duped husband? Or did she flagrantly defy his wrath, waving her reckless luxuries and confessing with pride her secret vice?

With the Priddle blouse under the tweed hat, I wasn't waiting to find out.

117

# 10

It was just as I parked the van at home that I realised why the weary farmer was so familiar. It was not his face – but what he wore. What might easily be the star of all Priddle persistence – the actual, original, highly-prized trench coat. I stopped in my tracks and half-turned back towards the farm. Then I pulled myself together and went forward with resolute determination to face what awaited me inside.

The kitchen door was open into the hall but the house was ominously silent. (Had the woman a secret store of Priddlemania?) I went to the foot of the stairs and called 'Anyone around?', threw off my coat and dumped it on the carved pew I bought for £1 from St Strabismus's Church Bazaar where some of the ecclesiastical fittings and furniture became confused with the rummage. There was pop music coming from upstairs, so I opened the front door and began to unload the van. (Or was she just better at jumbling than I was?) I carried the treasured blouse into the kitchen still inside the tweed hat, and with trembling hands (perhaps she had the capes, too, at home?) drew out the silk, so soft and light and with so many years of fond care behind it. At last, after all the hours, the miles, the dreaming and despair, I held one of the Priddle blouses in my hands. Slowly I let it fall from the shoulders and it hung, exquisite and elegant – but lop-sided and shamed, with one sleeve missing.

'That's nice,' said Ben behind me, 'when's the amputation?'

I turned and stared at him. He must have seen the look in my eyes, because he said quickly, 'Well, here's news to cheer you up. Demelza's having a saucer of tea, Emily's washing her hair, Phyllis has eaten your poinsettia and a copy of the Egon Ronay Guide for 1974 and I've made a cake for tea.'

'Good,' I said, 'I thought she was right off food.' I went upstairs and opened the door of the small spare room. Emily lay on the divan with a towel round her head reading a book. Phyllis stood defiantly on a heap of torn paper, a bit of poinsettia sticking out of her mouth. The water bowl was overturned on the floor.

'Em, darling, she's what you'd call restless, isn't she?'

'Ummm,' said Emily, turning over another page of somebody's old Mills and Boon. Shreds of praise for Brown's Hotel lay all over the rug.

'That makes it pretty clear she expects VIP treatment, doesn't it?' I said, putting my arms round the heavy neck and hugging her.

Emily said, without looking up, 'She's been sick, too.'

'Oh! By the way, I've got a Priddle silk blouse.' I felt myself smirk, sleeve forgotten. It scored as a Priddling win, anyway.

Emily looked up and I could see she'd been crying. I smiled, looked away and said, 'I'll get some tea, love,' and went back downstairs. I think she was picturing herself portrayed in the romance and was identifying Ben as well. There's nothing worse than being bothered in the middle of a fantasy, specially with a sponge cake.

Ben already had the kettle boiling. I said sharply, 'And what have *you* been doing all afternoon?' because I wanted them to be together and happy.

'Answering the phone, entertaining clients, being my usual charming self.' He put three mugs on the table and brought out the chocolate cake.

'Who rang? Which clients?' I grabbed the mug and a slice of cake. I was starving. Energy and emotions force the adrenalin to stir up an appetite. Slimmers should keep very calm, composed, cool and idle.

'Pa. Marsha. A Friend of Beowulf.'

'Oh, God! And who called?'

'A feller with a whippet wearing a fur coat.'

'Sounds as if the whippet was —'

'The whippet *was*. Still is, I expect. He's in the office if you want to see for yourself.'

I leapt as if stung. 'Why on earth didn't you say so before?' I rushed to the door.

Ben poured the tea. 'He said he wasn't in any hurry. He looked as if he could do with a rest. So did you when you came in.'

Ben was right, of course. The young man was slumped in a chair near the fire, eyes closed. The dog sat all over him, like a furry eiderdown. I couldn't think why Ben had referred to it as a whippet until I patted it and then I felt its bones against my hand and its ribs like corrugated iron. The man started to get up but I waved him back in the chair, and sat down in the one opposite, apologising.

'Honestly,' he interrupted, 'It's all right, really. It's so lovely in here. Peaceful. Quiet. Warm.' He spoke as if he regarded comfort as a rare treat, and I felt a rush of pity.

They were both in need of care. I went to the door and called Ben to bring us some tea. Then I said, 'What a super dog! What's his name?'

'Kip. I'm Jake Edwards. He's a Wheaten Terrier.' He paused, then laughed. 'But I'm a dead loss.' It was a strange thing to say so I took no notice. Ben brought in a plate of scones with butter running between them, and the cake. I crumbled a scone for Kip and the young man took another. They finished every scrap before the young man said, 'I wonder if you could board him for me? I can't pay anything in advance, I'm afraid, but he needs somewhere like this. Regular kennels would be too impersonal. They told me about you in the village. You see, if you can't have him, I'd have to . . .' Then he stopped.

'How long will you be away?' I asked, knowing what the end of the sentence would have been. I couldn't refuse to help, but I had to appear businesslike or we'd have both grown emotional.

'I don't know.' He looked as if he'd like to say more but felt it better to stay silent. I offered them both another scone. Kip glanced at his master for approval before I gave him one.

We had to fill the gap between us. 'I called him Kip because he, er, "kippers",' the young man said. The dog was looking up adoringly through a heavy fringe. His eyes were hidden but his whole attitude spelt devotion.

'Flat out, like a kipper,' I said. 'Sign of a contented dog.' Like collapsing with laughter into a chair, every limb relaxed. And that small thing which we both understood formed an immediate bond. Without an analytical assessment, intuition on both sides was satisfied. 'He can stay as long as he likes,' I said. 'Is he a good mixer or – ?'

'Or a bit of a mixer?' He laughed. 'He's all right. He'll mix the way that's called for. He'll be no trouble, I promise.' His thin hand strayed constantly over the dog's head, reassuring and yet somehow admitting defeat. He made a few excuses about not leaving a phone number or address. He'd just left one place, he said, and would have to find a new home which would take them both. I didn't ask any more, he seemed so vulnerable. He was no more than twenty and so sensitive I was afraid he might suddenly cry. I wanted to invite him to stay for supper, but it would have sounded patronising, so I took out the empty plates and cups and the bowl where Kip had enjoyed his own tea, and left them there, together and alone. I turned at the door, but they were unaware of me – just looking at one another, knowing so much more than I did or, perhaps, ever would know. I felt that neither knew quite how to cope with the enormity of the moment.

I found I couldn't mention it to Ben. I flipped about the Jumble Sale and the cake and the phone calls, and all the time I was aching with tears of sympathy for the drama going on so close. This, I knew, was no ordinary boarding.

It was twenty minutes before I heard the front door close. Kip was standing there, staring wildly, his legs rigid, body tense, facing the last sight of his master. Before I could reach him, he threw himself forward and began a high, shrieking yelp. It roused the other dogs all over the house in a frantic response, and however hard Jake Edwards was running, the sound must have reached him and broken his heart. And yet I knew he wouldn't come back. Kip hurled himself at the door, again and again, leaping and beating at it while I stood helpless. Then, just as suddenly, it all stopped. He seemed to deflate, crumple to the floor, where he lay panting and whining. I tried to comfort him but he warned me away. I left him and went back to the kitchen where Ben and I talked about it in shocked voices.

Kip just lay there and hardly moved. I took him some food and water, but he completely ignored them. I tried to put him on a lead and take him outside and at first he was reluctant, then enthusiastic, then disappointed and finally resigned. He knew, as I did, that Jake had gone and, from that moment on, Kip's place was in the hall, within sight of the front door, to be first to greet him when, finally, he came back. I felt the two of them must have been through a great deal together to share such single-minded faith and love.

The face of the young man stayed in my mind and haunted my dreams. I tried to push the whole incident aside, but somehow it was always with me in the dogged endurance of Kip. He eventually ate a little, lapped water thirstily, slept in a thick box with a big warm blanket, but more, I guessed, from a determination to be ready for his master's return than to sustain himself.

When he was settled, I began on the phone calls.

'What did Marsha want?'

'You to ring her soon as possible.'

'And Pa?'

'He'll ring again. He wished you well. He said he'd got it.'

121

'I know he's got it. He rang earlier and said he'd got it. But why doesn't he say what it is he's got?' I suppose we shall find out in due course. Did you take out Demelza or Pearl?'

'No,' said Ben uneasily and gave me a look that spelt trouble. 'Demelza wasn't keen to leave the cupboard, actually, and Pearl – was, well, not there.'

'Not there?' I stopped short at the cake tin, about to help myself to crumbs of comfort. Outside the snow had really started. After all those hints and nudges, it was thickening against the dark sky and I could see huge soft feathery corn flakes beginning to build up on the window sill. I never have been able to disregard signs of weather extremes with equanimity. I see the elements taking over – the wind that turns to gale that turns to tempest. The temperature that grows from 75° to 90° and to the eventual fiery furnace. And now the delicate gentle beauty of snow that would become a blizzard and a burial ground. I pulled the curtains. I had enough to worry about inside the house.

'Well . . .' Ben began but I interrupted, 'I'll go and see what's wrong. You're keeping something from me, aren't you?'

'I'm just trying to hand things over in their order of priority. First, you needed to relax a bit, then you had to see a man about a dog, now we can go into the rest.'

'The rest?' I moved the teapot and the cosy fell off the Aga and landed on Charlie's head. He wore it stoically, like a laurel wreath to taunt a loser. They had all been round to size up Kip, who ignored them. Rosie had sneaked the remains of his food but they knew, all of them, that we were a cottage industry and that we helped support one another. Fee-payers provided the style to which we were accustomed, much as the stately home throws open its doors to visiting Americans. No guests would mean no rates paid and therefore no rabbiting, varied social life and country sport.

'Demelza's been prowling around a bit. I think she's nesting. I gave her the *The Times Literary Supplement*. And Pearl . . .'

'Well?'

'I can't find her.'

'You *what*?' It was worse than the snow.

'Look, it's nothing to worry about.' (My God!) 'She can't be outside. The doors have all been shut and she's too small to try the chimney. I only noticed she wasn't there just before you got back. I've searched all over the house – every inch. She must be hiding somewhere. I was just going to try the game larder when you came in, but the phone's been ringing such a lot: look, I'm terribly sorry, honestly!'

I said, 'Ben, darling, it isn't your fault. How can it be?' It was mine, all mine. A punishment for greed. The Law of the Jumble. Win a silk shirt, lose somebody else's pug dog. And the winning only had one sleeve, at that. I'd never go to another jumble as long as I lived. I'd swear off rummages and sales of work and vicarage bazaars and church fêtes too.

Pearl was certainly nowhere in the dresser cupboards. Demelza, on the other hand, was indulging in a frenzy of activity. She had scratched up every square inch of newsprint and was now busy on the carton itself, ripping it apart like a demonstration of strength by Mr Universe with the A – D telephone directory. I mopped up the water bowl which had been swept out of the way in her effort to improve our accommodation for her precious litter, and then left her at it, after some soothing words and gentle persuasion to relax had been completely ignored.

Ben fetched Emily and we divided the house into three, agreeing to leave no area unturned. I stopped suddenly in the hall. 'Oh, Cheeses!' I cried, 'I left the front door open while I was bringing the stuff in. She could have escaped then! She could be half-way home now. She'd have to cross the motorway. She could have got under the gate where the wire netting got caught on the baker's van. She could have found a hole in the hedge. She could have –'

'Hang about,' protested Ben, 'you'd have seen her, surely?' He was leaning over the banisters and the old bronze chandelier, with one mermaid's tail missing, was set swaying ever so slightly by the vibrations of anxiety.

'Not necessarily.' I began to shuffle around the pile of old fur coats on the hall sofa, kept there through the winter to deter villains from attack: it looked like a permanent party was going on. Two sleepy moths blinked and went back to a good chew.

Emily joined Ben at the head of the stairs. 'She's definitely nowhere up here,' she said. 'I've opened all the cupboards, drawers, looked under the beds and even *in* most of them. Have you tried the conservatory?'

'I doubt if she could open the door. It takes me ages and a sharp knife to get in since it was painted. If she's managed that, she can come round with me and do all the windows.' I had to try and keep the drama from becoming a melo-one. Don't they say tragedy is comedy in a cloak?

'She must be outside, then. But she won't go far in this snow! I bet she's shivering on the back doorstep this very moment,' said Ben, but he didn't sound very convinced. He came down the stairs and put an arm round me. Only in high heels would I be taller now. His attempt at comfort made a lot of things startlingly clear. Ben had grown up and would soon go his own way: no one is ever completely independent of someone: and that if I didn't hurry up and find Pearlie-girl, she would perish in the porch.

But she wasn't there. We all stepped back in again. The snow was now thick and, away from the house, very deep in places. It came at us with the soft malign taunt of a sneer, daring us to challenge its power.

'You two keep an eye on Phyllis and Demelza,' I said, 'I'm going out.' I might have been Scott of the Antarctic.

They didn't argue: merely exchanged a look. Then Emily went off to the maternity wing and Ben put on his boots and raincoat. I added the dog walker over my jumble riding mac and found my wellies, but they were still wet and cold after the recent expedition so I put on the newly acquired size 8 aggi boots instead. There was enough room inside to accommodate a few mice as well as my feet, and it felt as if someone had, but I couldn't waste time with curiosity. Looking like a mature Yeti in scarf, gloves and beanie from behind the kitchen door, I joined Ben waiting for me with his head in a brown paper bag. I said briefly, 'You could have had the deer-stalker,' but he replied, 'Brown paper's supposed to be very good insulation,' and we stepped together out into the dark, stark world of night and snow.

'I'll cover the stables,' suggested Ben. I nodded. I wanted to do the drive and the front of the house because I was afraid Pearl might have headed back home in spite of the spartan diet there. It all seemed hopeless, anyway. I could barely see into corners and crevices where a small dog would take shelter. Tears stung my eyelids inside and a sudden sweeping wind round the corner of the house stung them from outside. I had to lift each boot with a physical effort before planting it down ahead. The expended energy helped keep me warm. I could almost have enjoyed myself if the object of the exercise had been a bit less daunting.

The front porch, too, was empty. I suffered a blow of sick disappointment. I was carrying in my mind a picture of the tubby pug taking refuge there, once she found how little the great outside world had to offer. I started off down the drive, calling her name, battling against the snow and wind. The air seemed to be dark purple, the sky non-existent. It was like plunging into white velvet, under water. Only occasionally, down where the motorway would be, I caught a glimpse of sickly yellow trying to claw its way out of the elements from the overhead lights. There was no way to see where I was going: I could have walked off the edge of the world without realising. I scrunched over flower beds, brick edging, a small fishpond and innumerable hibernating plants hoping to get a reassuring bark from my constant calling. I knew I was heading the right way for the road when I almost walked slap into a small car which rounded the gatepost and shot a beam of light into my eyes. The Police? Some kindly stranger carrying Pearl? Great heavens! please don't let it be the Pawleys! I stumbled towards the door and rubbed snow off the window to peer through. Bun peered back at me, nose to nose, eyes narrowed, pixie hood pulled well round over flushed cheeks. Wen looked across her twin from the passenger seat, frowning under a jaunty little peaked cap in home-knitting, with ear-flaps and a bow under her chin. Then she recognised me. She leant behind her sister and undid the door at the back. I had no choice but to get in.

'What*ever* are you doing, dear?'

I had to make a swift choice between the awful admission of truth or some ridiculous lie. I went at once for the ridiculous lie.

'Singing,' I said on the spur of the moment, getting in the car. It was just possible they might have heard my voice ringing out across the snow. I settled in the back like a hen scattering shoals of white feathers.

Bun put the car into gear and we trundled forward. 'We got caught in all this coming back from the Pensloe and Wensley,' she said chattily, 'and I said to Wendy, why not pop in on you for a nip and a natter till it clears a bit? You did say any day around teatime, didn't you?'

So I had, so I had. But not today, for God's sake, not today!

'Singing?' queried Wen, puzzled.

'It's difficult to practise in the house – the high notes and that. Specially when everyone's around. They do rather hate it, you know. Gets in the way of the Big Match on afternoon telly. Out here I can let rip. And of course it's a well known fact that acoustics are better in snow. Clarity of atmosphere.'

'I never knew that,' said Wen suspiciously.

'I didn't even know you sang,' challenged Bun, stopping the car at the back door.

'Not a lot, not now,' I blustered, peering sideways from the car through the windows, terrified they might grind poor Pearl to

pieces under their unsuspecting wheels, 'just for my own amusement really.'

'Soprano? Mother had a light soprano, didn't she, Bunce?'

'Isn't it awful,' muttered Bun, meaning the weather. She was
wondering whether it was worth getting out.

'You might say that,' I answered both of them and trying to
remember what range soprano implied. 'Sweet Lass of Richmond
Hill and, er, Sheep May Safely Graze,' which was ridiculous
under the circumstances. Goodness knows what put it into my
head.

It was then we saw Ben coming round the corner of the house in
his paper bag. 'Hullo!' I cried uneasily. 'It's Ben!' Just as if we all
sang together on icy nights in blizzards up and down the country.

Ben stopped in his tracks close to the car and stuck his head
forward, trying to see inside. I flattened my face on the glass in my
anxiety to reassure him it was me. He drew back terrified. I must
have looked pretty nauseating, but hardly that bad, I thought
crossly. I wound the window down a bit and shouted, 'It's Wen
and Bun, Ben,' and then, because it sounded so silly, I added
lightly, 'popping in for tea!'

I know it sounded snide, as if I were adding under my breath
'Heaven help us,' which in actual fact, I was, more or less.

We all went in, followed by Ben. I believe he thought I had news
of Pearl or why would I be driving about on the worst night for
years, chatting about tea? I couldn't think how I was going to make
it clear that I had to protect my reputation and business interests
by forgetting Pearl for the moment, nor how I was going to keep
him quiet if he didn't cotton on. There was no time for any specific
plan. But specific plans are often less reliable than tuning in as
you go.

'What a cosy den!' squealed Bun, recognising a similar
muddle to her own with relief.

'I do love a stove,' said Wen, warming her hands on top of the
Aga.

'Take off your coats,' I cried desperately, putting on the kettle
and watching both doors simultaneously, alert for Emily or Ben
arriving from opposite entrances and demanding news of Pearl
before I had time to wink, shake my head, say something significant, or just faint dead away and distract everybody.

'It's always the same at the Pensloe and Wensley,' sighed Bun,
regretfully. 'They put up a beautiful Griff for B of S, together with
a badly-docked Boxer with one testicle' (the docking must have

been a very hit or miss affair, I thought) 'and a lot of rubbish. You can guess who got it, of course, when I tell you Mrs Spagworth was judging!'

'The Boxer?' I suggested, though I knew perfectly well it was going to be a bit of the rubbish.

'A Maremma!'

It sounded like a South American thigh-slapping gypsy dance. A lot of stamping about, a flashing of teeth full of roses.

'Of course you know who owned him?'

'Carmen Miranda?' I risked, lining up the mugs on the table.

They both stared at me. 'Doesn't she do Pekes and Labs in Lincs?' said one of them uncertainly. I was relieved when Ben, who had gone out again when he saw we didn't have Pearl, stumbled back in, his paper bag sodden and clinging to his ears in shreds. I went forward with the idea of muttering a warning but the mice in the aggi boots made me catch my toe on a corner of the rug and I fell flat on my face. It was almost as good as a faint. Everyone ran forward and helped me up. 'I'm OK,' I protested, between laughter and tears of despair. The twins muttered uneasily, 'Rotten luck,' and 'Hard cheese, old thing,' and pushed me into a chair. I'm sure they thought I was drunk. Anyone singing down the garden in a temperature of 4° or 5° below, and inches deep in snow, had to be drunk or potty.

Ben took bits of brown paper out of his hair in soggy lumps. 'I haven't seen a sign of her,' he said despairingly.

I shook my head at him and raised my eyebrows and grinned inanely. As a message, it was impossible to decode.

'Are you OK?' asked Wen, anxiously.

'Fine, fine,' I muttered. And to Ben, 'Not to worry. I expect she'll have to wait till later, Ben. The weather, you know.' I tried hard to make him understand we must never reveal our awful secret.

'No one would travel on a night like this unless they had to,' comforted Bun. 'Perhaps she'll turn up tomorrow.' It was obvious she thought Ben had been waiting for somebody.

'It was quite a jolly morning when we left home at seven,' said Wen, as if that might help a bit.

'What do you mean? We can't wait till tomorrow!' protested Ben, sounding shocked.

'Elderly, perhaps?' enquired Bun sympathetically. 'They do get so obstinate. Dads did, didn't he, Wen? Wouldn't be parted from his bedsocks even in hospital. Sister said to me, once, 'Mr Finch won't take his sleeper unless he's got his bompers on.' Always called them his bompers, didn't he, Wen?'

Ben stared at her as though she'd gone mad. Wen said, complacently, 'Old people do take risks, though, Bun. Take Anona Wagg – Skyes, isn't she, Bun? She was at the Western and Pridwell Beaglers. Drove a hundred and twenty miles through the night – and she's eighty-nine!'

'Shids,' said Bun.

Ben and I tried not to look shocked.

'Shid Tzus and Lhasa Apos, though she *was* Samoyeds and St. Bunnies. Nice Sams she had. Won a fourth at Crufts in sixty-nine. It was sixty-nine, wasn't it?'

'*What about Pearl?*' demanded Ben in a frenzy of rage.

'My boots ought to come off,' I cried, despairingly. Wen grabbed one and Bun the other; I had to tip back my chair and cling to the Aga rail. The phone rang and at the same time, Emily burst in the door calling,' Phyllis is panting. I think she must be in labour!' as one boot hit the floor. A lot of screwed-up paper fell out, and I was so glad it wasn't mice that I burst into tears.

'Sorry,' I apologised with an hysterical laugh, 'but you could say it's just been one of those days.'

The kettle was whistling and the phone was screaming at me like a child of four with its finger stuck in a medicine bottle. I rushed across in a frantic sort of hobble in a bare foot and an aggi boot and attempted a calm 'Hi!' just as if nothing was happening. I watched Emily making coffee for everyone, chatting to the twins and Ben joining in and knew with a sinking heart they were betraying me. However unwittingly, the game was up.

Nothing came from the other end of the phone but heavy breathing.

It was all I needed. 'Look,' I said patiently, 'you're wasting your time. Nothing you can do is any worse than I've got already. You'll have to do a lot better than that. In any case, heavy breathing's a joke nowadays. Old hat. Go and try it in a cemetery. They could do with it down there,' and I slammed the phone down.

Then I turned and faced the music. Wen was saying, '. . . and this, er, Phyllis. Wouldn't it be wise to ring the doctor?'

'But she's another of them,' explained Emily, 'A lovely Great Dane. I've been reading all about it and so far she's acting quite normally. No need to panic.' She turned to me. 'Demelza's puffing a bit, too, but then she always does. I should think Phyllis will be first at the winning post.'

Ben said, 'I'm going out again to find Pearl.'

Wen and Bun looked at one another as if propelled unwillingly into a bawdy house wearing nothing but their pixie hoods. I didn't know how much had been said, but there's a time for truth, just as there are times for evasion, times for downright lying and times for doing a bunk and avoiding disclosure. This was truth-and-dare time. The truth was simple, but not very pure. There was no getting away from it.

'Phyllis, Demelza and Pearl are all pregnant bitches belonging to other people. I board over the delivery period. Pearl has vanished. I was looking for her when you arrived.'

'While you sang!' said Wen, much relieved. Singing as you look for a pregnant pug is understandable. Being careless is better than being eccentric.

'Yes,' I agreed. It was easier in the end.

'And she's still outside, the poor wee scrappie?'

'We don't know. She vanished from her box. I'm sorry, girls, but I'll have to go back out again. Do help yourself to biscuits,' I added, with a touch of the gracious hostess overcoming a lapse of the part of the butler.

'But we must all help. It'll be like playing 'Murder'. We used to have fun playing that at parties, didn't we, Wen? I'm sure we'll find her. Has she been gone long? Have you searched the house? Did she get out of the front or back door? I daresay she's somewhere quite close you've overlooked.' and she began opening the doors of all my cupboards with the same excitement she would have put into a party game.

Wen, who viewed life more seriously, took over. 'If you're sure she's not in the house, we'll all go outside and search. She must be found. Our Beauty Queen of Palmer's Green disappeared every time before she whelped. Never came to any harm, mind. Found her once in Mummy's drawers, didn't we, Bun? and another time — no, that was Lilybet-Lou, I think. She had her puppies in Daddy's tool-box.' They were like a double act, but I was grateful to them both for being a comfort, specially when Bun chimed in, 'They always find somewhere safe and warm. You see, they put the babies' welfare first and after all they only want to be independent and avoid the fuss. They feel privacy is important.' Don't we all? But she put a kindly hand on my arm and said, 'They never come to any harm.'

I watched them put back their coats in spite of my protests, and take a torch. I gave Ben mine and asked Em to fetch my own wellies so I wouldn't fall over and create another – yet another – diversion and drama. I was also looking for more torches. Wen, Bun and Ben went off into the night like Wilson, Kepple and Betty, leaving the stage clear for an instant. Naturally the phone rang.

Pa said indignantly, 'I was only kidding. Where's your sense of humour?'

'Somewhere in the snow outside. It's about six feet deep here and I've got stranded refugees, if you want to know. Heaving breathing isn't in my itinerary.'

'Snow? We haven't got snow up here. The night's quite balmy.'

'It's downright crazy here,' I said crossly, 'a pity it's spreading to the inhabitants where you are. We haven't time. Just tell me what you've got and add the final straw. This camel's got to stagger on . . .'

'Are you all right?'

'No!' I shouted, nearly in tears.

'I'd better ring back,' he said sadly. 'I never seem to choose the right time. I don't know why I'm trying.'

'I do,' I muttered under my breath. Then aloud, 'It really would be better if you could call back. I have to go on a search party,' and I put down the phone because there in the doorway stood Emily with my wellies, and Pearl.

Pearl was looking more pugly than ever. Rage and indignation were popping out of those absurd eyes. Rolls of fat began round her neck and went on and on, like Mrs Michelin. 'Where was she?' I cried, tears running down my face and tickling horribly.

'Behind the roll of old tennis netting in the hall cupboard. I thought you looked there?'

'I *did.*' The cupboard ran under the stairs, a long way back where we kept the cylinder vacuum that doesn't work but keeps the old carpet sweeper and three shopping baskets without handles from feeling lonely. Boots and golf clubs and a lacrosse stick, tennis rackets and the Christmas decorations in sundry boxes keep up the pretence of 'storage' instead of rubbish.

'She was in one of the baskets. Nice and cosy and dark and private and absolutely hopeless for puppies too. Perhaps she would have had them in the netting instead.'

I hugged them both. I kissed everyone, including Charlie, and Mattie, who sighed and looked away, embarrassed. 'I shan't need my wellies, then,' I said with relief. Then I remembered the others outside. 'I suppose I'd better go and call off the picnic out there, though. Poor Wen will have one of her turns if I don't get her back by the Aga soon.'

'I'll put Pearl back in her cupboard, shall I? And give her some milk? I think she deserves a ginger biscuit, too. By the way, all this paper from your aggi boot doesn't look like newsprint.' Emily handed over some pre-war scrunched up £10 notes. There must have been eight or ten in her hand. I stared at them and at her. 'It's money,' I said.

'Money?'

'Real money. The sort that used to buy real things. My God! Where did I throw the rest, from the other boot?' I rushed to the pedal-bin under the sink and dived about among empty Pusskins tins and orange peel, banana skins and potato peel, and extracted another half dozen.

'Put it all in a paper bag,' I said urgently, pulling on my boots and grabbing my coat. 'I must go on out. Shut the door so Pearl stays in her room from now on,' and then I plunged back into snow shouting, *'She's found!'* or *'We've got her!'* or something, right into Bun's ear. She was, I could see, quite nicely sheltered from the weather in the space between the porch and the wall. She came in, her nose 'bread and dripping' as my great-aunt used to say to her husband to draw his attention to certain needs during tea. I always wondered why she never offered us any.

Wen was nowhere to be seen, even though the snow was now falling more lightly and I could focus without difficulty. Every time I opened my mouth to shout, it filled with snow but I heard Ben call, 'Coming!' from the direction of the garage.

He followed me into the kitchen again where Bun was already making herself comfortable and asking questions. I got out a bottle of ginger wine. It was a time to celebrate and get a bit warmer. The wine had come from Ireen as a Christmas present and was a pleasant change from her sunflower cordial and Sweet William wine which no one had yet offered to try. We all stood round with our glasses, talking about Pearl and the money from the old boots while Ben counted it out at the table. There were seventy pounds from the left one and eighty from the right. Someone, at some time in the distant past, had hidden it away. The boots must have been kicking about in an out-house for years. I once found 37p in the pocket of a riding jacket, and sometimes discovered love letters I never could bring myself to read beyond the first fond words. Other things, too. An old camera for 10p with a film still inside, half-used. Once developed, it showed pictures of a coy young man over-exposed in more ways than one. I found the vicar's pen, a presentation from some earlier parishioners, in a suede handbag. The pen was inscribed 'God Go With You' but it appeared to have gone with the wrong one, because the bag had the name of Mabel Massingbird inside, together with Miss Priddle's fob watch and Mrs Netherleg's opal ring. Mabel Massingbird was the archdeacon's wife and what he jovially termed 'a great little collector' though I doubt if he realised quite how ruthless were her quests. I returned the plunder to the rightful owners anonymously and was relieved when the archdeacon conveniently carted Mabel off for an early retirement in Rome where she probably pinched the Pope's baubles.

'I'll have to trace the owner of the boots,' I said with a sigh. The money was nice just to look at, evocative of a time when we all had a respect for what it could mean because we really earned it. We sipped our ginger wine and discussed its origins. Emily thought it must have belonged to an old, old woman treasuring her lover's boots down the long empty years, never knowing that his life savings lay in the toes. Ben said realistically, 'But if he left her for someone else, what did he go in? Bedroom slippers?' Emily thought perhaps he'd died suddenly instead. Ben said it was more likely to be robbers' ill-gotten gains. He said the robber probably died in a shoot-out but his boots had been kept in loving memory by a sorrowing widow. I had to sniff back my tears, but then I have to be led out sobbing from Oxo commercials and Police 5.

It was then that Bun suddenly squeaked, 'Where's Wen, then?' and we all looked round. In the excitement we'd quite forgotten one lone searcher, maybe even at that moment sunk into some snow-drift and beyond help.

We all dashed back out again, happily fortified by the ginger wine, and Ben found her after ten minutes' anxious calling, with Bun in floods of freezing tears and me resigned to the worst with the house burning down as a finale.

Wen was asleep in the car. She said later she got in to use the headlamps to attract Pearl and she must have dropped off. She had thought, she said, that the poor little thing might run to the beam when she saw it sending its message of hope across the snow. Dogs often did, wasn't that so, Bun? It was a new theory to me and even Bun looked uncomfortable. Wen added brightly that she'd only been in the car a few moments and must have dropped off immediately from utter exhaustion. None of us queried her timing: we just finished the ginger wine and Emily suggested following it up with cocoa and cake. Ben thought a dash of warming rum all round might be advisable. Rum and cocoa, he said, was a well-known naval reviver after battle. Wellington had sworn by it. Nelson demanded it. It was used as an aphrodisiac for pandas in Peru, too, he added. The twins seemed eager to get at it when they heard that. They clapped their hands and giggled as if they'd been offered Knickerbocker Glories for breakfast.

I was a bit uneasy about the effects of rum on top of everything else, but I have to admit I was first at the bottle.

Marsha rang an hour or two later. We were all soporific and I was exceedingly mellow on cocoa and rum. I said, 'Hiya, Marshmallow!' and everyone round the table giggled.

Marsha said severely, 'You sound tipsy!'

'Cocoa and rum,' I said. She said she'd tried me before and I was always out, and when I *was* in I was odd. What on earth was going on? Marsha tends to think that no one living beyond the purlieus of Potters Bar to the north, or the plains of Purley Park to the south, ever has anywhere to go. She thinks we should all sit waiting, like troglodytes, for our city friends to make our lives less drab by coming to stay in our spare rooms.

I rambled on about the jumble sale. I didn't tell her about the money in the aggi boots nor about the blouse with one sleeve. It's hard to make that sort of thing clear and interesting in a few minutes.

'How's Ben?' she enquired.

'He's fine,' I said, surprised and ignoring his frantic gestures. 'He goes home tomorrow.'

'I thought he was ill,' she accused me. 'I was surprised when he spoke to me this afternoon.'

'He was ill,' I agreed hastily, 'quite seriously ill. Very ill, really. We thought he had appendicitis but it turned out to be a stitch from jogging. He's a great jogger, you know. Never misses a morning.' I was quite proud of that.

'You said mumps.' Now she was really cross.

'Of course. Appendicitis *and* mumps. Only the mumpish thing was due to his glands swelling from the jog, you see. It was all very nasty.'

Ben was nodding his approval. The rest looked puzzled. Bun put out a sympathetic hand and patted Ben's. Wen drew away uneasily. She had placed her pixie hood on the Aga to warm and it steamed a little. Em had gone to see Phyllis. Demelza had been chuntering away like Stevenson's Rocket. She'd kicked all her bedding out of the cupboard and was sitting square on the floor-boards, defiance written all over her.

'I must see you,' said Marsha, 'soon.'

'Well, you wouldn't make it this far for a start,' I said with confidence, 'They're using reindeer to find the motorway. Nothing short of a helicopter would get to us!' But she wasn't beyond using one of those if she'd made up her mind to invade.

'This is urgent. I don't think you realise, but it will soon become very urgent. I haven't had time to tell you *everything* but I read it in the ripples. You see, you're never able to spare me more than a few minutes on the rare occasions you're in. I find from the ripples that you and I are closely linked, *very* closely linked, and because we are chosen to bring The Power of Insight from God to the people, we have to *be* together a great deal from now on. I shall only need a small room with a southern aspect and you know I eat nothing, nothing at all.'

Oh Lor', I thought, she's been given notice to quit again. I bet she's been spending the rent money on Poly-whatsit.

'How about the boyfriend?' I asked bluntly.

'This thing is bigger than all of us. Polyflor has gone.' (Plus the piggy-bank?) 'I had my ripples read and they were most revealing. You and I are to get very close from now on.'

Marsha keeps several cats and cooks fish-heads all the time. Her flat is very small and I do try and keep my distance because the smell of cods' eyeballs steaming quietly on the stove clings to everything. I said, 'Terribly interesting, but I have some people here. I'll have to ring you back.' Then, curiosity getting the better of me, I asked, 'What ripples?'

'In the Power of Insight, we read water,' she said, 'the sea, if possible. Here in London we make do with the Thames or the Round Pond, or even a fish-tank when pushed.'

'But not too hard,' I said gleefully, 'or the fish will fall out!'

'I mean pushed for anything nearer natural resources,' she corrected me severely. 'We don't push the bowl, just tip slightly. Fish are definitely out.'

'That's what I was afraid of,' I insisted. 'It's all fascinating, Marsha, but I'll have to hear more about it later. 'Bye now.'

I put down the phone and turned. Bun had undone the top button of her blouse and her neck was very red. Frilly was nibbling the buttons on her home-knitted cardigan. Frilly had been known to swipe all the buttons off a dress without the owner being aware of it until she stood up and if fell off. But Bun wasn't worried. Her feet, in their flat lace-up Sturdies, were spread out and her head was tipped back sideways. Her face was scarlet. Wen, too, had her eyes closed. She wore suede ankle boots lined with sheepskin. Her stockings were ribbed and, because she sat upright, legs apart, one could see beyond the knee to its flirtation with the elasticated leg of her bloomers. I was right then. They *did* wear their school knickers!

Ben was knocking back the last of the rum. It looked like a Hogarthian cartoon. 'I'm going to have a look at Demelza,' I said.

Bun leapt to attention. 'Oh, do let me come too!' She bounded across the room a little unsteadily but with the excitement of a five-year-old at the circus. I wasn't too keen on anyone viewing our 'facilities'. A range of cupboards under a dresser might not be the professional's idea of suitable maternity quarters, but with Bun's past experience and know-how, her advice could be invaluable. So with mixed feelings, I led the way.

Pearl was asleep, but Demelza was busy. She was somehow doubled backwards, investigating what promised to be imminent proceedings, and for a shaggy dog that size, plus extra, it was a feat of no mean effort. 'Oh, looky!' cooed Bun coyly, 'she's calling out the first little feller! We're just in time.'

She clasped my arm and giggled. 'Call me dotty if you like,' she invited, 'but I do think she chats to the babies, calling them to pop out and say Hullo!'

I didn't comment. Words shrivelled inside me. But Bun went on, 'See? She's searching for No. 1 now.' Demelza certainly seemed to have her nose up the chimney. Bun knelt down close and endeavoured to encourage the action by singing to the tune of 'Rockabye Baby' –

> 'Hurry up, Baby; hurry up, do!
> All the world's waiting in here for you.
> Heave-ho, me hearties: first down the spout
> Get's a good licking the minute he's out!'

and as if it had understood every word, I watched the puppy appear, screwed up in its nest of gift-wrapping.

'I made that up myself,' boasted Bun. I didn't doubt it for one moment but if it had been sung to me, I'd have found my way back again at once. 'It often works, you know, music. And some encouragement, of course.' Then, abruptly, 'Do you handle?'

I stared, puzzled. She said, 'I mean, do you take over? Do the necessary? Take its nightie off and put the baby in a pot?'

It sounded like cannibalism. I said crossly, 'I don't know what you're talking about. I don't do anything. The bitch knows best, for God's sake. What pot?'

'Masie Pilcher pops hers in warm jam jars while she's seeing to the rest, but I don't hold with it myself. It's currently rather New Thought to take over, of course. Biddy Farquharson does everything. *Everything.* I said to Wen, it would be easier to mate *Biddy* with a Tibetan and let her get on with it. She grabs the puppy and fusses it about, pops it in the jam jar, snatches the placenta and won't let the bitch have anything at all.' She stuck her pointed nose right into the cupboard and almost down Demelza's ear.

'A boy!' she cried delightedly, 'I can see his spare part!'

I was incensed at the intrusion: it was a moment I had wanted to share in quiet community with the wonders of creation, not with a warbling audience. I said, 'Do go and tell the others! Maybe they'd like some more cocoa. Did you turn your headlights off? Could you let Frilly in?' (she'd asked to go out after the button incident, coughing a bit) 'and ask Emily to go and see Phyllis again?' If I could have thought up anything else to get rid of her, I'd have gone on.

After the second puppy was safe and warm, and its blunt nose snuffled deep into the great shaggy coat, I went up to see Phyllis. Emily lay on the divan watching her tear apart a few old copies of *Farmer and Stockbreeder.* Pa had invested in a regular order when he began to think of land values. Finding farms were for millionaires and Arab sheikhs, he went on to ruined mansions. We had a few of those, some smallholdings, nurseries and a deserted monastery. Then even mansions and monasteries began to be snapped up by Syndicates, Government Departments, Borstals, Trade Unions and Maharishis, for Summer Schools, Fringe Religions, Meditation and subversive political party retreats and Pa had to lower his sights to monstrosities, which he was now hunting down with the enthusiasm of a corgi for a Queen.

Yet somehow the *Farmer and Stockbreeder* went on for ever.

# 11

To my surprise, nothing else happened that night. Wen and Bun finally staggered out into the snow, falling over one another to thank me for a most exciting time and slurring their words a little. They scrambled into the Bounder and, waving and shouting, shot away into the night. The little car lurched and slipped, but the snow had banked up to cover their worst excesses. Wen's hat had drooped over one eye but her grasp of the wheel was as masterful as ever. I went inside and closed the door with a sigh of relief. Then I began to warm up some milk for Demelza. While I was standing at the stove, Ben drifted down. He was wearing the beautiful bathrobe.

'Em says Phyllis is straining,' he announced. Then, with more interest, 'Did you know the aggatibo in a remote part of Asia can turn somersaults by walking through its hind legs?'

'I feel as if I've been doing that all evening. Watch the milk a minute, will you? Funny Pa didn't ring again. Wen and Bun went.' I wondered why it was everything *I* said was so dull and factual. I made a note to try and throw in a few epigrams or profundities from time to time. I whisked an egg into the milk and, because I aimed to improve our overall standards of living as well, added a dash of sherry. Ben raised his eyebrows. 'A monkey got drunk in Saskatchewan,' he said reprovingly, 'and tried to make love to a snake.'

I worked at unboggling my mind to cap it with a gem of wit or wisdom, but I need time for that sort of thing. Instead I said briskly, 'A three-year-old rattler, actually, called Prince. He had a slight attack of hiccups.' Then I took the milk to Demelza.

She was sound asleep. Bun and I had put clean paper in the box and a hot water bottle wrapped in an old jumper at the far end. The puppies, tiny and vulnerable, but so incredibly an immediate part of the world, were already establishing their rights to the best positions. What hope was there, I sighed, for any kind of equality in opportunity when Nature herself operates on a power basis?

Demelza raised her head. She glanced past me anxiously, but

137

finding Bun had gone, managed a smirk of self-satisfaction. 'Go on,' I said, handing her the basin, 'it's a celebration.' She lapped the lot and smacked her lips at the sherry. Then she fell asleep again. I wished I could do the same.

Pearl, after all the earlier activity, had fallen into a sulk because no one was telling her how clever and smart and lucky she was. She had been out of her box to collect the tail of a long-dead mouse, probably brought in by Frilly as a gift to the babies. Pearl chewed it in a desultory way, like tobacco. It didn't seem the kind of thing to be hanging about in a maternity ward, but for her sake I ignored it and stroked her head. I promised to bring her a biscuit later in exchange.

Kip was still lying near the front door as I passed across the hall. His nose quivered to sort out scents underneath in an endeavour to find his master's. I switched on the hall radiator for him and began to go upstairs.

Ben followed from the kitchen. 'Suppose they get into a snowdrift?' he said accusingly. I knew exactly who he meant. I was feeling just as uneasy.

'Wen's quite capable of making her own decisions,' I retorted, though I wouldn't have been so sure about Bun. 'And I did suggest they might like to stay overnight, didn't I?'

'Not very enthusiastically, you didn't!'

'They had to get back for the dogs, anyway.'

'And they finished the rum, you know.'

I said, with some asperity, 'The snow's stopped, there's a full moon, it's a good road all the way – and they're not kids.'

'Not in years,' Ben went on patiently, making me feel awful, 'but in experience and judgement I'd say they were less reliable than Charlie.'

'They'll be all right,' I said half-heartedly, but I wasn't convinced. It was useless to get into a state of guilt or anxiety. I had enough to bother about going on elsewhere.

'Did you realise the phone was off the hook in the office?'

I stopped again on the half landing, where the high, deep window showed snow in ridges against the glass outside, and a thick wall of it battering like talcum from a giant puff. 'What?'

'The phone's been off the hook. Bun went in to dial the local weather forecast and she came back to ask Wen whether the recording was, 'No showers expected' or 'Snow showers expected' because the line was so bad. Wen took it on the kitchen phone, so the extension was left off. I've put it back now.'

138

I sighed. 'Then I expect Pa's been wondering why the line's engaged all the time, and the Bolsovers and Pawleys have been ringing, and Hetty's been trying to warn me of future arrivals and goodness knows what else.' I was really thinking with dismay that Ross might have given up trying.

By the time I got upstairs, Phyllis was asleep and so was Emily. I hissed at Ben, 'You said Phyllis was straining, didn't you?'

'Em said she was.' We stood for a moment just looking at the enormous dog and the slim girl, still and sleeping, two heads together. I whispered, 'Don't they look gorgeous.'

'Emily wouldn't go to bed and leave her.'

'She'll have to go now but I hate waking her. Do see her electric blanket's on, would you, and her bedroom fire, too?'

She woke when I touched her, and yawned. I said, 'Darling, you must get to bed. It's terribly late.'

She shivered suddenly and sat up. 'Have they gone? Is Demelza OK? How many did she have? And what about Pearl?' Amazing, the leap from dreams into a real world. 'Phyllis had a false alarm. All that straining – I got so excited. Turned out she wanted to be sick. Brought up yards of colour supplement – *Observer*, of course.'

She kissed me goodnight, then Phyllis, and last of all Ben who had come back and was standing in the doorway. She hesitated, then gave him another quick kiss and was gone. Ben said, smiling, 'Glad Adam's coming. Be nice for both of you.' Such arrogance! But I kissed him goodnight, too, and felt an extra warmth behind it for his casual adoption so suddenly of a man's world.

I finally got to bed wondering about Wen and Bun, but it does seem the majority of things go right, and that's why only the small proportion of things that don't, make news. When Lulu and I were aboard, I pulled the curtain round the four-poster and dreamed Pa was home saying he'd bought a derelict barge on the Grand Union Canal, and why not harness Bubbles and Jody? I was woken in the early hours by my efforts to drag Lulu over the side because she kept falling in the water, but I found it was Charlie who'd scrambled in and had his nose in my ear, one paw on my shoulder while the other had shot everything off the bedside table.

Sunday passed surprisingly uneventfully. The bad weather halted together with the action: it was very pleasant. Church bells rang more clearly through icy air, sun shone quite ungrudgingly, all the papers came as ordered (to satisfy my patients rather than to meet our search for truth) and time glided quickly into Monday.

I was up late, exhausted from the day of rest and with metabolism able to fall to its all-time low in consequence. By the time I reached the breakfast table, Ben was greeting me with a wave of toast and a quote. 'Hey, how do you find this? "Wilfred, a hedgehog in Chelmsford, got his head crammed in a bean can and a Mrs Cheeseman phoned the police because she heard him yelling." '

'I thought it was a rat with his head in a yoghurt carton?'

Ben stared thoughtfully at the dog-eared pages. 'That's funny,' he said.

'Funnier than most of the stuff you've been shooting.'

Outside the sky seemed clear and the day ahead quite promising. I wished Ben wasn't going. I decided to award myself some loganberry jam.

Ben put the book on the dresser. He was looking very spry, I thought; very jaunty, very chipper. He wore black corduroy jeans and a matching jacket, grey sweater and boots. I was impressed. I felt sure Hetty would be impressed, too, when she came to pick him up. Hetty always took Ben to the station on the day he was going home. I watched him glance in the mirror by the door. I was even more surprised when he said, more to himself than to me, 'I should have had my hair trimmed.' I made a great noise at the sink so I wouldn't have to answer. In the past, it was left to me to suggest regular ways of personal tidying which Ben, just as regularly, had ignored.

'What's happened to Hetty's husband?' he said suddenly. I put down the plate I was drying, and leant back against the table. 'He went abroad on some big engineering job. Hetty merely told me they were treating it as a "trial separation". He's been gone ages, though.' But I wondered a bit, myself. Ben could switch from canned hedgehogs to the sombre real world in an instant.

Adam was coming, Ben was going, Phyllis had demolished a small table mat and the Book of Common Prayer, Demelza was sorting out her puppies and washing them furiously every time I went in. Pearl seemed to have changed her mind about the whole thing and was only here for the holiday. Her early morning walk had included a roll on some smelly treasure in the stables. Pearl was a roller, mainly due to her size and shape and probably defiance and rejection of a life spent plastically wrapped. I had to bathe her the minute she got back, using my best shampoo in deference to her (possibly) imminent accouchement. She enjoyed the bath. I daresay she got scrubbed every morning at home, together with Mrs Pawley's knick-knacks and Mr Pawley's smalls.

I wanted to get the kitchen moderately clear before it turned into something like a passenger lounge at London Airport, but as I began the phone rang. Lady was in such a state of quivering anticipation that she made a dive for it at the same time as Kip rushed in, waving his tail like a fringed banner, and blundered into Charlie. I really would have to sort out the curtain in front of Kip's eyes, but for the moment a foot between the two dogs had to do. I picked up the phone and shrieked, 'That's enough!' meaning it for Charlie who retired, muttering threats, and protesting that he was only leaping to my defence.

Marsha said sweetly, 'Got a hangover, darling?'

I used my 'busy' voice. 'Just up to my ears in everything. Adam's due this morning and Hetty's fetching Ben.'

'Hospital?'

'What?'

'Ben. Is he going to hospital?'

'No. Home.' What *was* she talking about?

'Last thing I heard he had mumps and appendicitis and glandular trouble and jog-cramp and . . .'

'He's better.'

'*How* quick, darling. Must have been the boozy cure. But now he's going, I could have his room, couldn't I?'

'Marsha, I'm up to my eyes in pregnant bitches: I can't fit in any more.'

'If you're insinuating what I think you are, darling, you're quite out of the groove. Part of our philosophy is Contraception by Concentration. Never fails, dear.' And never needs to, I thought, appalled.

'No, I meant I'm chocka with dogs and so on. I couldn't concentrate on anything else till – well, about October at a guess. Look, ring me another day, would you?'

'We've been friends for twenty years,' she began, but the reminder was so awful that I shrieked, 'Oh, Lor' – the canary, but loose!' and put down the phone. We don't have a canary, but I daresay there's one loose somewhere in the world and Marsha knew all my other lies. If you have to tell one, make it stupendous and spontaneous. Like the chalked advice over the kitchen door, JUST GET ON WITH IT! which is the least subtle of any I ever put up and probably the most effective. It should be dangled in front of all committees, quangos, and debaters in the House.

By the time the phone rang again, Ben's bags were by the door

141

and he was making a final tour of the place to see what he'd forgotten. I said eagerly, 'The paperback, Ben,' nodding at the nasty little thing on the dresser, with its animal perversions, thumbed pages and the sticky bits where cookery had taken over. Ben called from the hallway, 'I'm leaving it for Adam. I've told Emily. She thinks he'll love it. Might teach him a thing or two about Nature.' I glanced at it with distaste as I passed. 'Your Body as a Precious Tool' was tucked inside. Passing on the phallic torch . . .

It was Bun on the phone. 'Wen and I want to say thanks ever so, dear. Such a jolly evening, wasn't it? All that boodle in the boot, babes in the boxes, and singing in the snow. We loved your cocoa, too. We shan't forget it for a long time.'

I said feelingly, 'Me, neither.'

'Is Demelza on Prigg's Potash?'

'No. The *Weekly Advertiser*.'

'Does it contain calcium, Vitamins A, E and F and wheatgerm?'

'. . . and the classified ads,' I countered. Why bother to explain it was a joke?

'Super. Now then, bobs and dews –'

It sounded like a good mediaeval oath. ('Stap me, Cynthia, by my bobs and dews thou shalt pay dear for this!') But she went on, 'Do it now.'

'Do it?'

'Get 'em off!'

I'd never tease Humphrey like that again. It was quite unnerving. I said, 'Hetty's coming up soon. I leave all that to her.'

'Fiddle-faddle. Wen and I always do our own.' I giggled. 'Honestly. You only need the veg. knife and some Friar's Balsam. The dews are just as easy.' She called over her shoulder, 'Aren't the docks and dews easy, Wen?' but there was a car drawing up outside my back door and a horn honked loud enough to drown the gory details which followed.

I said, 'Well, thanks. Someone's here. Can I ring about it later? I'll only get it all wrong if I'm distracted.'

So she finished, '. . . and then watch it!' or 'wash it', I wasn't sure which and I didn't want to know. Before I put down the phone she shrieked, 'Wen forgot to have a feel for Lulu!' But I pretended I hadn't heard.

Hetty literally swished in. She wore silvery leather with a big collar. Even her high boots were 'A' for fitting and elegance. She kept admiring them when she thought I wouldn't notice, but I never missed a trick where Hetty was concerned, and Hetty, believe me, was full of tricks.

'Ben's nearly ready,' I said. 'You'll make the 9.27 easily. He knows which platform and he's got his ticket.' I purposely tried to make him into a small boy with a label round his neck.

'As it so happens,' she murmured off-handedly, 'I can give him a lift all the way to London. I'm going up there as well today. Just a last minute business call, such a bore, but there you are. I'm leaving the surgery fully-manned, of course. Will you have Edyth for me? You know how she hates it there without me.' She handed me her prim King Charles Spaniel. I always felt she hated it here with me, too.

I said heavily, 'That's nice!' but what *was* all this? Had Ben known all along? Was there really something going on between them? Hetty, more than twice his age and amused at the admiration of youth, and youth bewitched and flattered by the glamorous older woman? It wouldn't be a very original story. Dogs don't give a fig for age provided it's active. Ben came rushing in. Did he seem uneasy or just harrassed? 'Hi,' he said, 'nice of you to be early.' He shot me a look which took me into his confidence with amusement and for a moment I was reassured.

'I was just saying, darling, I shall be going all the way with you.' Did the words hold a *double entendre*? I was back at the worry like a squirrel to a store of nuts. I looked at Ben. 'Fantastic,' he said cynically, and I was comforted again.

But Hetty was smart at getting what she wanted and Ben certainly hadn't sounded very surprised. Ben was going back to his last year at school: would the paperback 'fax' be enough to establish his new sophistication in the playground? How would nuclear physics stand up against anyone as challenging as Hetty?

For the first time ever, *Ben* kissed *me*. Kissing's an odd sport: the order of it, and the nuances. The interpretations and the hidden meanings. I knew from his approach – the light, voluntary contact and the new confidence, that he was telling me not to worry. He was independent, his own guardian, and our relationship would from now on have to be more free, less defined. I dropped most of my past responsibilities and hugged him. 'I know you won't write,' I said, 'but do ring sometimes and let me know how you are. And come down any weekend and, of course, half term if you want to.' By that time, his mother would be exhausted. She had once said to me in a faint little voice on the phone, 'Breakfast, my dear, he eats breakfast! Is that natural for anyone over the age of six, I ask myself.'

Ben was taller than Hetty at last. When he first came to stay, we had said patronisingly, 'Why, you're almost as tall as Hetty!' over and over again to express admiration. Now I wished he wasn't. Somehow it confirmed the tiny lurking uneasiness. But at last I felt it was their business and out of my hands.

Humphrey arrived just as they were leaving in the car. Hetty called out to him, 'Tell Ireen I want some of her Crab Quinine. I'll be in at the weekend for it.' Crab apples formed the basis of a few dreadful concoctions Ireen prepared. I'm sure they worked by sheer alarmist principles. Any goat, for instance, sniffing the bottle would take a new hold on life in self-defence.

' 'Er'll 'ave it in stock. Nip in ternight and 'ave a dram. My Willie's up!'

It sounded a very fair invitation. Willie was Humphrey's son who worked in a hotel at Penzance all the summer, fished through the winter, and drove a Jag with his initials on the bonnet. Hetty liked Willie. They were rather similar: ruthless, attractive, unusual and basically well-meaning beyond their own personal success. She said she admired his enterprise, but that wasn't all she admired. Willie was a big boy in his mid-twenties and quite unlike his gnomish parents. When he was home, he lounged around the Dun Cow in mean jeans and took Pretty Pawley's mind off her seduction programme and into his.

'Afraid I'll be back too late. Is he staying long?'

'Never says. Eem a close one, my Willie!'

I said to Hetty through the car window, 'How about docks and dews then?' but only in a small voice so I could say I'd said it. I don't approve of docking. If I let it go and she forgot and the owners never said anything, a few puppies in the world would maintain their normal wag and balance. Demelza and her litter were all right, of course, but Pearl's would present problems when they arrived. The Pawleys would probably consider it more hygienic. But I would protest that the docking leaves too much revealed. Such immodesty . . . Wen and Bun had their own sealyhams in mind when they reminded me, of course. If someone had presented them with a litter of mice, they'd have dutifully docked each one. I made up my mind there and then that whatever breed I bred, and however determined the owners, no puppy should leave without its tail. I would stick to my convictions and refuse to be dictated to by some stupid and sadistic trend. It made me feel a lot better.

Humphrey handed me some letters and we walked in together. The phone began to ring as if I'd stepped on a secret spring to set it off. It was Pa. 'Is that a private club or can anybody join?'

'Sometimes I think everybody already has,' I said grimly, 'why?'

'The line's been engaged solidily since seven o'clock last night.'

'Rubbish,' I said, 'we've hardly had a call.' I'd clean forgotten the phone off the hook and this morning's queue. I was staring at Ross's quick reply to my letter – his distinctive handwriting on the big white square envelope with the London postmark. 'Now do tell me what it is you've got?'

I turned the envelope over and wondered if he licked the flap or ran it along one of those damp rubber sponges, like elderly uncles' lips.

'Whaddya mean? What've I got?' He was joking, but he could have sensed my sudden distraction. I put the letter down quickly.

'You said you'd got something, and it's not laryngitis, is it!' Everything seemed to be on the verge of something. I felt very tense.

'Well, I heard about it just as I was going to the auction for the other one. It was being put up at the same time so as it hadn't had the same publicity I reckoned it to be a damp squib.'

'A *what*?'

'It could go cheap.'

'A poultry sum, you might say!' I thought that was very funny, but he said seriously, 'That's it – and that's what happened.'

'Gosh!'

'I snuck off to this bum sale when the high-flyers got launched and —'

'You *snuck*?'

'Sneaked. They say 'snuck' in some places.' I could tell he was playing Tycoons and Twisters. It took the place of Cops and Robbers or Cowboys and Indians via the telly, years ago. You hear it all the time in 'Playschool' and bus shelters. That's why adventure playgrounds are being turned over to computer centres. Pa finished triumphantly, 'And I got it.'

The pips went. The dialling tone took over officiously, like a bossy welfare worker. I put down the phone, inwardly seething, looked across at Humphrey with a forced smile and asked, 'Sugar?' as sweetly as icing runs off the edge of a lardy cake. It was the furthest extreme from the way I felt.

Humphrey doesn't take sugar. 'Causes baldness *all over*,' he used to warn me, dripping some of Irene's Beet Balm into his cup from a small bottle.

145

Emily came in wearing her dressing-gown. Humphrey tried not to look. He was one of those who consider a bikini passably decent, but anything that hinted of sheets, pillows and night, thoroughly disgusting. Emily poured herself some coffee and said, quite casually, 'Humphrey, has Ireen got a Great Periwinkle?'

'You mean for one o' them love potions?'

Emily shot me a grin that could have meant anything, and I went off wondering, to visit the patients. Demelza was still at the morning wash, dementedly up-ending each puppy in turn and belting it round the box to get at its crevices and corners, behind the ears and back again. Pearl was trying to catch sight of her navel and arrest something that had got there first. Phyllis was losing interest in the Christmas number of *True Story,* tossed it aside and turned to last Easter's *Woman.* I caught sight of a headline which read, 'Are You On The Pill?'. It seemed churlish to remind her she was a bit late for that.

Rajah was asleep in Emily's room, the sort of dog that begins to age at four and enjoys the opportunity to resign from active life. He had to be coaxed for walks. Lady was at Adam's bedroom window, paws on the sill, eyes glued to the drive. She knew Adam was coming soon: of course we'd all told her, but I think she'd have known anyway. I went back down to the kitchen, satisfied, and found Humphrey had gone. I think he must have been frightened off by Emily's dressing-gown and enquiries about the powers of the Periwinkle. She tilted her chair back when I came in and said, 'Sorry I'm so late. I saw Ben go. I was only just awake. Who rang?'

'Bun, Marsha, Pa. Adam should be here by ten thirty.'

She showed little sign of regret about Ben, and even less excitement about Adam. But she did come over and put her arms round me and murmur, 'You hate all this activity, don't you? You'd like us all here all the time. Well, I expect we'd like that, too!'

'If you were, I'd never get a look at the marmalade,' I said.

Adam had arrived at his own home, a mile or two away, the day before. He had just spent a week in France with his father and the rest of his time during Christmas holidays with his mother in Los Angeles. He had spent four days with us just before going to the States and would now have another four with us before going back to boarding school. In the meantime, his parents surged round the world separately, restlessly and never, it seemed, joyously. Adam was in a similar boat to Ben but whereas Ben was resilient and even seemed to be blossoming under the challenge of independence, Adam longed for a proper settled home life and looked forward to his times with us as just that. His aged grandmother and a living-in couple to look after him when he was in England during the holidays left him free to be where he chose.

I read my letter from Ross in a rare moment of pure sunshine, leaning against the conservatory window. Snow had backed away from the side of the house, and below me the reservoir was idle and colourless in the strong light. It was like a kid sulking in school uniform while everyone else was wearing fancy dress. Nothing moved, except on the motorway, and the occasional bird daring to come close enough for the food we put out.

It was a moment to be treasured: quiet, calm and beautiful. And then there was the most shattering yelp of excitement, and I knew Lady had seen Adam. The barking went on and on. I heard Adam laughing, Charlie yowling, Rosie joining in and even Connie screaming like a slate pencil from her perch. But it was Lady above all who could be heard, and I know no human who ever finds a euphoria as single-minded as that.

I hugged Adam. He always caught at my heart-strings because he was so vulnerable compared with Emily and Ben. He had a very clearly defined outline to his features, as if the contrast button had been turned up. His skin was like magnolia and his hair fell as evenly slatted as a Venetian blind. When it touched his face, he had an endearing habit of wrinkling his nose. Just about to enter his teens, he was eventually going to be one of those quiet, attractive men who, without any effort at all, appeal instantly to women. Adam was reserved, polite, considerate and kind. Yet he had an undercurrent of strength I admired, and his mother, I think, was beginning to fear.

'Had a good holiday?' I asked, as soon as Lady would let us carry on a normal conversation.

'Yes, thanks. Mummy sends her love and Dad wants me to give you his warm wishes, I think he said. They'd be useful at the moment, too. It was all wrong having Christmas in California, somehow.' He laughed. Last year he would have been silently rebellious, but lately he had become resigned, I thought. 'Lady looks in terriffic form,' he added.

Lady had boarded with us permanently by private arrangement with Mrs Adair, Adam's mother, when she found Adam had asked us to have her while he was away at school. He had seemed such a little boy then, seeking us out and offering us his pocket money in exchange for the dog's happiness. Adam's mother was beautiful and had real concern for the boy, but no idea how to motivate it without disturbing her own way of life, and that she would never do. He spoke very little about his parents but his silence told me a lot more than anything he might have given away.

'Daddy and I did some skiing again. It was nice. Grannie's going to New York next month. Can I come for half term and all Easter?'

'Darling, you've a room here, you know that. What more do you want – a mortgage?' We both laughed. 'You just missed Ben. He's left you a note and a book. He'll be up at half term. And Em's here, of course. We should all be together next time.'

Emily came in wearing her pink jersey catsuit, shown to me the night before with much pride. I was glad she wanted to look nice for Adam. Last year she would hardly have bothered to put a comb through her hair when he arrived, simply dragged him off to ride Bubbles and his pony, Bramble, now being stabled back at his own home for the winter months.

She hugged Adam and though he laughed at her enthusiasm, he hugged her back. Time was when he found it difficult to show emotion, but with us here, where emotions were always busy, he could relax. I love people who hug spontaneously. It's much nicer than the formal kiss of greeting. Hugs hold nothing back: kisses can be classified.

The two of them carried his things upstairs, chattering about France and flights and food. I went to the phone and rang Hosanna.

She was a long time answering and she mumbled something I didn't catch. I said anxiously, 'What's the matter? You sound drunk.'

'It's Harry.'

'It's not. It's you. I can tell by the lisp.' She had a mild trick with her 's's she pushed to extremes when she was upset.

'I mean it's Harry's fault.'

'What is?'

'Everything. From the thing that's happened to the cooker, to the EEC Agricultural Policy, if you like. He emanates trouble, that man. It always happens when he's around, anyway.'

'There's a man a mile up the road wearing the Priddle trench coat,' I said. Shock tactics were called for and I felt this was a time for sharing triumphs as well as disasters. I wasn't ready for a long tirade against Harry this morning. She forgot the lisp as well.

'*Who?!*' I could tell her whole body had suddenly clicked to attention.

'I don't know his name. His wife jumbles for pot plants, corsets

148

and party frocks.' I didn't mention the Priddle blouse. Triumphs are not all for sharing and anyway she'd laugh about the missing sleeve. I couldn't give her that satisfaction. I would now be on the sleeve trail, of course, at all future events. It's good to live with more than one purpose.

'We'd better meet,' said Hosanna normally and briskly. 'Come down for a drink about twelve.'

'I can't,' I said, 'you know how I'm placed. Can't you come here?'

'Harry's gone off in the car. I'll try and get a lift from Ralph when he brings the order.' We left it at that but I wasn't at all sure when the weekly order would arrive. They had to pick their moments, because PO Corner had to be manned continuously except for half day, and the grocery side kept open most evenings.

I put down the phone and went to the window. It was turning cold again. Colder than ever. The sky was leaden. I took the morning paper and sat on the Aga using a folded towel as a cushion and with my feet on the back of the chair and read Lynda Lee Potter.

It was just after eleven when I heard Phyllis. She was making the most peculiar sounds I'd ever heard – a weirdly strangled sort of whine. At first I thought it was Radio 3: then I dropped everything and ran.

She was sitting in the middle of the littered floor, howling.

I went over and put my arms round her. She stared at me crossly and then put her great nose in the air and gave a quavering moan. I was utterly terrified. The noise was unearthly. Suppose she had some terrible complication? Hetty was away and her locum was over at Barley Bottom where she had a second surgery. Her assistant might be available but he really was so terribly slow. I once called him in to treat a tortoise with a ricked neck but by the time he reached us, the tortoise, Shelmerdine, had vanished and was probably half way to the Royal Veterinary College because when she reappeared two days later, her neck was going in and out again like a piston.

I tried to soothe Phyllis with sympathy and kind words, but they were no substitute for Hetty's usual brisk reassurance and immediate diagnosis. Phyllis listened quite attentively, took time off for a quick scratch and then had a personal check round the Grand Canal. I relaxed a little, but as soon as I moved towards the door, she started up again.

Emily and Adam both came out of their respective rooms, looking worried.

149

'Listen,' I commanded unnecessarily. You could have heard the noise all over the county. On the coast it may have been taken as a fog warning.

Em rushed past me and I heard her murmuring to Phyllis. The noise grew less, then stopped and there was silence. It left a void that was even worse. Was she dead? These things happen. I would tell Killarney Green that we were with her to the end. I would swear no one could have done more.

'She had a claw caught in the rug,' said Em, running downstairs with the water bowl.

Half an hour later while we were debating lunch, Adam said, 'I've a letter for you from Mummy.' He gave me a thick blue envelope which, alone, must have cost as much as my entire box of manillas. When I'm rich, I shall buy only the heaviest and stiffest writing paper, use half the number of words I do now and allow only about eight to a page, and never – but *never* – use the flipside.

Adam's mother said she was enclosing a cheque for Lady's boarding fees 'with a bit over for the kids to have a day out' which would have taken them to Disneyland for a week. She hoped all was well in our delightful household. It was nice of her to add that because I could hear beyond it the sigh of relief that she didn't have to be part of it. She was ours sincerely and the cheque was too, covering rates for the next two years at least. She was nothing if not generous and I'm sure she never worked out a calculated figure. I reckoned I might even get a booster put in our feeble hot water system. The bathroom was like manufactured mousse – an icy waste.

Emily, too, had produced a letter from home. I remembered it was still on my bedside table unopened. So much had been going on that it seemed one of the few things able to wait. I left the debate over sausages versus fishcakes and went upstairs. After some polite introductory chatter, Em's mother wrote, '. . . so we think it's time she went to boarding school. Her leg has improved beyond our wildest dreams and so has her self-confidence since coming to you and the village school. But in September it would have to be the nearest Comprehensive or an independent school on the coast and we think the winter travelling, etc. etc.' I sat down on the bed with a sick feeling that my life was being chopped up and distributed to the wolves bit by bit.

But I had to see that for Emily it was better to walk away into a wider world. Time has a way of shuffling the jig-saw to make different pictures. Then, sometimes, you begin to wonder if you hadn't had it wrong the first time.

150

# 12

Pa rang on reversed charges just before Hosanna arrived. 'Darling, I've been longing for you to ring back,' I said, which was true, because in a changing world he was the only thing which remained stable.

'I didn't say I would, did I?'

'You didn't say you'd go on breathing, but I knew you would.'

'Why?'

'Jokey calls cost money,' I reminded him severely, and he hastily began getting down to business.

'I went to this other auction like I said, and there was hardly anyone there. About seven, including the executioner and a man who came in to get warm and snored all the way through.'

'Executioner?' I interrupted, puzzled.

'Auctioneer then. I feel they have a similar function. He was just starting – you know: '. . . ample accommodation, sturdily built, sound structure, three acres comprising garden, meadow and overgrown tennis court' – we always have an overgrown tennis court, don't we? – and the rest as per details. Only I hadn't managed to get any details because I'd come in on it so late. Still, it sounded good. 'Sound structure' means a lot these days. You get faulty roofs, woodgerm, blocked beams and you're —'

'Blocked what?' I asked, mystified.

'Drains,' he corrected himself hastily. 'Anyway, labour costs money is what I'm trying to say, and —'

'But what *IS* it?' It never occurred to me for a minute that it might be a house.

'I'm coming to that. So I joined the bidding.'

'You mean you didn't know what you were bidding for?' I asked, aghast.

'I told you. Ample accommodation, three acres, well built, structurally sound . . .'

'Yes, but *what* is? A factory? Park keepers' hut? Funny farm?'

He said uneasily, 'Now, don't get excited. The bidding began at two —'

'— o'clock or million?'

'Thousand.' It had to be a hen run. 'I joined in at eight – and got it at nine!' When all about us were paying forty and fifty thousand for rural semi's and double for anything bigger?

'So what is it?'

'I think I've got a snip.'

'Well,' I said grimly, 'that's marvellous. That's terrific. I've always wanted one of those. The Folks Who Live In A Snip. Wasn't that the old song? So romantic. Our Little Grey Snip in the West. Snip Sweet Snip. Yes, it's just what we always wanted.'

'OK, OK, *OK*. Kennels.'

'*Kennels?*'

'I knew you'd be pleased. You can just carry straight on doing – er – whatever it is you're doing. Built seventy years ago for a man who brought Keeshonds from, er, Kees. Lovely place. Lots of wrought iron railings, some splendid gates. Unfortunately, the house burnt down in 1969, but the kennels are in perfect condition: been maintained by a man who rented the ground and used them for breeding rabbits. They could easily be —'

'Kennels? You mean we're moving into *kennels?*' I shouted. 'We've *got* kennels!' There they stood, our kennels – unused, unloved, unlived in by even the most dastardly of dogs. And we were selling them to buy – more?

'They do have planning permission for extensions and though we would have to keep the period atmosphere of the solid wrought iron erection . . .'

'You can stuff your wrought iron erection,' I said rudely, 'and ask for your money back. I presume you put down a deposit?'

'Of course. Look, where would you get anything else at that figure? Even the roller rink fetched six times as much.' Suddenly rollering round the cooker with the kettle began to look quite attractive. But I didn't say a thing. I was winded with aggro.

'We might be allowed to put up a bungalow temporarily,' he said airily, as if he were offering me the Big Time and would pop along and do it this very afternoon, 'and later we could —'

'Move,' I said sharply, 'and that's what you'd better do right now – and quickly. I wouldn't even let my boarders live in kennels so I'm damned if I will. Though even that might be better than a bungalow. I've got kennels, I'm surrounded by kennels, I never want to see kennels again, though in point of fact I always did have a sneaky feeling it's where we'd end up. Where, exactly, would we be ending up?'

152

'A village called Long Brick. It's near —'

'Long *what*?'

'Brick. There's Little Brick and Bennett's Brick and Winter Brick —'

'Which isn't very big, I bet!'

'You'll just have to come and look at it. You'll soon change your opinion. You'll love it.'

'I can't wait.'

He paused. Then using a different voice, he said sadly, 'I suppose I might unload it at ten if I moved quickly,' but he was being defiant in the face of remorse which made me feel awful.

'Ah, well,' I said comfortingly, 'at least we'll feel at home there.'

Hosanna arrived as I put down the phone. She sank on to the only empty chair, unfortunately meeting Charlie's squeaky toy – a rubber chop – which let out a maniacal squeal. I said, 'I've just had a shock, too.'

Hosanna threw the chop at Charlie who caught it deftly and began to show off a bit by jumping on it, bashing it against the table leg and snarling and snatching every time it protested.

'Go on,' said Hosanna.

'Pa's bought somewhere at last.'

'Good jumble country?'

'Would you believe a village called Long Brick?'

'Long what?'

'It's near Little Brick and Bennett's Brick and Winter Brick.'

Hosanna collapsed. Charlie's chop squeaked its last as he bit through it. I went on, 'He says Winter Brick isn't very big but I've got to go and look just the same.' It was what we both needed – something childish and silly and giggly. A release from tension. Men guffaw, women giggle. Men drop dead from heart attacks far more often than women because even in laughter they don't relax. Golf and guffaws are no substitute for gossip and giggles.

At last, wiping my eyes, I said, 'Zanna, like I was saying earlier, remember the farm up the road from here that changed hands in Piggy's "Hullo and Goodbye" column?' The parish magazine was edited by a man called Nobby Hogg, know locally as Mr Piggy. He thought of himself as a clone of the late Lord Beaverbrook. Harry called his scandal sheet *The Drawsheet*. It was full of badly veiled hints and bits of local news too boring to be believed. We only bought it to count the number of words he couldn't spell and the number of times he began a sentence with 'I'. Everything in it emanated from Piggy's thoughts, memories and ideas.

153

'Do you mean after old Truscott died and his daughter went off to her son in Canada and sold out to a couple from Runton?'

'Gosh, did it say all that? I skipped most of it to get to the Star Bargains.' I told her about the woman, the lift home, the man in the trench coat and the whalebone.

'You're sure it's the Priddle?'

'Almost. There can't be two, just like that.'

'Do you suppose they brought it with them? From a Norfolk jumble?'

'It's possible. It would explain where it's been. You know how trash travels.'

'That's blasphemy,' said Hosanna. 'The trench coat isn't trash for heaven's sake!'

'But look at that photo of the Clover twins in drag! That went into the Scouts' Outing Tried-and-Trusty by mistake and the next thing it was spotted at the Young Mothers' Make-do's-and-Mistakes right over at Middle Latchett. Daphne Higson swore she saw it again in the PTA Pool-raising Fun Fair on the White Elephant a week later. That's a fifty-mile round trip. No reason why a gem like the Priddle trench shouldn't do a hundred.'

'Well, if it's come home to roost, it can perch next in my wardrobe,' said Hosanna, greedily.

I poured us some hot blackcurrant and dashed brandy essence into it. The taste turned to sweaty leather, but we were too enthralled to notice. 'We'll have to try and cultivate the family. I thought we could run our own Rummage and collect from up there. We could say we're concentrating on raincoats or something.' I could see she liked the idea. She said eagerly,

'What charity do we represent?'

'And where do we hold it? They charge £3 for the Scout hut and £5 for the church hall.'

I put my head out of the kitchen door for a quick listen, but nothing stirred. Adam and Emily were up the field with Bubbles and Jody, strawing down their shelter. Rosie was probably with them. Kip and Charlie were either side of my chair like book-ends. Treacle and Mattie conferred, heads together, by the Aga. Sniff and Snuff were worrying the broom outside the back door. They attacked it at any opportunity, convinced that because I used it to separate antagonists and settle strife, it should be dealt with. Pearl had enjoyed a good breakfast, Demelza was stupefied by contentment and Phyllis had a fresh supply of *Hotel and Catering* (from a time when Pa was into buying The Carlton Towers, a guest

154

house, 3 mins. sea with 6 bedrooms at Broadstairs) and last seen
happily ripping up advice on cold storage for cucumbers, and
Edyth had taken refuge from the rabble and was asleep on my bed.

I sat down again. Hosanna said, 'I'll have a word with Betty at
The Cow.' (The Dun Cow was often referred to by others as The
Serviced Jersey, but Hosanna, who naturally hated Betty, always
referred to it as 'The Cow'.) 'She won't dare say no. I've the same
sort of hold over Betty as the Middle East has with oil, and if she
doesn't co-operate, I'll sanction Harry. She's got that small dining-
room they used to use for weddings and things. I'll say it's for a
good cause. By the way, what is the Good Cause?'

'Animals?'

'OK. But which?'

I felt like saying 'Mine' but we needed something official. 'Could
we make up a name? Anything well known might bring in do-
gooders on the same field of operation. You know, the one-eyed
woman with the wig who works so tirelessly' (did you say 'tire-
somely'?) 'for the RSPCA. She always pinches half the jumble for
her daughter's villa in Monte. And Mrs Duckworth for the Blue
Cross.'

'I think she's got two really. It's just an eye patch to "give added
interest" as that speaker at the W.I. advised when she was lectur-
ing us on "Bringing out our Charisma". Could we just say "Needy
Friends"?'

'Any queue would be for the hand-outs later,' I said grimly.
'Butter's up again and Dennis told me tinned tomatoes would have
a halfpenny on this week.'

'It should be a registered charity, really.'

Kip wandered back to the hall. I thought of his master, the
appealing young man with the tragic brown eyes. There are no
charities for helping some people. No words, either. There was
nothing I could do to reassure Kip. Both of them seemed at arm's
length and in a different world altogether.

I could hear Emily calling Rajah and Adam shouting for Lady.
It was nice all four were friends . . . Friends! 'The Friends of
Beowulf!' I cried in an Excelsior sort of way. 'They'll do!'

'Friends of *Who*?'

'Don't ask me to say it again or who he was because I can't.' I
told her about Monica Sattersthwaite-Pells. 'She's got an electric
nose and was once dubbed knickers by her chums at Roedean.'

Hosanna wanted to know more but it was getting late. I said,
'Get Ralph to run off some circulars on his duplicator. Something

155

like 'Scrummage at the Dun Cow'. That'll draw attention, and the date – say Saturday week? We want raincoats, fur coats, egg cups, Renoirs, nuts, skewers . . .'

'Skewers?' said Emily coming in the door. 'What's a skewer?' She was carrying something wrapped in her woollen hat and holding it high above the dogs. 'A baby rabbit,' she went on, her voice edgy with tears. 'I think it's been caught and got away. Its leg's a bit damaged.' We don't use four-letter words like 'trap'. They're an obscenity.

'The weather's too awful for him out there if he can't get home,' I said. The laid-back ears and frightened eyes needed dark and warmth and privacy. 'I'll do something about the leg in a minute. Pop him in the airing-cupboard. There's plenty of room where we had General Distraction before Christmas.' (The General was a one-time sick squirrel, since released whole again.) 'Leave him your hat but get plenty of straw and some of Phyllis's paper shavings. Then he'd better have some warm milk, carrots, cabbage – anything his parents taught him to pinch from my garden.'

Hosanna got up to go. 'Can I see the pups?' she asked. I remembered I had to ring Mrs Bolsover, so I said, 'Of course, you know where they are. I've a phone call to make.'

But Mrs Bolsover was probably at her ladies Kitchen Club because nobody answered.

I heated up Demelza's hot water bottle and tried to stop Pearl from snoring by lifting her head out of the blanket. She snuffled a bit, snorted a few times and then, surprisingly because of her shape, lay on her back with her legs in the air, chortling to herself. I had an uneasy feeling she knew something I didn't.

Zanna came downstairs slowly. 'My word,' she said, 'you've got your work cut out with Phyllis. What's Pa going to say about the state of siege?'

'Nothing time can't cure,' I said uncertainly.

'Do you think she'll have many more?'

'Many more what?'

'Puppies, of course.'

'After she's had this lot, you mean? No. It was a mistake anyway.'

'I mean after the one she's got.'

'The one she's . . .' I stared at Hosanna. Then I rushed past her and raced upstairs. Phyllis was stretched out on an advertisement for tinned milk while the biggest new-born puppy I'd ever seen staggered blindly round looking for a share of the fresh stuff. It was dark brown, sturdy and looked thoroughly aggressive. Phyllis seemed perfectly satisfied though she was right about the divan and the seed box. They were quite useless. The floor was much more convenient. I'd have to fence her in somehow or the puppies would travel out of reach, but for the actual business of production, the entire floorspace was the only possible arena.

I urged her on with pride and admiration. I refilled her water bowl and replaced some of the more out-of-date newspapers. Then I went back to the kitchen. Hosanna was waiting for me, moodily turning the pages of my Accounts Book. 'You'd make a rotten auditor for the Scrummage,' she said. 'I'll have to do it myself.'

I took the book out of her hands. 'I have my own methods,' I said loftily. 'In code. Keeps it private when nosey friends call in.'

'What's the score?'

'Upstairs? Still one. She likes to get on with it at her leisure and without being bothered. I've often thought hospitals should run a simple Do-It-Yourself Maternity Department. "Just plug in here for gas and air, dear, and pop baby in the container provided" sort of thing. Scissors ready sterilized and a Teasmade on the boil. I know I'd prefer that to all the drama and heavy stuff.'

'So would I.'

'Why don't you give it a try, then?' which was the nearest I'd ever dare get to finding out.

She gave me a funny look. 'Harry hates kids,' she muttered.

'He said you did.'

'We agreed before we married that we couldn't stand the idea of family life.' Her own hadn't been very happy: I didn't know about Harry's.

'No one wants kids when they're wooing,' I said.

'Wooing? Harry and me, wooing? What a gorgeous, ridiculous crazy absurd word!' and she burst into tears. I was shocked. Horribly shocked. Hosanna was so tough. Everyone said so. It was being part-gypsy, they said. Quite insensitive, they said. And here she was, sobbing in my kitchen.

'Hey, what's up?' I said and put an arm round her.

'I dunno,' she said crossly. 'That fat puppy, that great sloppy Dane . . .' She sniffed. 'Sometimes I think everyone's got something going for them but me. Everyone's got something. Even Harry's got his pictures.' It's funny that she'd come to realise what everyone else had been saying to everyone else for ages, just by seeing Phyllis's face, all contented and end-of-the-line amiability.

'Go home and tell Harry,' I said.

'We're not speaking.'

'Then speak.'

She picked up her gloves and sighed. 'Do you think we could get Posy to give us a hand?'

She was back, I decided, at the Scrummage. Posy Pink lived with her dishy husband in an unpretentiously pretty cottage near the village shop. Posy wasn't her real name but Pink was. Her garden was the most beautiful I ever saw. Posy herself had the lovely face of a dew-kissed daisy. She also had a minute Yorkshire Terrier who wore a muffler in winter and was therefore called Dr Who, usually known as Bruiser. Posy would help anyone at any time and ask nothing in return, not even a trench coat. What's more, she was fun to be with; intelligent, witty and wise, and Dr Who was the biggest publicity stunt in four counties. He wore a bow made from a bit of J-cloth and knew exactly how to win friends and influence people. It let me out of all the organising, since I was going to be even busier than usual, and in the back of my calculating mind – which I prefer to call shrewd – I knew Posy would be terribly good for Zanna.

'Nine,' said Adam, coming downstairs just before tea. Phyllis was now nicely boxed in by two planks and an ironing board. She seemed quite satisfied even if it did look a rather amateur effort. She was out of draughts, had plenty of space, but was confined enough not to lose sight of the multitude gradually amassing alongside.

'I do wish she'd stop,' I said gloomily; it was as if she enjoyed it all so much she didn't know where to draw the line.

'They're jostling for position like racehorses.'

'I wish Hetty would hurry back. She promised right at the start that she'd always be on hand. I remember her saying so. It was all her idea in the first place. It always is. God alone knows where she is now.' Or Ben either. What would I say if his mother rang to ask where he'd got to?

'A Husky in Greenland had a litter of ninety-one.'

'Twenty-one,' corrected Emily, picking at crumbs falling through the cake rack where she'd just placed a batch of her own baking.

'Phyllis wants to beat that,' I said bitterly. 'You've been at Ben's book again. It should have been banned; it's utterly addictive, like hard drugs.'

'It's jolly interesting,' protested Adam. 'I bet you didn't know that the South African Leaf-Eared Mouse eats cochineal and has pink bones.'

I maintained a dignified silence.

'And cows in Cabanga have extra high yields.'

'High heels?' I queried, suddenly interested.

'Yields.'

I lost interest again.

'And earwigs lick their eggs to stop them going mouldy.'

'Legs?'

'Eggs.'

I was silent.

'And the favourite home of the deadly black widow is under the seat of a lavatory?'

'Look, Adam, shut up, will you?'

'Emily didn't like that one either.' Adam gave Lady a currant She ate it gratefully. Some dogs will eat bus tickets if offered by the one they truly love. It's not the food value, it's the token of affection. The gesture of giving is a less involved way of making love, if you think it through. You offer something of yourself for the pleasure of another, and in doing so gain your own pleasure. I once had a dog I adored called Henrietta. She and I were not unlike lovers. We would have given one another anything we had. She gave me her whole life and in return, at the end, I gave her the most I could – her painless, swift death when she was old and sick and weary. It was the greatest sacrifice I ever made.

There was a ring at the front door bell. The kids were having tea and feeding the dogs from the table. We don't have any rules against sharing at certain times. Connie leant from her cage to grab proffered crusts liberally buttered. The wireless was rooting around the Top Twenty. I resented callers.

Outside stood a pretty girl hugging a small brown dog. 'I'm sorry to disturb you,' she said apologetically, 'but the people at the shop said you might be able to board Sue-Ellen.'

'Come in,' I said, 'it's so cold out there.' It had started snowing again quite heavily. We stood together in the hall. I didn't want to extend the visit to any more comfortable area because I find people tend to hang on if you do. 'I'll be honest with you,' she said with a nervous laugh, 'I'm eloping. I can't take Sue-Ellen with me because we're heading for France, but I won't leave her at home because they'd be horrid to her and forget her peanuts.' She produced a large bag and dropped it on the hall chest.

'I won't forget,' I promised her. Already I was seeing myself as godmother to their firstborn. 'I'll do whatever I can to help.' Sucker for romance, that's me.

'So kind,' she murmured gratefully. 'We're madly in love, but our families are being so difficult. Dead against it. Keep saying we'll regret it. We'll never *never* regret it!' I nodded sympathetically. I remembered how it was to be eighteen. It hadn't changed much either.

'It's just for a week, maybe a bit more.'

'That's OK.'

'And she doesn't have to be outside, does she?'

'We've heaps of room indoors and she can share my bedroom if she likes.' I couldn't be expansive enough. These two young things, world against them, only me to rely on for support.

She turned to the door again. Then she held out her hand. 'My name's Milly, and it's wonderful of you to approve. No one else does.'

'My dear,' I said, putting on my counsellor voice, 'if you're in love and both of you are sure, that's enough. Love is what counts: not age, or class or colour. Love will overcome all problems, all the objections from others, the hostility and the misunderstanding. You can support one another through it all and I bet when you come back, they'll welcome you with open arms and admit they were wrong!' I almost added a blessing and 'God go with you, my children.'

I'm glad I didn't because she said, 'You're the only one who sees it like that. I wish you'd have a word with his wife.'

After a bit of a woof at Sue-Ellen from Rosie and a welcome and kindly sniff from Treacle, the latest forsaken sat gloomily near the sink looking like anybody's outraged wife. I got out the ginger snaps and shared them round. Then I went upstairs and found we'd reached the score of eleven.

160

# 13

Thirteen being considered unlucky, Phyllis rolled on the smallest puppy and another died during the night. I smuggled them out in a cocoa tin, and buried them under the hedge in the field. The ground was very hard and the spade loose at the handle and I wasn't sure whether I was crying for Phyllis, the puppies or myself, because I wanted to go to bed and sob there, if sob I must. I hauled a large frozen log over the grave, and then stood for a moment looking out across the most riveting view I can remember. You don't have to face the horror of airport lounges and tropical insects to catch a glimpse of heaven. The sun was coming up and the sky to the east was burning, and for a moment the ice and the snow and the wind were subdued into submission. I caught flashes from the reservoir again, but no solid shapes or outlines. Simply frayed silhouettes and diamonds. The motorway twinkled harmlessly with speeding lights, like the eyes of deer which I once watched at midnight coming down to waterholes on Exmoor.

Emily had burst into tears when she found the first puppy dead. Phyllis was completely unmoved, of course. Adam looked embarrassed, death being indecently personal. I comforted Emily, but she seemed set on mild hysteria so I gave Adam a small wink and Emily a large sob, and she immediately forgot her own distress to comfort mine. If you can't beat 'em, show 'em you're just as vulnerable.

The funerals were a bit makeshift but were the best I could do under the circumstances. I hoped most fervently that the rest would survive. I wasn't keen on getting into the undertaking racket, and there's a limit to the number of empty cocoa tins available at any one time.

'I think we'll have to rear the brindle dog on a bottle,' I said.

'Lovely,' agreed Emily.

'Not lovely at all. Every two hours, night and day? I've got plastic carriers under my eyes already.'

'When's Hetty coming back?'

'I should think she's on the way now. I rang the surgery first thing this morning but there's been no word from her. I'm not worried about Phyllis though. I daresay Phyllis could manage all eleven but the brindle keeps falling over backwards and the others stamp all over it, so it can't get back in. It's not as strong as the rest.'

I followed the interments with a hearty breakfast. I decided not to ring the surgery again unless I really needed help. I could manage on my own without Hetty, who usually confused me by making me feel thoroughly inadequate. Hetty never meant to underwrite my abilities, but she had so many herself that she left others aware of the absence of their own.

After breakfast, I began to cook a fresh lot of dog meat. It came in cartons like regular deliveries to a Spare Part Surgical Supply Stores – ears, trotters and tails plus enough strictly anonymous bits to remodel a herd of buffalo.

'Did you know ants have five noses?'

'They wouldn't want this job then,' I said grimly, closing the oven door.

'. . . and gorillas never snore?'

'I've known some who did!'

'And one British dog in seven has worms?'

I said, 'For heaven's sake put that beastly book in the bin. I thought the torment was over when Ben left.'

Emily said, 'I can't think why they put in all those *boring* bits about animals when every day they do more interesting things than the people who write them.'

But I was looking at Kip. He was terribly thin. Was it worms or a shortage of protein? His master had been thin, too. I wished suddenly I could care for both of them and that I'd never let Jake go so easily. I made a note to pop a worm pill in Kip's dinner and make sure he had as much food as he could eat. The trouble was he didn't seem really interested in more than keeping alive until life for him began again.

I decided to go back up to Buttocks Farm where the man in the trench coat might even now be plodding his weary way towards the moment of truth for us both.

Without Ben, I had to take drastic measures with the van, stabled overnight. I used an old hair-dryer I keep out there for de-frosting doors and windows and to blow nutshells out of the engine. Squirrels store winter reserves behind the battery and I always have to take a quick look in the crevices to see they're not back for a hasty snack before starting up.

162

My passenger from the jumble sale was bumbling about in the hen run. She wore boots, a headscarf, a man's overcoat and a vast shapeless garment that might have been a knitted doormat in ginger wool. It hung gloomily over the coat like a cloud over a bog.

'Gosh!' I said, going into my flattery act, 'what eggs! Such a size . . . and the colour!' I might have been admiring the Koh-i-noor's five nearest rivals.

She stared at me, but I went on, 'I know you won't mind this unheralded call, but we're holding a Scrummage Sale in aid of the Friends of Beowulf,' ('What's a Scrummage?') 'and we did wonder whether . . .' ('Friends of who?') 'you had anything to throw out?'

She shook her head. I said, desperately, 'A Scrummage is part jumble, part rummage. I expect you know the sort of thing – ?' But she didn't, of course, and she looked at me suspiciously. I began to think she had reason.

'I just thought you might have some bits and pieces to dump , since the move. Things you don't have any use for. Odds and . . .'

'No.'

'Raincoats really. We desperately need raincoats of all kinds. Absolutely any sort of raincoat. Old, tatty, worn out, dirty, too long – some are, you know, Army surplus, lined.' I stopped myself from giving a complete and accurate description of the one I wanted off her husband. But she began to walk away, shaking her head. Her feet squelched in the mud and the set of her shoulders told me to go home and do something sensible.

'I thought Mr . . . er . . . your husband, might have one or two,' I called after her. 'You know what farmers are!'

'Yes,' she said grimly, 'never throw out anything. It all goes on the compost, the scarecrow or their family.'

I laughed uneasily, and stepped on a hen. When the squawking had stopped, I said, 'Sorry, I expect she'll stop limping soon and it doesn't seem to worry them really, does it? No, as I was saying, we're having a special raincoat stall because men do need rain-coats, don't they? And one man's Pakamac is another man's Bur-berry, as they say.'

She didn't answer. We were clear of the hens, though the victim of my boot was still clucking in disgust and probably in some pain as well. I felt a real heel, but I had to try just once more.

'Tell you what,' I said with the air of a gambler putting all on his last throw, 'I'll pop in just before the actual day and see what you've got. Save you bringing it all to me. Raincoats can be so heavy! I've a pot plant I need some advice about. I'll bring it along.'

'No time,' she said, wiping her nose on her woolly mitten, 'and no raincoats. I'm a jumbler not a jumblee, any road. I don't give to 'em. I buys.'

I almost gave up then, but I did have one final ace to play. 'It's going to be on a give-and-take basis, of course. Did I mention that? If we take two old raincoats from you, you can choose a new and better one from what we've already got, *or* a pot plant.' I was making up the rules as I went along. 'Yes, we shall have a choice of pot plants to trade in for raincoats.' I sounded more like Widow Twanky in Aladdin every minute.

She stopped in the doorway and turned. I hoped for the offer of a cup of tea (and a glance round), though it was hardly likely. And indeed she just said crossly, ''E'll be in for 'is 'am,' and it was a warning.

The phone stopped ringing as I reached my own kitchen, and I glanced round the edge of the *Daily Mail* and saw, 'Pa rang twice. ringing again.' And further down, 'Sue-Ellen's owner rang.' (For my further blessing on her union, perhaps?) and then, in red ink, 'K. Green rang about Phyllis. You never said!' I wondered how much I was being accused of never saying and also how much they'd told Killarney Green. That reminded me of Demelza and I tried ringing Mrs Bolsover again.

'Hullo?'

'Mrs Bolsover?'

'Yes, dear?'

'Good. I did try you before but you were out, I think. Demelza's puppies have arrived. Four of them: three dogs and a bitch. All of them lovely.'

'Oh, that's marvellous! Wonderful! Has she quite recovered? Was it a difficult time for her? My darling Demmie! Can I come over right away? Who did the delivery? I'll drop everything and be with you in an hour.'

'*Tomorrow*, Mrs Bolsover,' I said firmly, remembering my role as Iron Matron. 'No visitors for the first twenty-four hours, remember? I suggest tomorrow afternoon, and do bring her something to show you're pleased, won't you.'

'But *of course*!' I could hear her mind ticking over angora bed jackets, grapes or the latest copy of *Tatler*. 'I'm so excited. I just don't know how I'll be able to wait that long. When exactly did it happen?'

If I told her the truth, she'd wonder why I hadn't told her at once. I could hardly admit I'd forgotten, and that Demelza had been a proud mother for over two days. So I said briskly, 'A very easy delivery. No complications. One might even say she did it all herself! She's proving a very good mother, very independent and capable.' One could almost see her whisking nappies on and off.

'And does she, can she, nurse them herself?'

'Adequately,' I said.

'So proud,' she murmured. 'Do you think a little cold chicken? some of her favourite chocky fingers? or fish, perhaps, steamed cod?'

'The chicken,' I advised quickly, 'that would be perfect. She's *very* hungry, of course. Eating for five, you know!' I was actually thinking that with a hot winter salad and plenty of garlicky bread sauce, Demelza would insist on us all having a share if the bird was big enough.

'Do give her my love. I'll be with her at three, tell her. Is she allowed her own blanket now? I've crocheted such a pretty one, pink, with her name embroidered in stocking-stitch – just a few forget-me-nots, and a bone. Would it be all right to bring a bottle of her favourite sherry so we can drink her health?' (I'd known all along she would be a secret sherry-drinker.) 'She does like a drop with me on special occasions.'

And so say all of us. I agreed it would be delightful. I would suggest she left the bottle with us, that the sight of the label would bring back happy memories of home and sessions with the sherry shared between them. Given enough kindly owners, I was going to be able to cut down quite substantially on the housekeeping.

Emily came in just as I was saying goodbye.

'You never said it was Killarney Green,' she accused me, 'so we never knew till she rang!' I hung my head. 'Adam says a boy at school has all her LP's and he'd give Adam a Flimsy Flummox autograph for one of hers. Is she coming over?' I was glad the days of Desperate Dan and The Devils or Gruesome Gordon and the Garrotters was giving way to another extreme.

Not quite though. 'She's touring with the Custard Cadavers, isn't she?'

I got a withering look. 'Who else?' she muttered, as if I'd stated apples grew on trees.

'I wasn't too impressed, actually. Well, I mean, I didn't see her perform, of course. In fact she barely moved or uttered. What did you say to her?'

'Well,' said Emily with the air of one who'd memorised every

165

inflexion, '*she* said "This is Killarney Green and I'm ringing about Mrs Phillidore Stossen." I knew she meant Phyllis because you'd told me that – but her voice! It's just like the *Daily Mirror* said – "Bitter Lemon and Ice". Sensational! She wears creations from sackcloth, you know, designed by Yuki and sprinkles her head with ashes. That's why her hair has that ethereal look. She burns all her love letters, fan mail, share certificates and contracts to get the right effect. It costs a fortune in solicitors, they say, but the same article said no other ashes had the same effect on her psyche.'

'I'm not surprised!'

'She asked if Phillidore Stossen had had the puppies, just like that. I said "Yes, eleven." I didn't say a thing about the two deaths because I didn't want to depress her in any way. Hardly fair before her appearance at the Littlewick Lido tonight.'

'Is that where she is?'

'And she said "Fine" and that she'd ring again sometime. I could tell she was deeply moved, though she was trying not to show it. Couldn't even trust herself to say more. Perhaps she'll write a sad song about it.'

'She's certainly a lady of few words,' I muttered balefully. 'I hope she can find a rhyme for Stossen.'

'But deep,' reproved Emily, ignoring the last bit, 'very deep. "Emotionally motivated" her notices said outside the Felixstowe Frivolity.'

'Emotionally nothing,' I said indignantly. 'She's not even sent Phyllis a card.' Then I added, 'And Pa?'

'Sounds terrific. Says we'll love what he's got. Says we must all go and see it soon.'

I said wearily, 'Let's have tea.' I was fed up with everyone else being so important everywhere – and there was still no sign of Hetty.

Pearl drank a great bowl of our strong Indian and went off outside to think it over. Everyone was being very nice to Edyth. I was glad to see a caring society operating around me. They followed her about attentively and Edyth, usually rather detached, was flirting a bit. Such a relief to see friendly relationships developing in a world mainly geared to hostility. Lulu would have been very jealous but she still maintained her purdah and dignity and her possible condition, which I prayed would be 'interesting', in my office behind the bureau.

Pa rang back later. He didn't reverse the charges. I guessed he aimed to keep the conversation short.

'All right?' he enquired, which means 'Are you in a receptive mood and not too wary or bad-tempered?' 'I was hoping to be back tonight but there's a lot to settle. I've been over the place again and we have a few problems to iron out. A word in the ear of the Planning Officer and that sort of thing.'

'I thought it had planning permission?'

'So it has, so it has . . . '

'So it has what?'

'So it has p.p. for a temp. dwelling: a 2b unit; bungalow, you know.'

'And . . . ?'

'It would be nice to extend the kennels to suit human habitation really.'

'The chances?'

He hesitated. We both knew the pips would go soon. 'Go on,' I urged.

'Few. Any construction on a permanent basis would be granted only to house more dogs.'

I could hardly believe my ears.

'Then where are we supposed to live?'

'The temp. dwel. 2b unit. The bungalow, actually. But it's only a technicality.'

'I preferred the snip.' Unless a technicality had at least four bedrooms.

'Just give me a few more days and —'

'I'll give you a broken nose if you don't drop the whole idea, grab your money back and come home. Do you honestly mean to say we're landed with kennels, and then more kennels and a 2b unit, and that's it? No home to go to? Thank God, we haven't sold this place!'

There was an ominous silence.

'We haven't, have we?'

'I did accept a deposit from Knickers Sattersthwaite-Pells, actually, based on an offer which —'

'— you couldn't refuse,' I snarled, beside myself.

'— was very generous and just in time for a deposit on this.'

Sympathetic as I felt towards Knickers' proposal to use my home for quarantined dogs, self-preservation came first. I cried angrily, 'Send it back, get the other one back, and get back now!'

'I more or less promised —'

'Then more or less break your word and skip. We've changed our minds and we're staying.' The pips went. 'We're *staying*!' I put

167

down the phone, quivering.

Adam, standing in the doorway, said timidly, 'One of Phyllis's puppies feels a bit cold.'

It was lying on its side on a page of *The Lady* with a few suggestions on how to combat boredom. It was sub-titled, 'Something New For You To Do', and showed how to work a lazy-daisy stitch on a tray cloth. I snatched up the puppy and pushed it unceremoniously inside my jumper and from there inside my bra to hold it steady, and ran downstairs. The movement surprised it enough to feebly fight back a bit. I was encouraged. I heated some milk to luke warm and added a drop of water from the kettle and a drop or two of brandy. I found the old eye dropper which had come with Ireen's 'Stye-stemmer'. I sterilised the dropper and began to tempt the puppy with a drop at a time. Its little legs waved weakly and its wide mouth opened and shut as if it were gasping its last, but it swallowed and seemed to enjoy the attention. An early imbiber if ever I saw one. Nothing given away by the eye, mind, but a broad and bucolic grin. He looked like a drunken slug.

Greatly encouraged, I pushed him back inside my bra and hunted out some baby food I recalled seeing at the back of the larder, left behind by a friend who stayed a weekend of forever with a three-week-old monster which had looked to me to be in even worse condition than the puppy, and if that one could survive, so could this one.

It was then I thought of Demelza. If she'd just mind the little thing while I got on with routine stuff – act as baby-sitter now and then – I could have my bra back. I went in and knelt beside her. 'You've heaps of room,' I said, 'and you actually enjoy the job which is more than I do. I don't have as much time, you see. You've got chicken and sherry on the way. You're a lucky lady. This is the least you can do.' I rubbed the alien puppy in her coat and against the smaller ones, peacefully snoozing between meals, burping now and then, or hiccupping like the last evictions after Closing, and then let Demelza sniff it. At first she looked a bit puzzled and shoved it away. I rolled the indignant puppy all over the smelly newsprint and in the smelliest areas of Demelza's coat. Then I smeared it with some of her own milk. This time she began to lick it. She half sat up and glared at me. The glare demanded to know what on earth I was doing with this prize pick of the litter. Then she began thrashing it around with her tongue. She was probably horrified at the way it had grown since the day before.

She washed it until it was to her entire satisfaction and then nosed it bossily in among the rest. I watched it begin to hunt for food and to my relief it quickly found what it was looking for, the others being knocked flat as it got them out of the way. Demelza settled back with a sigh and I crept quietly and with triumph upstairs to reassure Phyllis.

But Phyllis was sound asleep. She looked like a horse that had fallen over a fence in the Grand National. Ten puppies scrambled over one another to be in the best places but she seemed oblivious to anything. I suddenly panicked and gave her a quick poke in case she'd had some ante-natal collapse or something, but she merely shifted a little, sighed deeply and carried on dreaming. She seemed as unconcerned about the puppies as her owner. I was about to steal away feeling more than usually smug about my successful career, when I noticed another occupant on the 'Something New For You To Do' page. It looked as if it was being slowly but determinedly trampled by the others. I could hardly bear to make a closer inspection. It was even less active than the last victim. The feeble leg-waving was down to a very occasional twitch. The blind and restless movement of the head, to a weak collapse. And there was just the same terrible and failing ability to hold on to life. I picked it up and cradled it in my hands and a shattering possibility took away my own breath. Was this to be one of those 'fading' litters one sometimes heard about? Would they all gradually falter, weaken and die? Come Back, Hetty! I cried soundlessly, All Is Forgiven. But in the meantime, I had to salvage what I could.

It was hardly fair to push another half dozen into Demelza's nest, like cuckoos, but where else could they go? I sighed wearily and stuck it up my jumper. A 34-inch B cup seemed to suit it very well. Thank goodness the rest of the litter so far appeared perfectly satisfied with what they'd got. Even Barbara Windsor could hardly accommodate that lot.

I heated up the baby food mixture again and began to set up a second survival system. The puppy was lethargic enough to accept anything, and I quickly dripped half a teaspoonful in the side of his mouth. He looked a bit thoughtful, so I tucked him back in my bra and started to clear up the kitchen. Adam and Emily had gone up to the field to make sure Bubbles and Jody had enough hay. For a moment everything was peaceful. I began to consider washing my hair and having an early night. The puppy would need feeding every two hours anyway. I creamed the make-up off my face, pinned my hair on top of my head and made a turban out of a towel. A face mask while I stretched out in the steamy water would do wonders.

I forget we rarely have any steamy water until I run the tap. The aged pipes are furred, have to run too far, don't really try very hard, and if hot water happens to get in one end, its always lost its enthusiasm by the time it reaches the taps. Anyway I could forget it, because the front door bell rang.

Hetty! It had to be Hetty! Thank God. I rushed into the hall and flung open the door. Outside stood the vicar, a man usually distinguished by his regular absence from all local activities. For one awful moment, I thought he'd been sent with bad news. We stood and stared at one another – he as hirsute as a yak and me bare-faced, bald and shining.

'What is it?' I begged hoarsely. 'What's happened?'

'Happened? Why, nothing that I know of: nothing disastrous anyway. Not to my knowledge.' He beamed at me, his eyes, overhung with a surplus of eyebrow, glittering through bifocals and his mouth obliterated by a surprisingly active moustache. A really amazing land-mass of beard hovered elsewhere. A truly biblical figure; a Soloman, a Joshua, a Jacob at least.

'Come in,' I said.

We stood together in the hall. I was uncomfortably aware of the puppy shifting position in my bra. I just prayed he wouldn't lose his grip and fall down my trouser leg. The vicar said it was nice to see me again because he knew most of his – parishioners by sight but I was one of the more elusive ones, ha-ha. And I said ha-ha, too, and added that he had been very elusive at the Christmas party in aid of the crumbling steeple. Odds being even, he cleared his throat and announced that he understood we were proposing to run a Jumble Sale.

I cursed Hosanna for giving my name instead of hers, though I could appreciate she might want to keep the Rev. out of Harry's hair. Harry was an uneasy agnostic yearning for final conviction either way. It lead to endless argument. The vicar said he had been approached for old surplices and I remembered Hosanna had once said she liked the idea of going to bed in ecclesiastical robes.

'I'm a sort of sleeping partner,' I tried to explain, thinking how like a commercial we looked for Before and After using a depilatory, 'Hosanna and Posy Pink have promised to do most of it.'

'I did wonder if, from the goodness of your hearts, you would care to donate a percentage of takings to the rectory roof? Dire

170

straits, I have to confess, dire straits . . . '

The towel round my head blocked my ears and I thought he was saying 'wire slates'. I began to mutter comforting noises about the possibility of enlisting Mr Treddie's help. Mr Treddie was our local builder and since his recent marital problems ended in divorce, he'd been rushing in and out of the church as if trying to prove to the Almighty that it was all to the Glory of God and not to Elfrida Hossack, who cleaned the altar brass.

The vicar, however, went on without listening. He mentioned the leak in Mrs Vicar's sewing-room and the damp patch in the parlour. He bemoaned his stipend and Mrs Vicar's agency work. 'Everyone wants a job as a domestic these days you see,' he told me, 'but no one can afford them any more. It's all "remember the days when the gentry knew how to give a girl a good time in the panty?" instead of whining about the deprivations they suffered in the cellars!'

I was quite startled. But he went on, 'Old Gladys Connor would have taken work as a kitchen maid anywhere last Christmas: she said she often looked back longingly to the days when Her Lady-ship permitted parties in the servants' hall, and how they all got tiddly on the best Burgundy. You can't get a real hangover on Supermarket Surplus. And as for the food . . . They miss it, you know, they miss it.'

He stole a glance at himself in the hall mirror. He tilted his head to admire his profile, woolly as it was. I stopped feeling self-conscious about myself because he wasn't even aware I was looking and feeling as if plucked for the oven. He wouldn't have noticed if the puppy had been barking in my bra as well as lumbering round like a squirrel in a stocking-top. I put a hand over it and nodded my head.

'As for the proceeds from our Scrummage Sale,' I said, drawing his mind away from the Good Old Days, 'I'm afraid it's spoken for and you'll have to excuse me, because I've got to do the baby's bottle.' I couldn't think of any other way to get rid of him.

'Have we had the christening?' he murmured, puzzled.

'No, no,' I laughed nervously, 'they're Danes – well, not en-tirely. A mixed parentage. I believe the father was a Maltese or something . . .'

However, he simply nodded and smiled and patted the back of his head like a customer approving a new hair-do, and said, 'These Danes – lovely people – but rather a permissive trend, I believe. All that pornography. And, of course, the Maltese, too, are, I understand, extremely sensual people. An au pair my wife interviewed last week, I found to be . . .' He shrugged. I felt sure he'd found her to be something he preferred to leave to my imagination and his own memories.

He only left when I opened the door and the snow flurried in warning us both that a blizzard was beginning.

Adam and Emily came back minutes later smothered in huge white flakes. I told them about the vicar and the bounding Dane in my bosom and, in exchange for a moment's hilarity, they offered to get the evening meal. I produced the puppy, which was duly admired, fed and tucked back in the B cup, and I started again towards the stairs. I would keep the jumper intact and simply have a quick wash, do my face and hair and put on a skirt. The puppy seemed to like the old tight lambswool. He was more relaxed now and quite greedy at the second feed. Another hour or so and he could have some more. Contact with living and loving security, careful warm handling, and my own regular pulse steadying and encouraging his own, was as vital as food and sleep and together they added up to a tighter hold on life.

I was half way up the stairs again when I heard a car. The headlights flashed through the windows on either side of the front door as it turned. Hetty! Surely this time it would be Hetty? Or had the vicar forgotten something? I turned and trudged back wearily, impatiently, even furiously enough to scare the wits out of anyone waiting. I opened the door with a scowl of rage which didn't do much for my greasy face and turbanned head. And then I froze. It wasn't the icy wind, the belting snow or the frosty air. It was Ross.

We stared at one another like Gog and Magog while the puppy fidgeted at the quickening of my heartbeat. The first time Ross had called, two summers before, I had been alone but had lined up six mugs of coffee to give the impression of a house full of people. I'd even armed myself with a tennis racket. Now I was caught completely unawares and as vulnerable as a mouse at a cat show.

Everything was wrong for the moment I'd dreamed of at regular intervals since we last met – my face, my hair, my jumper, my jeans, the weather, the time, the place and the puppy heaving about in my bra like a trainee on a trampoline. Worst of all, perhaps, was my lack of eyebrows. I have very anaemic eyebrows: very pale, very sparse, much too low. I have to supplement with a cosmetic pencil or I look bland and empty, like a box without a lid.

I have to have those few strokes on my face to show I'm alive.

I put my hand across my forehead automatically while resting the other on the puppy. Ross came in and passed me. I kicked the door shut with my foot.

'Goodness,' I said, 'I had no idea . . .'

'Well, neither had I. Do you mind? Have you got a headache? You're not sick, are you?' I must have looked very pale without make-up, like someone suffering a turn, with my hands at strategic points of combat. The turbanned head could have meant a high fever, but the pallid cheeks denied anything so simple. I immediately rushed to another extreme.

'No, no, no. Not *sick*!' Raving mad, perhaps; drunk, even. But not *sick*! 'No, I'm fine, fine. Terrific form. Marvellous. Super. Couldn't be better.' Stop it, shut up, don't go *on* so, I told myself. Relax, be casual, show you're above eyebrows and the rest. 'It's very nice to see you again.' And that sounded as if it would be even nicer when he left.

'I meant to stop somewhere and ring,' he said, turning to face me full frontal. I thanked God for 40 watt lamps in far corners. 'I was heading down the motorway to the airport to meet a plane and found myself almost within sight of you, and I just couldn't resist. How could I?' If he had been able to see me from the motorway he'd have driven straight on across the English Channel.

The hall was as cold as a Bejam freezer. OK for vicars but a bit daunting for a lovers' meeting. I felt like anything but a romantic moment without my eyebrows. I led the way to the office where a small and self-effacing fire burnt ready for the evening when the kids and I would migrate from the kitchen as a gesture to TV and more gracious living. I stumbled across the dark room towards the table lamp, determined not to put on the centre light and reveal the appalling all in a full 150 watts.

Lulu had crept out of her basket and was lying by the sofa. I caught my foot on her in the firelight and she shrieked like a banshee and shot into the firescreen, which fell over and sent a shower of ash into the air.

'Are you all right?' asked Ross, keeping close to the door for a quick getaway.

'Fine, fine,' I reiterated, every move belying the word. I put on the small lamp at my desk and turned. The puppy yawned and stretched, and my breast heaved about like the rising tempest. I could only hope Ross would think emotion surged in my bosom and nothing more positive. I decided that if I could get him to agree to some coffee or something, I could unload my burden, add my eyebrows, brush down my hair, find my lipstick and return with a merry laugh to put the record straight. I began, 'Let's have a . . .' but he interrupted, 'Look, I can tell this is terribly inconvenient, isn't it? Shall I go? I should have had more sense, but where you're concerned I can be very impulsive . . .' And that, I thought, sounds pretty thin from someone who manages to drop in once a year when passing.

I tried to head for the door but he moved forward to stop me and in the shadows caught his knee on a small table, knocking off a box of fondant creams. He stooped and Lulu, from her proper place again behind the bureau, shot forward and grabbed at his finger at the same time in mistake for a raspberry cream. Ross straightened up with a little gasp of pain and side-stepped into the fender. I saw my chance and moved like a coy virgin behind the sofa. Thus skirmishing in vain attempts to cover the embarrassment of the moment, we still continued to exchange pleasantries.

'I was meeting someone, you see,' he said as he squelched on two Coffee Kisses and narrowly missed Lulu's foot, 'but because the forecast was bad, I left home early so I'm still ahead of time.' He edged along the rug, following the outline of the furniture carefully to avoid further accidents. 'Don't go!' he cried, as I saw my chance and headed straight for the door.

'I must get you something hot!' I insisted almost hysterically, seeing self-preservation ahead in my handbag. 'It's so cold!' The anguished movements had caused a small log to come alive and throw out a few flames. This provided almost enough extra light to reveal everything, flaws, warts and all.

'No, no,' he protested. He might have been expecting strychnine. Anyone watching would have been moved to tears by the melodrama. My hand was on the door, but the other rested on my heart like Dame Nellie Melba about to break into a song of thwarted love and passion, only she never had to contend with a puppy struggling to get its paw out of her upholstery.

Reluctantly I went back and sat on the arm of the sofa, my head back out of the firelight and my feet up to the knees in squashy fondants. I noticed that since our last meeting the elegant Ross had grown a small beard. It was gold flecked with darker strands like his thick curling hair. He was tall and broad and tanned and he looked more than ever like a buccaneer from the Spanish Armada. Men, of course, never have to consider their eyebrows. Maybe that explains why they've been top dog so long.

174

'Come here,' he said softly, trying to draw me up to stand close. The puppy gave a squeak and shifted its position rapidly; on one side, I looked like a nest full of fieldmice while on the other the usual bath bun lay dormant.

'A drink,' I cried, 'to celebrate. We must have a drink!' I moved off again, this time to the cabinet where a few forgotten bottles lurked uneasily behind supermarket labels. Ross fell silent, probably with sheer exasperation. He let me go and stood where he was, with Lulu dodging round his ankles. Either excessive warmth or the brandy was causing my passenger to roll about like a sailor on shore leave, and hiccupping to boot. I gave it a little slap and it heaved over and fell silent and still. Oh, God! I pleaded, don't let it die in there, please don't let it die! Well, not yet, anyway.

The sherry bottle was empty, of course. Mrs Bolsover had seen to that. There was only enough gin to drown an earwig, and an empty bottle of Schnapps which had stood there since we moved in. We could choose between a collection of miniatures from the Christmas tree or half a bottle of Vodka. 'Vodka!' I cried with triumph, pouring it wildly into champagne glasses which were the only kind likely to have been unused. 'Here's to you and me . . .' and Bonzo the bra-baby, I added fervently. It had suddenly struck me that he might have suffocated, even if the earlier smack had been harmless.

Ross took the glass and put it down carefully again. He chose the desk, which seemed reasonably stable and unlikely to disintergrate, and then, as I turned to close the door of the cabinet, caught me when I surfaced. I was totally unable to move without looking as if I suspected him of rape or rabies.

'You're avoiding me,' he accused. I may have heard more brilliant deductions but rarely one more accurate. I nevertheless muttered, 'No, no, of course not . . .' and tried out a short laugh but it sounded more like a honk from a wounded goose. Ross put both arms round me and drew me very close. Very, very close. So close that I was uncomfortably reminded of the squashed chihuahua. In sheer desperation, I gave Ross a hefty shove against the sofa. It was a small sofa as sofas go, and as sofas go, it went, crashing over and scaring Lulu half to death. She yelped and leapt into the hearth, scattering fire-irons. Ross landed on top of the cushions, unhurt but undignified.

'I'm sorry,' he said icily. He wore the look of a man who'd misjudged the traffic lights. After the letters, the phone calls, the few brief but beautiful contacts over the past two years, he must surely have felt a right to something more than a seat in the cinders.

He got to his feet and began to wrap his enormous camel coat round him again, turn up the collar, demonstrate a man's independence and pride before making an orderly retreat.

I could recognise a moment of truth when it came. I went to the door and switched on the centre light. I switched on the desk lamp and the standard in the corner and took the towel off my head. And smiled at him painfully without my eyebrows. Then I hitched up my jumper and said boldly, 'It's all because I've got a puppy in my bra,' and fished it out.

He said later that what he admired most about me was the sheer unpredictability of what I was going to do next. I demurred, and wrote it off to my appealing mystique. We didn't mention the other facts and that I smelled more of Ostermilk No. 1 than Chanel No. 5. The puppy seemed happy enough with a drop of Vodka to be going on with, and a roll on the cushion. Lulu sulked behind the bureau. But Ross and I stayed on the upturned sofa a lot longer than the ten minutes he had to spare before heading for the airport again.

When he left, he took the puppy in the palm of his strong hands and laughed gently at it. 'A cuckoo,' he said, 'a cuckoo in the nest. I'd like to buy it, please. It'll be ours. Can you fix it?'

I looked in the mirror when he'd gone and suddenly my face had stopped needing eyebrows to come alive.

Supper was ready. I took the casserole out of the Aga and said, 'It's snowing again. It's pretty thick outside.'

Adam began serving the mashed potatoes. 'Did you know a horse called Whizzer jumped into an apple tree when a motorist backfired?'

'Happens all the time,' I said absently.

'Took the Fire Brigade to get him out.'

'Always does,' I said.

'And a puppy in North Carolina was born with two tails.'

'I know just how he felt,' I said, grinning.

# 14

It went on snowing. It grew colder. The Aga wouldn't draw. Adam upset Emily. And I found my gold mouse was missing. My gold mouse had been given me by a long-past lover and had actually stayed with me a great deal longer than he did. It hung round my neck (much as he had, to my irritation) on a gold chain and had one emerald eye. Because he'd become an embarrassment before he ever gave me the mouse, and had left me shortly after, I considered the charm to be very lucky. Now I needed it badly because suddenly everything was going wrong. The wireless warned me that further up country the roads were blocked. Weather forecasters joined in gloomily about possible blizzards, threatening hurricanes and definite falls in the temperature to well below zero. Losing my mouse now seemed a lot more significant than it would have done during June.

I'm usually pretty sanguine about losses. I reckon if you've had something and enjoyed it, then break or lose it, that's fair. You've no right to whine. Nothing was meant to be permanent – neither daffodils nor childhood nor dinner plates, gold mice or lovers. But mine had been a mouse with a meaning. Every Christmas I get things to put round my neck, and I start the year smothered in Paddington Bears, Snoopys, gold ingots or silver hearts. I've had St Christophers, lockets, Poohs and Piglets and during the following twelve months they either fall off, or apart, or simply from grace. They vanish into hot baths and cold swims, they get caught in sweaters, scarves and other people's ties. I'd always been left with the gold mouse until I reloaded round him the following Christmas. That mouse had been more than a mere mouse to me. He was a staunch companion, a permanent fixture, an extension of myself, charismatic, a talisman, magic, a token of faith in the future. Stability, if you like, and that's a rare thing. Now he'd left me. 'Who's dogging?' I asked. I put on the dog walker and looked around

'I've some more unpacking to do,' Adam said and left the room. I heard him run upstairs. Adam never ran upstairs unless he was upset. I glanced at Emily. She said quite simply, 'Goodnight,' and left me. I knew then they were too tied up in their secret war to seek a peace with me. I would have to undertake what Ben called The Last Post, alone.

Deserted. Pa, Ben, Hetty, Ross, Adam, Em and mouse. Even Marsha seemed to have stopped ringing. I quite missed her. Hosanna was happy bickering with Harry. I wanted to turn to someone and say, 'Ah, well, it could be worse,' which really means it's as bad as it can be because anything that was worse would be beyond inclusion in the same league. But there was no one to listen.

I called to the dogs, 'Who's coming out?'

None of them moved. Et tu, brutes, I thought bitterly. I put Sue-Ellen on a lead, hoping the rest would follow, but she started shivering with fright at the very idea of being led out to face the elements and in the end I just carried her there alone, waited until she'd ruined the unblemished snow, and whirled her back upstairs with Edyth, disciplined by Hetty to a final run much earlier, and tried the rest again. I pleaded with Mattie, explaining carefully that I wanted to go to bed early and they'd be uncomfortable and regretting it all if they didn't go now. Mattie finally sighed, lumbered up grumbling, protesting that she could always wait till morning and it was these youngsters who needed to learn self-control. The other dogs gradually got to their paws with a show of indignant reluctance, stretched, yawned, and ambled behind me. I had them all gathered at the back door before I opened it. I didn't want to keep the cold air blowing in any longer than was necessary.

But now it wasn't just cold air: we were into one of those blizzards they had warned about. A complete wall of snow. We staggered back as one, and I shut the door quickly again. Some of the dogs smirked a bit and hurried back to their boxes. Mattie gave me an 'I told you so' look and bumbled back to the Aga. I hesitated a minute. Then I went alone to face the worst night in years. Only obstinate defiance kept me going. I felt like Captain Scott. I hoped someone would say of me 'She was a very gallant lady' though I was more likely to be remembered by my mobile bra in some quarters. I envied the pup, left in a cotton-wool padded chocolate box on the top shelf of the dresser. I grabbed a spade from the potting-shed and began to shovel a path of sorts towards the back gate. If anyone ever tried to reach us again, at least they'd find a route to the door with our Red Cross parcels. But from the way the snow fell thicker and thicker, covering all my efforts behind me, I began to doubt that they would even try.

I worked for ten minutes, and all the time I was battling against the elements they were doubling up with laughter behind me. But I cleared a patch for the dogs. I went inside again and spoke with enraged authority and this time they shuffled forward like a row of prisoners on exercise duty.

They were back within seconds. Pearl, Demelza and Phyllis, unaware of what was going on outside, came willingly but in a hurry and barely noticed what was happening in their eagerness to get back. Pearl sneered at Phyllis, which was rather foolish considering the contrast in sizes, but Phyllis roared back at her and I shrieked at them to shut up and get on with it. Pearl withdrew, sulking, to pee under a bush, one baleful eye on the others. I suppose she was envious of their success in the puppy stakes. She hovered under a bush heavy with snow and would only come back in when Phyllis was out of sight. The floor was covered with wet pawmarks and dripped coats. I might as well have let them all stay in. It couldn't have ended up wetter.

Rosie, who usually kept much to herself and was always outside minding her own nefarious business, had discovered Sniff in her box during the week. Sniff and Snuff had now been collected and gone home, but Rosie still smarted from the retaliation of both when she quite rightfully turned Sniff out. She was seething for a revenge on somebody else – anybody else. Edyth and Sue-Ellen spent most of the time in the office with Lulu or upstairs in my bedroom, all girls together. I could usually keep the peace easily when the dogs were outside a lot of the time but in winter tempers grew edgy. Mattie wouldn't stand for any terrorist activity and everyone recognised her no-go area. But tonight I could feel tension and knew that the slightest alien vibes could trigger off trouble.

When I'd tidied up the kitchen, I went upstairs to see if the same sort of uneasiness had cleared between Adam and Emily. Another day of sulks and snow would be too much. Adam was in bed, reading, clothes neatly folded, fire out. I said, 'Goodnight, darling. Everything OK?'

'Yes thanks. Goodnight.'

'The snow's thicker than ever. Hope it stops overnight or you and Em won't get to the village tomorrow.'

'We weren't going.'

'I thought Emily seemed a bit quiet tonight. Anything wrong?'

'Not that I know of.'

'Goodnight then.'

'Goodnight.' And nothing about red-nosed raccoons, their mating habits and the one that swallowed a box of elastic bands and sprang to attention ever after.

I went into Em's room. She was sitting by the fire, writing a letter. I said, 'Goodnight, darling. You'll go to bed soon, won't you?'

'Of course.'

'The snow's thicker than ever.'

'Yes.'

'Adam seems a bit quiet. Is he OK?'

'I expect so.'

'Goodnight then.'

'Goodnight.'

I went back downstairs fuming. I looked out of the conservatory windows. Snow piled itself high, it was everywhere. Only the bare branches could reach beyond it and they seemed to be appealing to heaven for help. I shivered. I rarely feel very cold, but this was the shiver of shock, the kind you get when disaster threatens, fear stalks you, the unknown lurks. From outside, the insidious snow was made worse by the silence, and even when I took the fuel hods to get anthracite, the silence was still there together with a rising hurricane which whirled and curled the flakes at me like a bombardment of feathers.

The kitchen was warm and still and it was a relief to riddle the Aga and then make lots of noise with the anthracite. Riddling's a rather splendid word. It expresses the sound and the action. There's a lot of therapy in the old-fashioned riddling of a range. It's comforting. How can anyone find solace in a switch?

I covered Connie, closed the game larder window to keep the worst of the weather from Atilla (neatly perched with her head tucked under, beady eyes watching me through her feathers) and unplugged radio and record-player. I bolted the back door and made sure Frilly was in, rewarding her with some shredded Cheddar.

By the time I could congratulate myself that the Aga was showing a bit of a glow, and I'd fed, cleaned and stuffed the Cuckoo back in my bra for a few moments while I remade his bed, it was well after midnight. With the lights out, I could see through the kitchen windows that we all stood a good chance of waking in the morning to find ourselves snowed in, under and over the top.

Charlie and Kip followed me upstairs. Charlie to guard me and

Kip, perhaps, to keep an eye on me in case I could lead him to his beloved master. I rather wished Jake Edwards *was* in my bed. Times are, when company alongside is more attractive than a visit from Casanova.

I undressed quickly. It was obviously unwise to keep the Cuckoo in my bra so I placed him to sleep in his Lindt chocolate box with a small brandy flask of hot water (for comfort, not boozing) under the cotton wool and the bit of blanket. Another bit of blanket I drew across half the top of the box. Then I popped the box in my bedside table drawer and left it ajar. The puppy wore an expression of bliss on its chubby face, as well it might. I think mine was rather different as I wearily set the alarm for 2 a.m. Edyth and Sue-Ellen shared a corner under the eiderdown and Pearl settled down opposite, leaving me just enough space to manoeuvre. Pearl wore the expression of a self-righteous Oxfam helper putting her own twenty pence in the till for a tattered tea towel.

At the first feed, I groped through a mist of sleep with vacuum flask, eye-dropper and puppy, administering drop by drop from a small measure. The puppy slurped and sucked until food ran out of the opposite side of his mouth; he then rolled over and waved his feet. He was much stronger already. I tucked the top blanket round him this time and he went straight off to sleep still making sucking noises. I adjusted the alarm for 4 o'clock and wondered if, by saving the puppy, I'd probably perish myself.

At 6 a.m. I was shattered awake for the third time, fed the puppy, got up and fell down. My head ached and my muscles felt leaden. The silence in the house was like a muffled nothing when you blow your nose and your ears block. It felt eerie and un-nerving. I picked up the phone to dial the weather service, and there was no dialling tone. I made some coffee, black and very strong. I was so tired I couldn't focus: so bewildered I couldn't think. I toasted bread, checked the puppy, let out the dogs (who edged past me nervously) and refuelled the boilers. Adam came in yawning and I announced that we were snowed in.

'This may be your last meal, dear boy, so make the most of it!'

'I heard bells ringing all night,' he complained, still yawning.

'My alarm – and my death knell. The puppy's fine. I'm beyond exhaustion. Can't send for help, the phone's off. I wonder if we could persuade Demelza to take another lodger?'

It was my last hope to save the sanity I needed to combat the siege conditions. But Demelza was outraged. 'I never came here to foster drop-outs,' she cried, hurling her own smallest half way down the box in an effort to get at its tail end. Her expression was rebellious. She resisted the introduction almost as much as I would, knowing what I now knew of the trouble involved. I took the orphan away and tucked it back in my bra. He looked so lonely and unwanted in his chocolate box, like a rejected hard-centre with toothmarks.

Adam was a bit apologetic about the night before. 'Emily was a bit bothered last night,' he volunteered.

'Umm.'

'She was talking about Ben a lot.'

'What about Ben?' I'd just remembered the money from the aggi boots. I would have to keep it till the snow cleared. I felt as if I were hiding contraband.

'She says he's changed.'

'Changed?'

'Grown up.' It meant 'joined the opposition'.

He put on his gloves, heavy things in angora and rug wool, a gift at 10p from the Rectory Good-As-New stall.

'Well, yes,' I agreed, 'I suppose he has in a way. He's got to do it sometime.'

'Em doesn't like it.'

I laughed. 'Maybe Ben won't in the end, but he's still Ben.' I knew what they meant – Ben had slipped from their side of the generation fence over to mine, unobtrusively – almost unobserved. But he hadn't climbed over or broken down any part of the dividing line: just found himself where time had taken him.

I thought the snow would be less deep outside than it looked from the windows, but it was worse. It came up to our knees and any shovelling from the night before had long since been covered. There would be another day without Humphrey, milk, baker or butcher's van. I hoped Edyth could eat pineapple chunks because we were going to be reduced to tinned fruit in a few days.

We gloomily surveyed the dim outlook: snow still trickled down but the sky threatened heavily for the rest of the week. Adam said, 'Did you know a penguin flew over the North Pole in 1891?' but it was no more than a brave try.

I said sadly, 'Penguins can't fly,' as we went back in.

'Would you believe a – hmmm – duck?'

'If you go on making them up, you'll have enough for a second edition of your own.'

He grinned. 'Think Em'll be OK today?'

'You said she was OK yesterday,' but I could see the thaw was as far from happening in the house as outside.

'You know what I mean.' Adam was trying to tempt Connie out of her cage, but nothing ever had or ever would. She suffered from agrophobia, we reckoned. She had come to us in a cage and she was going to see the thing through in a cage. Her previous owners had taught her just one thing, sit firm and say nothing. We thought they were probably members of the Mafia. Charlie and Kip were bickering over Edyth's favours. Edyth, like so many strict spinsters, could be primly provocative.

During the morning and the shared drama of survival under siege, Emily dissolved. She even offered to do all the cooking for the next few days – 'if Adam helps a bit?'

'I'll have a look through Delia Smith if you like,' said Adam, flushing with relief and gratitude.

'I'd sooner have Ben's recipe book,' said Emily. I agreed it was more original: you got actual lumps of the dishes suggested on most pages and some of our comments at the bottom. Under 'Fish Blancmange' for instance, you were told it made a good starter. 'Specially for a sprint to the nearest Chippy,' someone had added.

Adam went upstairs to fetch Phyllis's dish for her porridge. 'Em,' I begged, 'do be nice to Adam. He's worried about you.'

'Why?'

'I don't know. I bet you do.'

She looked at me with the cool eyes of a female challenging interference. I muttered, 'The trouble is, you're all growing up,' and recalled my own children suddenly doing the same thing.

Outside it went on snowing, dense clots which immediately filled the way behind us as, together, we set forth to clear a path.

'I bet we never see human form again,' said Adam, once we were back inside.

'Do we ever?' retorted Emily. I was silent. It all seemed too likely at the moment to be hysterically amusing.

'We'll have to ration bread a bit,' I warned them. 'Eggs are running low, too.'

'I'll make what we can't buy,' offered Emily, 'and we'll get Connie and Atilla back on egg production.'

'Low in flour, too,' I muttered, wondering why it was I never buy in bulk or invest in a deep freeze or attempt the role of organised housewife.

'You ought to have a freezer cabinet,' said Adam, whose home probably had as many as Sainsbury's. Emily agreed. I'm sure her's had as well. They suddenly found a point of contact; stories were swopped, opinions shared, rival manufacturing concerns compared. My own dismal lack of forward planning made a splendid point for restoring harmony. I always claim I prefer eating food fresh from the ground, bush or tree when it's in season, and deplore the whole idea of being a cross between a squirrel and the worthy Pawleys, who discussed endlessly the best way to pickle prunes and where to put your ripe bananas. I've never had a thing out of anybody's freezer that didn't thaw as sloppy as tripe. But the truth was, I'd have given all my convictions for a deep-freeze full of food at that precise moment.

'How about the dogs?'

I said bravely, 'Look, it's not going to last long, all this snow, and we've loads of, er, Bisto, custard powder, orange segments and at least fifty-four teabags!'

'We could survive forever then.'

'I intend to.' I felt like a good cry, but it was frustration more than despair. Somebody would alert somebody eventually and helicopters would arrive with reinforcements.

Emily was preparing to make something for lunch and she was unloading supplies as if there would be no tomorrow. Don't think like that, I thought.

'Look,' I said to Adam, 'you make a complete inventory of what we've got, then we can sort it into rations for, say, a week ahead.' I hoped it would have the effect of stopping Emily breaking eggs as if hens had forsworn industrial action for all time. 'Ralph is due up with a delivery tomorrow and I bet he'll make it somehow.'

They looked at me witheringly. I added weakly, 'Well, the next day then.'

But at lunchtime the snow was still falling.

The Cuckoo stayed in my bra most of the time because even with his brandy flask full of hot water, he didn't seem all that happy in the box. He needed to feel close to someone, and that was understandable, but you can't shovel anthracite with a puppy in your undies, and I decided I had to find a Mother substitute. After looking around without an idea in my head, I decided on the rug-wool-and-angora gloves because they had the consistency of a shaggy coat. I stuffed one with old tights, popped a small fishpaste jar of hot water inside, and wedged it in a corner of the box. It looked like an ageing haggis or tartan bagpipes, but the Cuckoo snuggled against, and almost into, it and made little contented gobbling noises before he fell asleep.

As the daylight began to go except for the sullen glow of piling snow, we listened more and more closely to the radio weather reports. News readers, too, were brightly predicting the worst, warning of roads blocked, cars abandoned, drivers perishing, trains halted, planes grounded. It seemed impossible that roses had ever blossomed round the same windows now frozen in weird patterns, or suntans been sought on the snowbound terrace. The reservoir, once rippling like cut crystal, had completely vanished days ago behind a screen of silver, and the motorway, usually speeding sea-bound cars like gems on a shimmering chain, was nothing but a memory.

Suppose, just suppose, the snow went on and on and on? Agonies of tragedies haunted my mind and wouldn't go away. I felt sick with anxiety and could only eat a little of Em's Ranch-hand's Roll. The two of them polished it off with the garlic spinach and mounds of mashed potato. I slipped my share of jam tart to Charlie, who rather pointedly went on chewing it for a long time under the table.

And as darkness finally wrapped around the house and grew pitch black behind the blizzard, the lights went out.

I felt a thread of panic starting. It mounted when Adam stepped on Kip who immediately leapt at Charlie. Charlie snarled and Rosie flew in for the kill. I grabbed the torch I'd been using to find coal and anthracite and called for order quite calmly but with heart thudding and fingers shaking. I picked up Charlie, and Emily hauled Rosie away.

'Let's stand just where we are for a moment,' I said, like a Cub Mistress at the end of the Annual Outing. 'Now, anyone remember where the candles are?' I tried to imply that I did but was just testing their own powers of observance.

Adam moved forward catching the jam tart and sweeping it off the table on top of Treacle. Mattie moaned about this sort of thing being just too much, and Rosie began to clear the tart out of Treacle's short coat at record speed.

Em cried, 'They're in the blue shoe box near Atilla's perch, marked Dried Peas in red ink. Shall I get them?' She moved forward and a bottle of milk joined the jam tart. Treacle sat grimly silent and enduring while Charlie struggled out of my arms and defied Rosie for prior rights. I said, with exaggerated tolerance, that maybe we should move one at a time and only with the torch, and perhaps Adam should do the main reconnoitering. I really wanted to scream and stamp and hit everyone and then go to bed and put my aching head under a pillow. Adam navigated the steps, doors and other hazards and came back with candles and matches. 'Matches!' I cried ecstatically, as if he were bearing an Olympic Gold. 'That's marvellous: let's go mad and light four candles at least. Then I'll find the oil lamps.' When we discovered there were only four candles, my enthusiasm was heard to waver a little.

But somehow we did manage to get organised. The candles flickered in jam-jars and I made enough baby food from the hot water in the kettle to fill the vacuum and see the Cuckoo through the next twenty-four hours. The dogs settled down and, apart from annoying Mattie again when I stepped in the water bowl, nothing went really wrong. At the time of Armageddon, Mattie will take offence and refuse to have any of it.

Atilla had followed Adam up the steps into the kitchen. She perched a bit insecurely on the jug of seed next to Connie's cage. Connie shrieked jungle obscenities and fell off her perch, scattering shells and dust all over everything. Tilla clucked disapprovingly, but was otherwise unmoved. Charlie barked and Phyllis bayed from upstairs, aware that somebody needed attacking. I ground my teeth and prayed for peace in our time.

The snow kept on falling.

Without electricity and radio, telephone, heating upstairs, and any light other than candles or oil, we began to realise the extent of our isolation. Light shed from oil lamps may be very gentle and romantic, but there's no comparison to 100 watts when you're working, when you want to find a thick vest at the back of a deep cupboard or navigate your way through seven sleeping dogs. Maybe the Victorians led tidier and better-organised lives. Maybe they had servants to do the blundering, toe-stubbing and wick-trimming: and maybe they even appreciated anything which blurred the features of the unmarriageable eldest of nine daughters. But I literally tripped round the house seriously threatening a holocaust.

Time dragged on: we ate a miserable meal of sardines and soda bread, followed by tinned tuna fish because, in the bad light, Emily misread the label. The Aga ovens offered our only hope for cooking, but they were old and slow and any meal would have to be planned a day ahead and left in overnight at least. The kettle whimpered on the hot plate and refused to boil. We drank quite-warm coffee. Adam and Emily played a dismal game of Scrabble until they argued over the 's's in 'desert'.

'Two *are* OK,' protested Emily, 'they just make a sandy waste into a pudding.'

'Like yesterday's sponge crumble?' Which was rather an unwise crack because it had been taken from one of Ben's own original recipes and copied faithfully. Emily sulked until the entire game disintegrated when Frilly shot across the table after a shadow and the letters disappeared on to the floor. Some of them hit the unfortunate dog bowl and in my effort to retrieve them, I sent most of the water over Emily's feet. It was the last straw in a rapidly emptying glass of bitter lemon. I said I was going to bed.

'It's only eight o'clock,' said Adam, shocked.

'I don't care what *time* it is. I'm cold, tired, chilled of the foot and hot of the temper. I don't care what you and Emily do, but if you've any sense you'll try sleep too. I'm sick to bits with walking on disagreeable dogs and dabbling in dog bowls. Good night!'

The dogs had been out earlier: I had the vacuum ready for the Cuckoo. I looked in on Demelza and found Pearl sitting anxiously by the door. When I picked her up, I found she was shivering, so I took her with me and popped her under my eiderdown again. We all needed company on a night like this, I thought.

Outside the windows, as I pulled my bedroom curtains, it was still snowing. I stood a few moments watching, wondering if by morning the wall of white would have reached the shutters.

I put on Pa's pyjamas, for comfort as well as extra warmth, and I put the chocolate box and Cuckoo in the drawer of my bedside table. Edyth, Sue-Ellen and Pearl distributed themselves happily enough under the eiderdown with some shuffling and snuffling and deep sighs before settling, and Kip curled up on his rug near the fire. I kept a coal and log fire going in my bedroom instead of an electric radiator, and Charlie decided to sleep on the armchair near it instead of in his usual basket. I set the alarm and blew out the candle. Joy, I hoped, cometh in the morning. But I really didn't have much faith in that at all.

I heard Adam and Emily come upstairs half an hour later. I heard their doors close and, a little later, a short sharp bark from Mattie in the muffled distance. Then silence and sleep . . . and outside, the falling snow.

# 15

I missed the ten o'clock feed and woke with dismay at 11.30 – not by the alarm, but by someone ringing the front door bell, again and again and again. It could only be Pa, distraught with anxiety for our welfare. Or Hetty, perhaps, her conscience struck by neglecting me in my hour of need. Or Wen and Bun on their way to the Bagshot and Barnet Boxer and Beagle Show? Even Jake, missing Kip as much as Kip longed for him to come back? I threw on a thick old dressing-gown (St Mandrake's Family Fair in aid of the bishopric or something) and ran downstairs, candle in hand.

It was only as I reached the hall I realised it might not be anyone I knew at all. Wasn't this an ideal night to rob and pillage and rape? A mere woman, in a phoneless situation? But why – and even how –, struggle through so much snow for this place when there were so many others much handier? Maybe the villain was after my valuables? What valuables? Pa's christening spoon – which prevented us from leaving the house empty at any time and would have been a challenge even to Securicor (because Pa had forgotten where he put it) – was all we had worth a hallmark. I would have welcomed any robber prepared to find it. And at the same time, he could have a look for my garnet brooch, the missing mouse, the book on hair care which gave a recipe for dried blondes, and one blue sock of Pa's which had escaped in the wash the week after Christmas. I knew there was a pair of inlaid opera glasses in an old plimsoll (left foot) and my gold watch on top of the pelmet in the lavatory. Beyond that, only Pa knew where other treasures were laid up, waiting for their value to rise above rubies.

I stopped at the foot of the stairs and looked across the hall to the windows on either side of the front door. A figure moved as if trying to keep warm and a torch flashed on and off. Do rapists carry torches? Was it some poor traveller who might freeze to death while seeking shelter? I went to the kitchen, woke Rosie and Mattie (bellow and bulk) and dragged them unwillingly into the hall. Then I shouted, 'Who's there? I have two trained guard dogs beside me and more behind me. They attack on command. I want your name and business!'

The torch flickered and I heard a low laugh. Then a voice I knew muttered, 'Come off it! Open the door for God's sake, it's me, Ross.'

I was only aware of the St Mandrake dressing-gown and Pa's striped pyjamas as I opened the door. No one expects eyebrows as well at midnight.

Ross hugged me, candle and all, while the guardians of my safety and honour shuffled back to the warm kitchen. The big camel overcoat was sodden with snow and his face was ice-cold. I set the candle down on the kitchen table and poured the last of the brandy. I hesitated about bringing forward the Glenfiddich. Loyalty dies fairly hard in extreme quarters.

'I waited all day at the airport because the flight was scheduled very late due to weather conditions. Then, because they cleared a runway and seemed uncertain which plane would get lucky, I booked in at the hotel and left messages. One or two flights came through but by four o'clock I'd had enough. I left more messages and started for home, only to run into the most awful pile-up on the motorway with a mile or two's tailback because of conditions.' A pile-up? Hetty? Pa? I squeaked for more information. 'Two great trailers, one skidded and overturned and the other hit it. No one hurt, just complete chaos.' I sighed with relief. 'Traffic was at a standstill both sides of the motorway – police cars, barriers, haulage, the lot. After moving at the rate of fifty yards an hour, I got my car to the side of the road just before your turn-off and decided to try and get up here and beg a few hours on a sofa till daylight. I didn't realise how blocked with snow it was going to be. It took ages.'

I hung his coat on one side of the Aga. Mattie grumbled a bit about it dripping on her but I hissed at her fiercely to show some sort of mild hospitality, so she snorted, turned round a few times and shot a small dry bone out towards us. I suppose it was the best she could do.

'Could I use the phone? Just a couple of calls,' Ross asked. He moved towards the dresser, neatly avoiding Rosie who was angling for a ginger snap. My own hospitality was pretty meagre, but mostly due to necessity.

'We don't have any connection at the moment. No electricity either. You don't think we're sitting by candlelight for romantic reasons, do you?'

He looked properly shocked. In towns they have tilly lamps, Citizen's Advice Bureaux and a Minister for whatever it is. I

189

added, 'You must be starving. Will it be tuna fish? tinned prunes? or some prawns in aspic left over from the jubilee?' Adding rashly, 'Anything you fancy!'

'I wouldn't deprive you. I had a splendid lunch and luckily I was taking back a box of cream cakes from the patisserie so I ate those in the car.' He might have saved just one for me. Suddenly, and for the first time since disaster hit us, tears rose to my eyes.

'I am rather tired,' he added. But wasn't I? And who had he been waiting for so diligently? and who was to be the recipient of the empty patisserie box? and who the hell was I to be the mug providing the sympathy? But I said, 'Of course. You can have Ben's room.' If he had anything else in mind, it was better put out of sight at once. 'I stripped the bed this morning but there's plenty of blankets and an eiderdown and a sleeping-bag, too, if you like.' He only wanted to sleep, I told myself, not hibernate until spring.

He said it sounded lovely. I led the way carrying the candle, and for the first time glad I couldn't have any more revealing light. The staircase was as frigid as a virgin mermaid. Teeth chattered in rhythm with my heart. I showed him the bathroom and we went together to get the blankets. Two luminous eyes peered from the depths of the airing-cupboard and made Ross take a step backwards, perilously near the top of the stairs. I grabbed his arm to avert instant death, and hastily reassured him. 'It's only General Hiatus, Em's damaged rabbit,' I said. 'Strays she brings in for home comforts until cured usually occupy the bottom shelf – there's been General Nuisance, General Chaos, General – sorry!' I almost winded him with my elbow as I retreated with arms full of bedding.

He said faintly, 'Is there anything I can do to help?'

He might have meant to restore sanity to the home, help towards installing central heating or advance my fare to escape from this primitive living, but I said there was nothing at all, thanks, and was not one wit astonished at my lying tongue. I left him holding the candle next to a pile of blankets on Ben's bed, and said goodnight.

Back in my own room, I threw two small logs on the fire and climbed back into the dark Gothic four-poster and drew the tatty velvet curtains. With the fur bedcover, and in the shadows, the scene could have been from a set of Garbo in 'Queen Christina'. I wished I had a sable wrap and thigh-high boots instead of the St Mandrake dressing-gown, but I daresay I was more comfortable the way I was. The puppy was shuffling about in its box, probably very hungry. I fed, tidied and comforted him and he got back close to the glove and fell asleep again. I was so tired I would have accepted a heart attack as a holiday. Under any other circumstances, this would have been a night to remember.

But outside the snow went on falling, so I put my face in the pillow and sobbed myself to sleep.

The alarm crashed through the still night at 2 a.m. and so did Ross. I heard him mutter a curse outside my bedroom door as he fell over a chair, and wondered if he was trying to make a quick getaway or find the christening spoon. I threw on my bathrobe which is less warm than the dressing-gown but looks more flattering for surprise appearances, and went out to the landing carrying my candle. Ross was crouched against the bannister rail, rubbing his leg. I hissed, 'Where are you going now?' I immediately wished I hadn't used the word 'now' because it sounded irritable.

He hissed back, 'Looking for the loo,' and added, 'Sorry I woke you: think I've twisted my knee.'

Well, that was all I needed. If he'd broken his leg, I'd simply emigrate at once, snow or no snow. I helped him up, finding it funny how romance rarely stands up to reality, especially when you've got a puppy in a drawer waiting for a midnight feast. The nearest room was mine, of course, and had the only fire still going, other than the kitchen. Somehow we managed to get there, like a couple staggering home after the pubs close, and I dropped him with relief in an armchair. The puppy was rattling about in the drawer like Larky Larrie. I knew my priorities and prepared the next feed at once. Ross watched in peeved astonishment as I fed the little thing, tidied him up and tucked him back. 'I never knew a woman like you,' he said, but it wasn't entirely a compliment.

Kip had allowed us past with a low growl of warning. Charlie came and sat next to me, alert and watchful. Edyth and Sue-Ellen slept on, but Pearl was true to her Pawley principles and I could hear her shuffling around under the eiderdown with embarrassment and disapproval. Or it might have been fleas, of course. I hoped her susceptibilities were more moral than physical.

It was quite a homely scene in the firelight: me feeding the Cuckoo and Ross massaging his knee. Ross glanced round. 'It's quite the most remarkable room I ever saw,' he admitted, choosing his words carefully.

'It's best by a very dim light,' I said, not much caring for the word 'remarkable' which, interpreted, means what you want it to

191

mean. My red woollen ski under-pants were clearly visible on a chair, knee-length long johns which, under jeans, were pretty cosy but, once revealed, looked pretty unromantic. I like to keep things where they're handy and it really puzzles me why we're supposed to hide even the most attractive things. I *like* to see the pure silk embroidered wrapper (Penrose High School Junk Jamboree in aid of heat for their pool the previous August) hanging by the door, together with six or seven others in designs such as Joan Crawford satin-tailored, down to pink rosebud cotton-dimity circa early Thirties, all of them treasured trophies from our Saturday afternoon circuits of village halls or scout huts. My huge patchwork bedcover and valance may have been drifting apart in places – a large square from great-grandmother's wedding dress having parted company from aunt Eleanor's widowing weeds – but it had a dozen generations of family history behind it. Everything in that room had a bit of history (local or personal) and deserved better than to be concealed. Even favourite scarves, furs, belts, night-dresses, shawls and underwear waited to please the eye of those few who might have entered, flung over an antique screen. But it occupied tonight's visitor and distracted his attention while I put the puppy back in the drawer and refilled brandy flask and fish-paste jar from the small red camping kettle heated on the open fire. Then I sat on the edge of the bed trying to decide what to do with Ross. If only I could have boxed and disposed of him as well, maybe I could have got some sleep.

'Would you like to stay here in the chair by the fire?' I finally suggested. I gave up wondering whether it was wise, moral, hospitable, silly or just plain convenient. I merely yearned for sleep. Contrary to current supposition, the body demands food or sleep way beyond anything else, and sexual gratification lingers a long way behind, like an optional extra on a Bentley. At that moment, it was the last thing I needed.

Ross didn't answer. I went across and began again. 'Ross,' I said, 'you can stay here by the fire if you like, instead of —' but he was already sound asleep. It gave the lie to the loo alibi.

I put some logs on the flames, and some coal to keep them going, and crept back into bed. I was asleep, too, the moment I got there. Two glorious hours before the next puppy feed. I began to dream of summer.

But it wasn't the alarm that woke me. It was Ross. He was standing by the bed when I opened my eyes, aware something was moving in the room, and it wasn't one of the dogs. Pearl, as usual, was scrabbling away under the eiderdown, but that was as much to be expected and ignored as the snow still falling outside. Neither was this an extension of the summer dream: when I sat up, the cold air reminded me of everything I'd have sooner forgotten.

'Is anything wrong?' I asked, through a yawn. 'Is it your knee?'

'I'm rather cold,' he said politely, like a weekend guest begging an extra blanket over breakfast, 'can I come in?' It came out in a shout as he caught the yawn and couldn't stifle it in time.

The reason for joining me was hardly the one I'd have chosen, though at that precise moment there wasn't any reason I *would* have wanted. It did gain sympathy, though. I muttered, 'Why not go back to Ben's bed?' but it merely sounded provocative. Coy, even. I added, 'Or make up the fire,' because it had burnt right through. I huddled in the striped pyjamas, my mind as thick as a boiled jumper, and tried to say what I was thinking without sounding bad-tempered or ill-mannered.

But he was already half way under the blankets. I moved over a bit. How could I tell him to go away when he'd made his reasons and need for warmth so clear? He was a pathetic sight, with the limp, the shiver and the sudden demolition of all status. I said, giggling a bit, 'You've still got your tie on,' because he was an Old Harrovian and very pleased about it.

Ross took it as a challenge. Within a few moments it was off, together with shirt and trousers. It was then, of course, I should have made it clear this was no invitation, merely a possible way of saving an injured man from frostbite, but I can now understand why Eskimos are supposed to offer their wives as a hospitality gesture to visiting travellers. It's all a part of compassion, like giving the best balloon to the kid who didn't win the raffle. But you don't expect them to demand an orange as well.

Luckily or not (as the mood takes you), the alarm went off at that minute, right in Ross's ear. He shot upright again and glanced nervously round. I went off him a bit. In fact, I was going off Ross rather a lot. Any really seasoned and devout Casanova would overlook such trifles, and though relieved to see him distracted from Casanova's usual pursuits, I would have welcomed a bit more savior faire. I struck a match to light the candle, watching at the same time for his next move, misjudged the wick and set fire to the lampshade fringe. I do believe Ross wondered for an instant if I was defending my honour with arson.

The lampshade got into the spirit of the occasion and began to flare. I knocked it on the floor, leapt out of bed and hit it madly with a pillow. The alarm continued to trill and Charlie growled but was too lazy to help me now. Most of the dogs were eager enough to leap to my defence during daylight hours, but sleep often took precedence, I noticed. I stamped on the last of the singed fringe in my Quicknit bedsocks (Vergers' Vacation Rummage) and the air filled with the scent of frizzled fabric. Though my feet were, obviously, now quite warm, the rest of me was rapidly icing over. Ross was clinging to the sheet and his piece of territory like a squatter in Park Lane. I had to choose between moral indignation in the armchair or my own rights to the bed and moral disintegration where I wanted to be. The disintegration might be a mere technicality, I reasoned, so I got back, fixed the candle in silence, took the puppy from the drawer and asked Ross to hold it while I prepared the feed.

It was hardly, of course, the role he had in mind, and men are notoriously sulky about anything which interrupts a display of masculine skill, or what they hope will be masculine skill. I'm not at all sure he was any more confident of achievement than I suspected. The pup took its food from a doll's feeding bottle now, managed a few slurps and a hiccup, and then had to be cleaned up before I could put him back in his box. I made a few jokey comments, but Ross said absolutely nothing. I expect it was a different outcome from the one he'd had in mind.

Once the Cuckoo was back in the drawer, I blew out the candle. I was so exhausted that my head felt like a very old satchel. To my annoyance, Ross put an arm round me and drew up close, as if parking two cars in one meter bay. I was far too tired to make a fuss and it seemed reasonable commonsense when we were both cold. I was almost asleep anyway. I'm quite clear about rights, wrongs and simple conventions. If someone attacked Frilly with a pitchfork, I'd have been a great deal more outraged than being told Pa had gone to bed with the barmaid. The first would be a Wrong: the second an Unwisdom. It's all a case of knowing your own priorities. Cruelty or injustice are a great deal more shocking than sharing a blanket, and if Ross meant to lead the situation to its routine conclusion, it might be an eventual Unwisdom, but not much more. And it would have gone according to plan if his elbow hadn't caught the Cuckoo's half-open drawer and shut it with a bang. Charlie leapt up barking, Kip growled, Lulu fell off the bed, and Edyth ran all over us . . . '

I showed my first real enthusiasm. 'Hold on! I shouted, giving Ross a push. On no account could I allow the puppy to risk

194

suffocation just to indulge a house guest. I noticed Sue-Ellen's halitosis as she rushed for comfort to my pillow.

It was probably Sue-Ellen's dental problem which put paid to any protest from Ross, because he shrank away rapidly and turned to face the windows. I, of course, whipped open the drawer, far too preoccupied to care what he was doing, and was horrified to find the puppy making spluttery noises. They could have been burps but to be on the safe side I snatched him up and waved him about in the air. The sheer surprise cured him at once. I peered into the bland face, so like the underside of a big toe, and he brought back a few drops of Ostermilk down Pa's pyjama jacket. By candlelight, I mopped us both up a bit, bedded the Cuckoo down and left the drawer wedged half open with a matchbox. Then I made up the fire, sprayed myself quickly with an aerosol talc and, by now wide awake and almost enthusiastic, hurried back to my lover.

He was sound asleep. I shone my torch to make sure, but he didn't move. He wore the look of a man who's had his bicycle stolen. I began to feel cheated, deprived, invaded and insulted. He was taking up most of the bed. Sue-Ellen had been pushed over so he could annexe my pillow. He had his mouth half open, like the drawer, and he breathed noisily. I edged on to an icy bit of sheet and fumed. I began to wish I'd never let him in my bed, my room, my house. Yet at each point, what else could I have done? You don't prefer death (even somebody else's) to dishonour any more. We had both lost some of our sense of humour, too, which was the only disaster so far because this would have been a very good time to use it, but I couldn't have raised so much as a smile at that moment to save my life.

I woke an hour later, aware of nudges in the small of my back. Not *now*, I thought wildly, aching with the urge to sleep on, but it wasn't Ross. He slumbered stolidly, almost obstinately, as well he might with most of the comfort and none of the interruptions. I turned, and found Pearl close behind me, licking and fussing. I tried to push her away but suddenly sleep deserted me. I lay for an instant, rigid with disbelief. Then I began to giggle: it was as much hysteria as genuine hilarity but once I started I couldn't stop. No wonder she had insisted on coming upstairs with me – a proper Pawley, bed was the place to have babies, and mine if no other was convenient. The bed and I shook with all the energy of a major earth tremor.

I laughed so much I was surprised Ross didn't wake. But it was just as well he remained oblivious of what was going on because I had grave suspicions that the bed could have been full of Pawley pug puppies. Finally I pulled myself together and slid carefully to the floor. It was a high mattress and I landed on Charlie: Charlie yelped, and struck out into the darkness to defend me, barking wildly. Kip rushed both of us, under certain misapprehensions about what was going on, and Edyth bit Lulu who jumped all over Ross. Ross turned over and murmured something romantic, probably thinking it was me.

'It's all right,' I whispered, mainly to myself as I lit the candle and hissed for hush elsewhere, wiping tears from my eyes, 'just a small interruption in our night of mad, passionate love . . . sleep on.' Obediently, Ross slept.

'Three,' I announced, bringing in a tray of tea. 'Two bitches and a dog.' Ross was still half asleep. I pulled open the curtains and let in the sunshine. The snow had stopped falling at last and the surfaces outside glittered like cut steel. Near the blazing log fire was Pearl's carton marked 'Mother's Pride' and she was dozing contentedly inside with her three ugly pugs. They looked to me, having spent the best part of the night searching the sheets with a torch, as beautiful as treasure trove. I put down the tray, opened the drawer, and took out the Cuckoo. I prepared the food and fixed the bottle and poured the tea.

'Suppose you broke a leg,' suggested Ross, leaning on one elbow, 'what would happen? I mean, who would cope? What would you do?'

'I'd sleep. Sugar?'

He shook his head. 'You never relax,' he complained.

'You should see me in the bath.'

'Nothing I'd like better.' We both laughed. It brought us back together again. Then there was a long amiable silence as I settled the puppy, half-closed the drawer and poured us both some more tea. Ross reached for my hand.

'Another time, another place, perhaps?' he said gently.

'Maybe. I'm sorry it all went wrong.'

'You're not.'

'We didn't stand a chance.' But he was right, of course. 'We were both tired, preoccupied, everything. Struggling to survive really.' The clock downstairs struck seven. I could see the drive from where I was: untouched, sugar icing on the cake before the birthday, trees standing like candles, sober reminders of time passing. I

196

said with a sigh, 'Breakfast in ten minutes,' because he had to get back to the airport.

For an instant he pulled me towards him, raising his eyebrows, asking, inviting, suggesting – but not for a moment did I imagine he meant it. In bed he looked a complete stranger, trappings fallen away and leaving him quite vulnerable. A man puts on more than a covering with his clothes. Each bit makes part of the armour women don't seem to need. I suddenly felt rather sorry for him, though I wasn't sure why. The loss of his demanding dignity, perhaps, and unfamiliar surroundings which left him helpless. I was like a dishcloth having the edge over an ancient manuscript, practicality superceding intellectualism or something. All I knew was that the moment provided the future with a different relationship – even a better one.

When he came down, I was able to give him bacon and eggs and toast and coffee because the electricity was back. The way out was just about navigable and tomorrow was another day: it might even have a delivery from Dennis in it. We sat at the kitchen table, anchored after the storm.

'That's an incredible bed you've got,' he said ruefully. 'Never slept better.'

I wished I could have said the same.

'A bit squeaky though,' he added, surprised. 'Never noticed it last night but when I got up this morning it did seem to protest a bit.'

I laughed. It must have been Pearl's puppies in their box. That bed hadn't squeaked for the last three hundred years. I was enjoying his bacon rind and crusts from the toast.

'Sounds as if the mattress is full of mice.'

I gave myself more coffee. 'Never noticed it myself.'

'As I went out of the door . . . ' but I'd stopped half way to the table, staring at him. He grinned. 'This bacon's ter-rific. Nothing here seems quite like it would be anywhere else. What is it?' But I had stopped listening. Boggle, boggle went my mind. Connie made a noise like a chair being pulled over the floor and then another like water rushing into the bowl, with splashes as a side-line. I said, 'Excuse me,' put down the cup and rushed up the stairs, two at a time.

I dragged off the eiderdown, sheets, blankets, pillows and lifted the mattress. The squeaking was faint now but I could still catch it from time to time as I worked. The puppy, very small, very flat and very flimsy, was carefully wedged between the mattress and the headboard on the ledge. It looked very, very poorly. It was so cold, I tucked it into the ever-ready bra and went back down-stairs. The vacuum flask was still bounteous and the eye-dropper lined up patiently on the draining board.

Neither of us needed to comment until I was dripping baby food and brandy with expert accuracy in the right direction. Then Ross said, 'It can't survive, surely?' He was getting ready to leave. He wanted to be at the airport when the first flights began to come in. I still had no idea who it was he felt it so important to meet and I wouldn't ask. Maybe because I didn't want to know: it might be a wife or a lover without a bed full of trouble. I think he had made up his mind to fall for a pigeon-fancier next time. At least they kept their nesting-boxes outside.

'Of course, it will,' I protested, hiding the doubts. The puppy kept opening its mouth very wide as if oxygen was going out of fashion. Its tiny helpless paws paddled feebly. I felt tears in my eyes and exhaustion halted any control. The poor, sad, discarded little thing – what had Pearl got against it, anyway? Or had she let it slip accidentally and couldn't get it back? Sensibly moved further down the bed to have the rest? Had we both been so tired we never felt her movements behind us at the pillow end of the bed? I made sure at least two or three drops stayed put and didn't escape from the weak jaws, and then put it purposefully back in my bra while I kissed Ross goodbye at the back door. It was, even now, a chaste clinch for the sake of my passenger.

'Don't cry, darling,' he whispered. 'Next time nothing, nothing at all, not even pugs and Danes will come between us.' We laughed together again, as he traced my tears with a fond finger, once more the masculine strength. Why point out the tears were for the puppy if they sent him away reinstated in his old image?

It was time to feed the Cuckoo again. In half an hour, the children would be down for breakfast. Responsibilities mounted round me. The dogs wanted to go out, the horses would have to be checked early and given a hot mash, the boilers done, the other fires started, the day – in short – faced again. Jumbling was a thing of the past, sleep a forgotten dream, and as for love affairs and romance, I could just remember these were for ladies of leisure and those of a non-enterprising disposition. I lay back for a moment in the rocker, one puppy in my bra and another about to go back in its box, weeping like a waterfall. None of it would ever have hap-pened to Hetty: but what *had* happened to Hetty? I could only suppose some terrible accident – and Ben? What had happened to Ben, too? And Pa? If Ross could get here, surely Pa could have tried? Was he involved in some lonely snowdrift or some appalling pile-up? The Cuckoo was shifting about, looking for something: maybe he needed the same closeness, reassurance and security I, too, had lost. I picked him up from the box and stuffed him inside the spare side of my bra. Then I leant back and began to laugh.

I was still laughing and wiping tears from my eyes when Adam came in. He said, 'The electricity's back.' I waved a hand airily at the bacon and coffee-pot. 'You've had a good breakfast,' he said, glancing at the plates and pots, 'sleep well?'

'So-so,' I lied, and told him about Pearl. I shared some more toast and coffee and remembered I had to ring Mesdames Bolsover, Pawley and Green. Self-pity vanishes with company and the smells of breakfast which probably raise more hope and delight than all the perfumes of Arabia. I placed the Cuckoo back in his box and put the Pawley puppy in with Pearl. Suddenly, I felt anything could be made to happen so I went in, spoke to her rather firmly, and pushed the little thing between the others. Pearl looked a bit indignant at first but I perservered in a commanding tone, so she sniffed it once or twice, obviously disapproving of the brandy fumes because she boxed its ears and then slapped it bossily up and down the carton before nosing it back in with the rest again.

'But why down the back of the bed?' asked Emily, a bit later when she joined us.

'It was very small and weak. I daresay she thought it better disposed of early. Or perhaps she was going to stack them all down there out of the way and I caught up with her too soon. Remember how she chose the cupboard under the stairs first?'

Adam was looking out of the kitchen window. 'I can see foot-steps from the back door to the lane!' He turned and faced me, his eyebrows raised.

'I went out to get logs.' (Had Ross managed to reach the airport? Start his car? Meet his friend? And would he ever get in touch with me again? Most of all, did I really care any more?) I added, 'Try the phone and see if it's working yet.' But it wasn't.

At midday, Humphrey turned up, nobly walking the last half mile to bring us a catalogue for thermal winter underwear with a six-week delivery date. He came in and accepted some hot black-currant juice. 'You've 'ad a h'intruder,' he announced smugly.

'Really?' It was those footmarks again.

'Funny you never 'eard 'im. Was you sleepin' sound like?' His able eye pierced me like a skewer. The plastic one had shifted a little to the south-east and looked a bit sulky.

'Oh, yes, very,' I lied.

'Ireen's 'Ogsbreath, most likely.'

'Well, no: unfortunately, I don't have any, but I manage quite well by just closing my eyes. It's an old family method. We can all do it.'

'Footprints down the back yard.'

'She went to get wood,' volunteered Adam.

'But these don't come back!' Everyone turned and looked at me.

'Then it couldn't have been an intruder,' I declared triumphantly, 'the prints were all going the wrong way!' Luckily Atilla chose that moment to demonstrate her resentment of Connie's constant sneers; she flew down and stalked all over Emily's Pumpkin Pamplemousse. Emily let out a scream of anguish and Atilla flew on to the rim of Humphrey's glass and clucked in disapproval at the chaos.

'If you want 'er neck rung, I'll be 'appy to oblige,' growled Humphrey.

'Thank you, but no. She's one of us, is Atilla,' though barmy to boot: and hadn't she been with us through our time of strife?

'Black Magic, them 'ens. Devil's daughters.'

'Not Atilla,' I said firmly, putting her back on the top of the cupboard. I wrote out a list of groceries for Dennis and asked Humphrey to take it down for me. I added, 'Soonest snow permits, please. Love in exile, and kisses postponed.' Then I did a note for Hosanna. 'Snowed in: no phone. Please tell Pawleys, Pearl's pupped (4, all OK). Pray for heatwave by Saturday.' There were two jumbles on Saturday, one of which (the annual Floralweaving Club's Trash'n Treasure) had provided me last year with a Hell's Angel black leather jacket, studded 'HITCH BITCH' on the back, so it wasn't to be missed.

The snow was quickly slipping away, like an embarrassed guest who dropped the tray, leaving everything wet and dripping. Patches of gravel gradually reappeared in the driveway; floods threatened in other parts of the country. Now the reservoir could be seen again, full to overflowing. The motorway revealed a panic of cars escaping hostage held by the elements.

Pearl had accepted her problem pup, but it was still half the size of the others and had to be watched. It kept falling over backwards, lying helpless, the tiny toes waving in the air like an upturned turtle. I kept on running to put it back myself and coming away wondering if it was already feebly signalling for help, and that worried me all the time – but it was nice to have my bra back.

The day passed without any threats and when Humphrey returned at teatime, I was singing 'Strangers In The Night' with a strong undercurrent of meaning just to taunt him a bit about the footmarks. He brought all my groceries from the shop, together with a note on pink paper with roses round the printed heading. It read, 'Darling, nil desperandum and Well Done! We were sending a helicopter anyway. Have a drinkee with us. Love and kisses from your Friendly Neighbourhood Stores.' There was a bottle of Beaujolais sticking out between the loo rolls and the Vim, and not a mention of it on the bill.

Hosanna's return note read, '*Inundated* with raincoats already. Fancy a Coxswain's Cape? or do you prefer pink plastic? Nothing Priddle so far. Have booked at Betty's for Saturday week at minimal outlay (Harry).'

It was nice to get back to normal.

# 16

'I don't think I've got it yet,' said Hosanna gloomily. It was Friday.

'I don't think I've got it after all,' said Pa. (The phone was working again.)

'I don't think *I've* got it, Emily,' said Adam, searching through the kitchen drawers for Ben's dreadful book of animal fax. I didn't let on that it was hidden under a saucepan out of sight.

We sat at the table in the kitchen eating cold pheasant, drinking wine and looking forward to sherry trifle. A bottle of champagne waited in the cellar for later in the week and there was another in the fridge. Mrs Bolsover had turned up with a chicken and the trifle. 'Demzy just loves rich creamy things,' she confided, 'so I've bought a box of éclairs, too. They're her favourites. I made the trifle myself and it's loaded with Madeira. I do think that's nicest, don't you? I'm so grateful for all you've done.' She had placed a fond kiss on my cheek.

Phyllis's spare puppy, nursed by Demelza, had been explained over the phone to avoid shock. Mrs Bolsover said she was proud and glad the little darling had so generously adopted a foster-baby. She was boasting to everyone at her Kitchen Club. I was a bit afraid Mr Bolsover would strongly object to getting a non-fee-paying interloper on his final account, but it appeared he, too, was going round swanking about the Great Dane who couldn't manage what his rare Scottish Shag had had to take on instead.

Killarney Green sent the champagne. She also ordered a steak a day for Phyllis, the way Interflora dispatch flowers.

The Pawleys had been up to see Pearl. 'Proper' Pawley had been carefully tended by her anxious husband (known as 'Rather' – the father). He helped her from the car and she made her way into our kitchen holding a Hermes scarf over her face so she wouldn't risk breathing our foul air, I suppose. 'Flu,' Rather whispered confidentially. It might have been a social disease of appalling origin the way his voice dropped. 'Temperature rose three points last night – wavering this morning.' I fully expected 'outlook unsettled' but he concluded with pride, 'Brave little woman insisted on coming out, though.'

Not that Pearl appreciated the visit. She looked positively apprehensive. It might have been uneasiness at her condition being finally accepted, or the fact that the puppies had a distinct hint of ginger Pom, but she hastily pushed forward the smallest to gain instant sympathy and it worked. Proper Pawley got down on her knees, putting aside 'flu' and Pearl's moral downfall, and tenderly touched the sleek, warm coat. When she got up, there were tears in her eyes and she announced briskly that she would be keeping that one. She left the Hermes scarf on a chair when she went, and she snapped at her husband when he mentioned his sinus trouble. She even said she would like to take them all home just as soon as I thought advisable. She would enjoy caring for them herself. And next day there was dover sole, best mince, and a home-made and pink-iced walnut cake delivered in Humphrey's Extras.

Hetty had arrived back contrite but triumphant. She swanned in with the thaw around teatime. There was a hamper in the car from Fortnum's. It revealed the pheasant and salad, fruit and cream, gateaux and chocolates, fondants and sherry and a white wine full of summertime. We all stared at her, because she was laughing and glowing and glittering and happier than for ages.

Apprehension made me a bit sharp. 'Well,' I said, 'Hullo and Welcome. I thought you'd deserted the snowbound ship.'

'Darling,' she said, 'I've brought you some goodies. Would I ever let you down on purpose? It must have been hell here, cut off from civilisation all that time. Ben and I were horrified, mortified when we spoke together on the phone an hour or so ago, after I got back and found how bad it had been here. All the time we were away, we kept thinking about you in utter horror as we listened to the news or read the papers.' She sat down and stretched out her long legs. She wore new black boots and a huge Burberry which had been lined with a soft sable imitation. I had once tried to line an old raincoat with an even older musquash and the result made me look like a pregnant wheelbarrow.

'We survived,' I claimed proudly, 'though we had our moments.' I went for kettle and mugs.

Adam said, 'Hey, fondants – can we open the box?'

'Well, you're not keeping the lot for the next snow-in, are you?' said Hetty. 'Open anything, eat everything now if you like. I'll opt for a drink. No, darling, *not* coffee. Get the glasses – oh, *any* glasses,' as I dived about hunting up the right kind, 'and we'll both tell *all*.' I knew she was dying to start. She threw back her coat and swept Frilly off the rocker, instantly taking her place. Frilly glowered for an instant then got her own back by leaping on her lap. I found ginger ale for Adam and Emily; the fondants left the box in rapid succession.

Hetty leant forward and said eagerly, after we had toasted one another and ourselves, 'Shall I begin then?' and didn't wait for an answer. 'Well, the drive up to London was fine. We had coffee on the way and lunch at Barbie's off the Mile End Road. It's well worth a slight detour. The underworld meet there to eat, you know, and the rest of us go there to peer. Ben adored it all – lots of Thirties Fedoras and chalk stripe suits with dark shirts and white ties. Very Humphrey Bogart. I'm sure they're really all out of work, bit-part players getting free meals in exchange for atmosphere, but it's better than the West End or Chelsea. We thought we'd spend the afternoon shopping. Ben wanted to get himself a few things before he went back to school.' She laughed. My God, I thought, Charvet ties? Silk shirts? an Asprey watch? 'He'd left behind a certain book for Adam and was beginning to regret it, you see.'

'I regretted it too,' I said, shooting a baleful look at the saucepan.

'None of the shops had it. We were all afternoon trying to track it down and then we were advised to try a tatty little place off the Charing Cross Road. It was there, all right. Ben was delighted. We went for tea at the Charing Cross Hotel. It's so dignified there, darling, I always feel like a duchess. And we thought we'd book seats for a theatre.'

'But what about his mother? She was expecting him home.'

'Well, yes, that was it. Such a naughty boy. He said if we rang her, she would demand he came home right away, so we ought to book first. We were lucky to get two returned seats for "Bombay" (you know, the sexier sequel to "Calcutta") which he said all the boys in his year wanted to see' (so much for being into nuclear physics this term!) 'when we found the precious paperback was missing. We had to scoot back to the hotel and there it was, still at the same table but being avidly read by this absurdly gorgeous man.'

'An elephant's penis is five foot long, blue whales even longer. But fleas —'

'What's that?' asked Hetty, diverted for an instant.

'It's all in the book. It's animal facts,' said Adam.

'Dairy produce?'

'Facts, not fats. Its about things like —'

'Go on,' I interrupted, addressing Hetty and frowning at Adam.

'Ben's always keen to learn, I'll say that for him,' approved Hetty. I wondered just what she'd been teaching him: but she went on, 'Ben went up to the man and explained and asked him if he'd got to the bit about cobras, and the man said how about mating giraffes? and they both got going on the lenses in flies' eyes or something. Did you know they have —'

'I know everything I don't care to know about every animal in the world. If I knew half as much about those under my own roof, I'd be really laughing!'

'I just wasn't all that intrigued, except by this devastating man. So I had to interrupt and suggest Ben got us a cab because it was the rush hour, and Igor – that's this heavenly man's name – said he would be delighted to lend us his Porsche if we would allow him to act as chauffeur, and there it was, would you believe, bang outside on a double yellow line with CD plates discreetly revealed.'

'So?'

'We took Ben home. After all, it was only fair on his mother and he had all his gear to park. His mother's quite a sweetie but terribly possessive, you know.' (I did. I had told Hetty this quite often.) 'She was all tearful when Ben said we were going to a theatre. Apparently she had this special meal ready and was planning a quiet evening round the fireside for chatting. Just the two of them. So negative, I thought. I handed over the theatre tickets with my blessing and took my leave.' She paused for applause.

'I'd just like to know what she thought of "Bombay"!'

'Well, duckie, I was a wee bit disappointed to give up my evening treat, but there! Youth must be served, as they say, though I'm never sure quite what that means. But then I'm just a country Vet. Igor was so sympathetic, and most impressed at my generosity so he suggested we should dine together. We had a simply fantastic evening ending up in a club behind Wiggers Street, of all places, very Cosmopolitan (in the glossy sense, of course) and we didn't get to bed till after four.'

'Where?' I asked rudely, but it was only too obvious and no affair of mine.

Hetty ignored me completely. 'Then, of course, the snow began and it wouldn't stop and lines came down (telephone ones) and others got blocked (train type) and I had to stay where I was. I knew they'd be OK at the surgery. Toenails and tonsils wait surprisingly easily when the weather's bad.'

'And Igor?' I poured more sherry. I was thinking that my own

205

story would have compared much as Benny Hill would to Hamlet.

'He's coming down at the weekend. He wants to buy a farm round here. I'm going to look at a few with him, act as adviser.' The whole of south-east England was going to be populated by Hetty's lovers, farming away like crazy.

'So how about you?' she asked, suddenly feigning interest.

'Us? Oh, nothing much happened *here*. Well, nothing quite like that. Nothing romantic, exciting, unexpected or worth talking about. I mean, literally nothing. The phone went off, the electricity went off. We almost ran out of food, we had no heating to speak of and nobody could reach us. Demelza had four puppies, Pearl had four (she buried one alive under the mattress) and Phyllida had thirteen but two died. She's managing nine quite nicely. A tenth is with Demelza and I've got Lucky Eleven in my bra. The Finch twins came over, got stranded, went home boozed up on rum and cocoa and we found over £100 in old notes in my jumble aggi boots.'

I stopped short. There was a silence. Then Hetty said, 'It was, in fact, usual run of the mill stuff and dead boring?' and we all laughed.

Adam said, 'And we had an extruder.'

'A what?'

'Some mysterious stranger who left here without actually arriving.' I suddenly wondered if he knew more than he was admitting. I dared not look towards him.

Hetty said, 'Why was Pearl in your bed that night?'

I said lightly, 'Well, you know how it is: everyone shares my bed at one time or another.' Never would I admit that Ross, too, had been there, or the outcome.

Hetty was really nice about my success.

She rewarded me with a promise to bring along a pregnant Bassett Hound called Fiona, as well as a furious Poodle who was rebelling against motherhood and who would need sensitive handling. She was quite witty, too. We need to be very happy in order to dig out the best in us and under all her brains and efficiency Hetty was really quite a lonely lady. So I was glad about Igor. I hoped he would stay around for ages.

Adam was due to go back home and get ready for school. Because of the bad weather, term had been put back a few days, but even so he was reluctant to say goodbye. I always felt especially close to Adam: I admired his independence and his pride and his reserve and I did wish I could make Emily care a bit more about him and hanker a bit less after Ben.

I decided to give Adam the ship-in-a-bottle which my grandfather had made and which Adam had always liked so much. He was mad about the sea. I took it to his bedroom just before he was due to leave and found him standing by the window with Emily. I stopped short and, being unobserved, went hastily into reverse. He was holding Emily's hands and I could see they were back to their old early relaxed relationship again. I went downstairs and waited until he was about to get into the taxi before giving him the present. He thanked me, but I was glad he was really looking at Emily.

The two of us ate gloomily at the kitchen table when he'd gone. I was still wondering why Pa hadn't got 'it' and where we should be this time next year. 'I do wish he'd ring again,' I said fretfully. 'He just said he didn't think he had it after all and he sounded absolutely shattered. I wish now he could have it. I don't want it myself but I want it for him more than I ever wanted anything in my whole life.'

'Maybe he's on his way back.'

'He said he had to see someone about something else first.'

'He makes it all sound very mysterious. I wish he'd stay on here.'

'Emily darling, wherever we go, you'll come too, of course. And Adam, and Ben for holidays.'

'Mummy wants me to go to boarding school.'

I looked surprised. I had no idea she'd been told.

'There were some brochures around at home about places abroad as well as in England.' Is this what had made her edgy lately? Emily had always been so happy at the village school and done so well.

I said gently, 'I know. But nobody's going to insist; they would talk to you about it first.' She shrugged, so I added, 'They just think it might be best for you.'

'For me? Or for them?' I could see she was going to put up some resistance. I wondered whose side I would be on: whether I was secretly glad she would fight to stay. The idea was just as sad for me, too, but deep down and beyond wanting to keep her, I also realised it would probably have to happen sooner or later.

To my surprise, she said, 'I guess they're right. I'll be here until the end of the summer term anyway, and then I could stay here through the summer holidays with Ben and Adam and go home leaving enough time to get ready for the new school.' I was amazed that she must have been thinking it all through like that.

'There'll be half-term holidays: you'll all be here at the same time always.'

She laughed. 'That's what Adam said. You see, I told him how worried about it I was when he came this time. I was determined then not to co-operate and that's what we quarrelled about. He said I was being selfish and silly and failing to grow up. It infuriated me. But of course he was right.' She sounded resigned but contented, too. 'Nothing lasts for ever.'

Neither of us spoke. She said finally, almost to herself, 'I'll be here when he's here and that's what matters.'

Did she mean Adam or Ben? And what about me? It wasn't very flattering but it was what I wanted to hear, just the same.

'We're in with Knickers up to our knees,' said Pa gloomily over the phone. I couldn't think of any comment that wasn't downright flippant. 'She's holding us to the sale now. All we can do is stall the date of possession.'

'Like Christmas in the year 2000?'

'You were right about a bungalow being inadequate, of course.'

I couldn't think of a comment that wasn't exasperated.

'There'll only be us, though, now,' I said mournfully, 'and the dogs, of course.'

He caught the note of wistful regret and said he'd be home as soon as possible, but that wasn't what I wanted. I liked him being busy and crazy and chasing his own rainbows. I wanted to eliminate the past year altogether, so we could live it again. Nothing lasts for ever, OK?

Hetty had taken Edyth, ringing me later to check that I had realised she was coming into season and had of course, taken the necessary precautions, hadn't I? Remembering the close and courteous attentions I'd so admired from Charlie and Kip, and some possibly more blatant ones, too, all of which Edyth had obviously appreciated, I merely muttttered in reply. It was far too late now to do anything about it and why should I try and do myself out of another customer in nine weeks' time?

I told Pa and it gave him something to laugh about. Trust a vet, he said. Honestly, talk about the cobbler's children! I didn't point out that for a professional speculator, he wasn't doing too well either.

'I've been thinking,' he said, 'and now you've rather confirmed it's a good idea – why not open a dogs' brothel? I mean, it's only a step from what you're doing now!'

208

'A retrograde step,' I cried. 'It would ruin trade here for me.'

'Easier though. Make a fortune, and you'd be a smashing Madame.'

I told Hosanna when she dropped by. We sat over the last of the Caraway Cocktail Ireen had sent us at Christmas which appeared to be the final alcoholic support left in the house.

'But why did he pick on kennels there when you've got kennels here?' she asked when we'd exhausted all the possibilities of dogs' brothels and cat-houses.

'Dirt cheap, he said.'

'And so it should be,' said Hosanna, 'it always is. But what did they want for the rest of it?' She added that she'd found a love letter in the pocket of one of the raincoats. It was from Stan at the garage to Betty at the Dun Cow, and she'd shown it to Harry. Had she, did I think, done the right thing? I asked about his reaction and she said, 'Thoughtful. Bang to rights goes his vanity and he's gone off beer a bit.' So we decided it was a stroke of fate. There had been 3p in another pocket, a plastic pixie hood in a third and an unused bus ticket to Parsley Mow in a fourth. There were also raffle tickets and a hair-net, two shopping lists and a lipstick to boot. She thought we might, in time, do as well out of pockets as we would out of jumble.

She read me the shopping lists because I've always been interested in the study of other people's requirements which differ so much from my own and account for those strange articles you see in other people's shopping trolleys. In fact, I used to collect shopping lists. I pasted them in an album and they became quite an absorbing study. More interesting than picture postcards or even old photographs: a great deal more revealing than autographs. Rather like a diary or family tree. 'Mum's Rolls' could have been of royal origin, and 'New balls for Harold' indicated a quick call at the human spare part surplus stores. 'Weedkiller for Mrs T' spoke volumes, and 'Enquire about old Women for sale' had a touch of the Sweeney Todds. People care little about accuracy in making their lists over the toast at breakfast. 'Back Numbers available' is a phrase they might use in the newsagent's but the actual translation from what they have in mind starts there. Shopping lists as a psychological study are completely neglected, yet they're full of clues to character, tendencies and hang-ups.

Hosanna said Posy Pink had been fantastic, an enormous help and real morale booster. Between them, she reckoned the Scrummage would be an all-time success. She said Posy had the small blue teapot she needed to go with her breakfast china and Hosanna herself would be hanging new curtains ('inside out, Petal; I'm not having Lady Thrake recognise her cast-offs when she drives past to church') and already had 2 cms. off her thighs from an old discarded exercise bike handed over by Stan at the garage. I pointed out it had done little to move any of his sixteen stone, but she waived that as irrelevant. Stan was another of Betty's admirers and spent much of his time making excuses to customers for the delay caused by leaning over the Public Bar and leering at her cleavage.

Emily was back at school. She left home at eight-thirty and was in by four, but the day was echoing empty. There was plenty to do, of course, but doing can't replace sharing. I began listening to the radio again, glancing at the TV screen, reading the news-papers. Rain had swept the country in the wake of snow, leaving floods. Bubbles and Jody drooped near the trees and hedges, bowed by the elements. I longed to fetch them in to the Aga with the rest of us, but they even rejected the strawed-down shelter, preferring martyrdom.

Eating toast and marmalade and balancing the local paper between me and the teapot, I saw on an inner page, the photo-graph of Jake. The eyes I remembered so well gazed back at me under the heading, 'Wanted for Fraud', and underneath I read that Jake Edwards, aged twenty-three and out on bail, had gone missing. He was under instructions to report regularly but nothing had been heard from him for the past two weeks. It added that he had no known relatives and anyone with information should call a number, presumably the police, which was given in the caption.

I stared at it for some time, going very still, even in my mind. It explained so many things, there was no need to think. I looked round for Kip, as if he should be told, but there was no sign of him. I went out to the hall, but he wasn't there. I made a systematic tour of the rooms, calling all the time, my fear growing. I grabbed a coat and ran outside, my voice rising in panic, but I knew it was useless. Kip had followed the instinct to find his master, and gone.

I had to do something, look somewhere, however hopeless. Out there, in that dreadful weather, together or still apart, they would be needing shelter and warmth, sympathy and love. The ground was heavy with mud, and a steady downpour pushed by great gusts of icy wind was doing its best to turn the house into an island, I struggled through to the stables and garage, sheds and out-buildings. At last, no place left to search, I stood in despair and gazed through the pouring rain down towards the reservoir and knew, at once, where I had to go.

I only hesitated a moment, then I began the steep climb down over the fields. On a summer day, hampered by nothing more than buttercups and daisies, the descent was easy, but now every discouragement winter could find was being thrown at me. Cold cut my face, rain penetrated the bottom of my sleeves, wormed its way into my turned-up collar, seeped uneasily into my boots. The ground was sodden and I was sucked in at every step, only to slip and slide as I struggled painfully to get free. Several times I stopped, almost forced to give up, but something stronger than my own survival drove me on. Gasping, shaking and fighting with every breath I took, I finally reached the small footpath leading to the locked iron gates in the high linked-wire fence. My eyes stung with tears of self-pity and despair and were blinded from time to time by sudden wild squalls which took my breath away.

I leant against the gates shivering, soaked and sick at heart. What, after all, if Kip had gone to the motorway instead? I was only following an intuition, nothing concrete. No hint or clue of any kind. Why head for the water, that stretch of sinister steel which, from a distance and under other circumstances, could look so deceptively gentle? And even now Kip might be waiting by the back door, aching to be let in.

But I only knew I had to go on. I forgot the bitches and their puppies left behind me; Emily due home from school at lunchtime; the over-active telephone, the keys I'd forgotten to turn and Pa's precious christening spoon. I forgot the Edwardian kennels ahead and Beowulf's Friends close on our heels. I forgot trivia that would eventually right itself in favour of an urgency I couldn't ignore.

It was painful and laborious, climbing the gate in mud-covered boots. They slipped where they should have gripped and I caught my coat on the jagged edges, leaving a long tear and a cut on my leg. Once over, I felt I could cope with whatever else was left as a challenge. I tried to recall where and when I had last seen Kip, but he was such an unobtrusive, single-minded dog that it was too easy to take him for granted.

The reservoir was bursting its banks and I had to edge my way carefully round the water to save slipping in. Wind whipped my freezing face and at close quarters the whole place loomed dark and threatening. Why had I ever thought it beautiful? Close to, ripples became tidal and sinister forces took over. A strange, still soundlessness brooded behind the noise of rain and wind.

At one point along the bank, trees gathered close to shelter a small hut used by workmen on regular visits. It was little more than a lean-to, but it was there I found Kip, soaked through and through, shaggy head resting on soggy paws. The long thick fringe had become bedraggled and matted, and the brown eyes were sick with despair. He let me kneel down in the mud and rest my tired head on his while I tried to find comforting words because, near him, drenched and dirty but neatly folded, was his master's jacket.

I stayed with him there a long, long time, oblivious of the weather now I had to face a greater disaster. After a while, Kip seemed to become aware of me, aware of my sobs and weariness, because he turned slowly and licked my face. Then he appeared to take matters in hand. Stiffly and awkwardly, he staggered to his feet, shook once or twice and then slowly went over and took one last, long look at all that remained of all that mattered to him. His head was held low and his tail dragged in the mud. And when he came back to me, he stayed standing waiting for me to move as well.

So it was Kip who took *me* home. It was Kip now determined to look after someone foolish enough to crouch there, suffering the worst of all weathers, but someone he recognised as caring for his master as he had. I think it was at that moment he adopted the new allegiance which was to last the rest of his life.

Gently he urged me to follow him back to the gate, watched patiently while I clumsily struggled over it, and then slipped easily throught the narrow rails himself. He was so thin, thinner even than he had been when I first saw him, and I wondered how long he had been there and when his master had waded out into the deep water and how Kip had known and a hundred other things which would always remain unanswered. It took us a long time to get back to the house, each preoccupied with our own thoughts. Had I fallen a little in love with the tragic young man who came into my life, strayed into my heart, stayed on in my mind, only to leave again silently, sadly and for ever? Otherwise, why was I caring so much? As for Kip, his concentration was now on getting me home safely and when we reached the welcome of the kitchen and the warmth of the Aga and I was able to rub him down and persuade him to have some warm milk with a dash of brandy, I took the opportunity to trim the draggled fringe over his eyes. I knew he accepted it all to please me rather than for any personal reasons. Only food was apologetically rejected.

The rest of the day dragged by heavily. The other dogs held back, curious but understanding this was a time for withdrawal and silence. Funny about Kip's eyes, I thought, as they followed me about the kitchen. They were suddenly different. Not just because they had been hidden so long and were now revealed, but they seemed lighter, clearer, more intent than before when I'd parted the fringe to find them. The fringe, I told myself, would grow again, of course it would. But as I rocked in the rocking-chair I hoped it wouldn't – and oddly enough, it never did. But Kip's eyes changed; they grew softer, less tormented. It only dawned on me days later that the eyes watching me, sometimes smiling, always expressive, were the eyes of Jake himself and that his were the eyes which would always be following me.

The police had to be told. They dragged the reservoir, but we kept well back from the windows. Not that Kip would have cared – any more than I did. We both knew his master wasn't there. He was a part of Kip – and Kip and I would belong together from now on, for always.

# 17

Hetty resumed her role of bossperson after spending the previous weekend with Igor. 'Now,' she demanded when she next came to check the puppies, 'what's new?'

'Nothing much,' I said, 'only a card from Ben.' She didn't comment and I wondered if she, too, had had one. I took mine off the dresser and passed it to her to read. Behind a picture of Buckingham Palace luridly floodlit, Ben had written: 'Hope you all survived snow. Wish I'd been there. Love Ben. PS Take care – a woman called Gladys Piggott in Diss had a heart attack when a thirsty mole popped out of her sink waste: I'd stop washing up if I were you!'

Hetty handed it back without comment. She wore a small secret smile which had nothing to do with the card at all. I suddenly guessed she'd had a letter and scored over me yet again.

'I've got a book for him,' she said softly. '*Animal Relationships*. I think he'll like it.' Her voice changed to her usual teasing tone. 'Courtship and mating, that sort of thing.'

I guessed she was trying to get my reaction so I said enthusiastically, 'just what he needs, dear, a lad of his age. Guidance from a mature woman of experience.'

So she asked about Demelza.

'The Bolsovers want me to keep the puppies till they're ready to be delivered to new homes. Mr B doesn't really want them to run amok among the Cyril Lord and the Conran. Funnily enough, he's almost as potty about them as she is. He agreed at once when she said she wanted to keep one herself. As for the foster-baby, he's gone around boasting about the Great Dane in the basket and how his Haggis Hound or whatever it is, keeps it in order. And they're not asking £50 apiece after all. They're *giving* the puppies to close friends on certain conditions, such as being allowed reasonable access at all times. It was Mr B's idea. He says they've got a duty . . .'

'Wow! Don't people change. Killarney G wants you to sell her First Eleven (that's what she calls them – didn't know she could be funny). Of course they're crossbreds (I bet Mr B didn't know that: a bastard among his babies would be unthinkable!) but they should go rather well. I've a lot of clients who need large impressive-looking creatures.'

'Such as Igor?' Nobody was more impressive-looking than Hetty.

'Actually yes, for one. He's making an offer for a farm here and putting in a manager. Managers need good guard dogs. I've a cheque for you from Killarney for the full fees and she wants you to keep the proceeds of sale. She says if you like, she'll organise an ad. in *The Stage*. That way she can vet some of the buyers and keep in touch afterwards.'

Shows how you can misjudge people, especially singing jiggers. A fortnight ago I'd have been amazed, but people, as Hetty said, change under altered circumstances. Or are we all soft as butter when we're under the grill? Killarney had sent all kinds of things for Phyllida but only two words, 'Miss you'. They spoke more volumes than all the Bolsover babble.

'And Pearlie-girl?' Hetty asked,

'Biggest surprise of the lot. She and the litter go home on Sunday. The Pawleys are transferring their hypochondria to ante-natal care, I think. Anyway, Mrs P's flu has flown. They're longing to dose and fuss and kill them with kindness. They keep on ringing up to warn me about sterilising dishes and administering a good opening medicine regularly, and their eyes aren't opening yet. Did you know Pretty's leaving home?'

'That'll mean evening classes again for the local layabouts.'

'She's got a job as a belly dancer in Kennington.'

'And the parents agree to it?'

'They thought she said a ballet dancer in Kensington.'

Hetty asked again about Edyth. I said I'd watched her very closely. I didn't say what I'd seen. Sometimes I like to feel I've put one over on her.

'That's OK then. Can you manage without me for a couple of days?'

I closed my eyes in exasperation. 'I'll try,' I said sarcastically. Hadn't I managed a lifetime of drama without her?

'Fine. Terrific. Only I'm going to town on unfinished business.'

Ben? I didn't even ask. I didn't even *care*.

'Is Pa home?' she added, after the short pause.

'Been – and gone. He'll be back in a day or two. I'm alone at the moment.' I was suddenly back with the old wish for somewhere else to be.

'Of course,' said Hetty, 'I'd forgotten. Emily's gone for the new school interviews, hasn't she? I'll stay overnight if you like. Or I could ask Wen and Bun. Maybe Hosanna or Posie or . . .'

'Or?'

'Where's Ross Washington these days? I'm sure he'd be happy to keep you company any time.' We laughed, but mine was a bit hollow.

'It's OK,' I said, 'I'll be fine. I love being on my own. It's such a change, such a relief. It's like a holiday. Marvellous . . .'

And I was only lying a little bit.

Atilla had moved into Connie's cage. Connie had moved out after taking offence at Tilla's clucking and occasional forays round the room, sometimes landing back right over Connie's beak on the brass ring of her roof. Connie, after years of persuasion sternly ignored, had made up her mind a bit late in life like a spinster to seduction, and taken refuge on the handle of the portable TV. She refused to be budged.

It was very inconvenient because her food and water cups had to be balanced at either end, and Anna Ford was likely to get a peanut shell on the nose during the News. Tilla strutted in and out of the cage like a squatter sure of her rights. Frilly was now in residence on top of the cupboard where Atilla had been. It was like musical chairs.

I was quite relieved when Marsha rang. It made things more normal.

'Dear Friend,' she began dramatically as if writing a begging letter, 'such ages it's been, but things here have been quite fraught.' She often talks as if it's written down in front of her.

'Oh dear,' I said.

'The weather. My dear, you wouldn't believe! London was besieged, but *besieged*. Snow. We had snow. I never saw such snow. Do you know I've lived, but *lived* in my Russian boots? Very sensual things and quite splendid with my new wolfskin cape.' (Social Security gone up again? or alimony paid at last?) 'This sweet man, Igor, insisted I had his when my little blue sandals failed me in Kensington High Street.' Marsha takes a size 7 as I know to the cost of my borrowed brogues.

'Sandals in snow do sound a bit strange,' I muttered.

'Have you seen the price of leather boots in Harrods?' she demanded piteously.

'No, but I know how much wellies are in Woolworths.'

Marsha ignored cracks like that. I wondered if her Igor was the same as Hetty's. I'm sure there were lots of Igors in London, but were they all the boot-bearing kind? And hadn't Hetty worn new ones when she came back?

'Very dashing. Fur-topped, lined and thigh-high. Cut a splendid dash in Frognal.' She was positively purring.

I wondered if Russians had fringe religions. 'What's his angle then?' I asked suspiciously.

'Angle, darling? Angle? I don't understand. He's very strong on Levellism, of course, but aren't we all? One world, one people, one level. It's very elevating.' Surely a contradiction somewhere? 'You and I and our friends on the football terraces and the criminally insane and royalty – all with one goal, to march forward into the greater glory together. Boots are the symbol. It's very exhilarating, very . . .'

'Erotic? Sounds to me as if he's suffering from a fetish,' I said suspiciously. There had to be more to it than the same old People's Power Game, Equality for All, Sharing and What's Yours is Mine, to attract Marsha.

She giggled. 'Well, he does have beautiful eyes, and very *unused* hands. But then his father's a diplomat and his mother the last remaining Romanoff, he says. He has a house in Wilton Crescent and hopes to buy a place in the country. As a base for the Revolution, of course.' Did Hetty know that?

'We must all rally behind him to change the world as we see it.' It *was* the old, old story under rather more fancy boots, I suspected.

'I don't think I want a very different world, just a few changes maybe. I rather like things a bit haphazard.' I glanced round the kitchen, my world. The rates demand lingered on the dresser leaning limply on a tax assessment form. Muddling Through, my mother called it. No neuroses attached, anyway. 'Has he got a Porsche?'

'What's that got to do with it?' But she sounded uneasy.

'Not much levelling there, then?'

'Anyway, I had to contend with the most incredible weather. One morning, I couldn't even get my bike through the snow!'

I gave a little shriek of delight. 'Bike? You've got a bike?'

But she ignored me and went on, 'Now it's cleared quite a lot, I thought we might cycle up and stay a week or two.'

'Lovely,' I heard myself saying, 'just do that.' She'd never get as far as Hampstead Heath.

It completely took the wind out of her tyres. There was a silence. Then she said in a disappointed voice, 'Did you get any

217

snow at all?' But she badly missed the blast of battle, I could tell. Could it be that was all she had ever really wanted and I'd fallen for the bait every time?

'Snow? Yes, yes, we got snow too. Now it's cold and wet.' But my heart wasn't in it or I'd have said sub-zero Arctic with cloudbursts.

'Maybe I'll leave it till spring.'

'Do that,' I agreed, 'but don't bring Igor.' I think we were both sad the spirit had gone out of our exchanges.

I took myself to the village shop. Dennis and Ralph were wearing white turtle-neck cashmeres. The Bargain Baskets swung on white ribbons. 'Snowflake Fingers' were being offered at twopence off the large size.

'My word,' said Dennis, 'you've lost weight!' It was the nicest thing I'd heard since I won the Sunday School Prize for Best Wild Flower arrangement with a lavish display of cow parsley backing dandelions when I was six.

Ralph came out of PO Corner and said, 'I love the toga effect. Terribly tomorrow, ducks. They'll all be up and down Sloane Street going Roman next week. Right little trend-setter, you are.'

'Methodist Bring-and-Buy in aid of Toads on the Roads. The sleeves had moulted. I took 'em out to wear as a fur jerkin but one shoulder gave way just now as I got out of the van.'

'I bet all the best designers work that way,' comforted Dennis, admiringly. 'Heard about Hosanna's latest?'

I shook my head.

'A shop, darling, she and Posie. Now, what was it? *Not* the green back; I really couldn't recommend it. You're safe with Danish smoked streaky, though, I promise you. And I'm going to pop in some of our new sage sossies. They're scrummy. No, dear, they're just to try. You can buy some next time if you like them.' No wonder they were doing so well. Hadn't someone told me about an extension at the back for car accessories, and tables with umbrellas in front for ice cream or fruit drinks in summer? Moving into the Fortnum range.

But Hosanna? I decided to call in on the way home. She was standing on her head in the back porch. 'Come through, come through,' she called impatiently when she saw my mouth fall open. 'Ten minutes of this and I'm able to dock an hour off my sleep pattern.' She went into reverse, landed unsteadily on bare feet and followed me in to put on the kettle. 'Mind if I do some ironing?'

I shook my head. I'd never seen Hosanna do anything before.

218

'What's this Dennis tells me about a shop?'

'Posie's idea really. We're going to open a Permanent Jumble at Betty's. Twice a week in the Dun Cow dining-room. Want to come in on it?'

I shook my head. It was their racket. 'Go on . . .'

'Well, you know how everyone's gone jumbling mad since inflation? Once a week, and all four timed for 2.30, seemed to leave the field wide open for speculation. We're moving in on a bonanza, like a private oil rush. Oh, it's all there, just waiting to be developed, you know. We've got hold of half a dozen old market stalls – trestle tables really – and we'll have one each and rent out the rest for lessees' own jumble. I am going to concentrate on Kitchenware and Sundries. Posie's doing Unwanted Gifts and White Elephants. It's going to save people bus fares to get into town for junk, you see.'

'Where will you get stock?'

'My dear, we've all got loads from past jumbles. And we're not opening on Saturdays, so we shall cover village halls, scout huts and church bazaars all over the county. We're very organised.' She made short work of a shirt, and flicked back the collar, folded it professionally and did up all the buttons. I stared in astonishment. 'Posie says we must present things properly, so we shall sort, wash, repair and display.'

But in that short sentence, she had killed the entire enterprise. It's where so many have gone wrong: it's the very risk and confusion of jumble sales, the possibility of a 'find' amongst the mess, the excitement of the search and the triumph of discovery, that keeps the queues forming.

'What's Harry think of it?'

'Ask him.' She passed me his mug of coffee and I went into the studio.

'Zanna seems excited,' I ventured tentatively.

'Notice the house? It's reasonably clean and tidy: notice I get my coffee now? Did she tell you she's actually reading recipe books? I get meals all the time.' He looked chuffed as anything. Poor Betty! But if the Dun Cow showed a loss on bar meals, it had Hosanna's stall to compensate. 'I told you she needed a purpose,' he said complacently.

'You said she needed a baby,' I reminded him.

He looked at me cryptically. 'You just wait,' he said. Maybe one would turn up with the jumble.

*    *    *

The Schnauzer was booked in and Hetty had news of a corgi and a hairless Mexican mated accidentally with a Springer. I said, 'Whoops! we'll have a team of bald hurdlers for the next Olympics!' and Hetty said, 'Better than a Boxer with a Pinscher, they'd all be disqualified!' and she laughed and laughed, so I guessed Igor was still hovering in the background.

Posy rang me later in the day and suggested I called in for coffee: she also let drop a few bits of interesting local news. Posy knew everyone, partly because of Dr Who, and partly because she was the kind of person everybody wanted to know. She told me that Hetty's farmer friend from Italy, Tony-of-the-Bugatti, had recently gone home, his confidence shaken by the snow, and did I know Hetty's husband was coming back?

I said, 'No. Does Hetty?' and she said, 'Of course' and I understood then why Hetty had found her own joke so funny. Hetty always laughs easily when she's really happy. I was enormously relieved. It was only later I thought it might, after all, be because Igor had already told her he was coming down our way with a friend, hoping to unload Marsha on us. Nothing short of another blizzard could save a situation so fraught with *real* dangers.

Something was happening for everyone. Lives were readjusting, were improving, were developing towards better days. For everyone except me. I tried to avoid indulging in a sniff of self-pity. I looked round my sultry kitchen and wondered how long it would be before Knickers Sattersthwaite-Pells began tearing the place apart. The earnest Friends would never fit in here. Knickers would think Humphrey disrespectful, Dennis and Ralph ridiculous, Hosanna strange and silly. Tears blinded me. She would fill my funny, shabby old Wrecktory with streamlined kitchen units, wall to wall carpets and bidets. She would scrub my reassuring words off the walls and put in brand new heating systems which would be so well lagged that rabbits couldn't recover in airing-cupboards, or so efficiently controlled by thermostats that the kitchen became merely a technician's laboratory and factory workbench instead of the heart of a home.

I knew then I had to do something. Too much character is destroyed for the sake of comfort. Whether it was a good thing or a bad thing is a matter of opinion. It just wasn't my thing. I couldn't allow it. I went to the phone and dialled her number, inspiration responding to desperation.

That conversation probably doubled the telephone bill and cost me half a week's housekeeping, but didn't everyone else ring *me?*

and wasn't this the final chance to win back my home? Even if it became threatened again later, there would at least have been a breathing space for discussion next time.

When I finally put down the phone, I hugged Treacle and Rosie and kissed Mattie between her untidy ears. She grumbled under her breath about all this excessive emotion, but she smirked as she sank back by the Aga. They all watched me tolerantly. None of them were a bit surprised when I got out the Glenfiddich.

# 18

I sat with my feet up on the Aga, surveying the Priddle trenchcoat. It drooped from a hook behind the door in a way the original owner would never have permitted. I was wondering uneasily whether even Jason found he'd suddenly gone right off the Golden Fleece when he eventually caught up with it, and if the Holy Grail seemed a bit less holy, perhaps, when it finally sat on the mantelpiece waiting to be polished.

The Scrummage Sale, organised by Hosanna and Posy, had come and gone, and what a splendid occasion it had been! The lady from Swallows Farm had shrilly demanded a campanula in exchange for her old shiny Vinyl, and Betty Tidy had bitterly regretted her generosity and loudly voiced her objections to the strong smell of rubberised raincoats and well-worn wellies by then pervading the pub.

I had, of course, been there. Not queueing with the rest but making a late and impressive entrance wearing – the Priddle Trenchcoat. Hosanna and Posy had stopped dead in their tracks and stared. Hosanna, a great surging tide of superfluous storm-proofing and rain resistance on the stalls in front of her, had gone a deep shade of red.

Wallowing in my moment of glory, I went over and said, 'Humphrey had it. He said some time ago he had something for me but it was only yesterday he actually dropped it in. He hoped it might be in time for the Scrummage though he'd really meant *me* to have it when the bad weather began, to wear when I went up to feed the horses. He didn't think much of my old dog-walker coat. We'll share of course, Zanna. I suggest a week each. I'll drop it in Monday if you like.'

Hosanna said haughtily, 'That's OK. I happen to have found myself a genuine Burberry in all this lot; it's almost new, too. There's a 'St Laurent, Rive Gauche' label in another I've kept back. I don't think I need the Priddle any more.'

It served me right, of course. 'Where did he get it anyway?' she asked, unable to restrain the same curiosity that had been my first reaction.